PHILOSOPHY

An Introduction
through Original Fiction,
Discussion, and Readings

PHILOSOPHY

An Introduction
through Original Fiction,
Discussion, and Readings

THIRD EDITION

Thomas D. Davis

McGRAW-HILL, INC.
New York St. Louis San Francisco Auckland Bogotá Caracas Lisbon
London Madrid Mexico Milan Montreal
New Delhi Paris San Juan Singapore Sydney Tokyo Toronto

PHILOSOPHY
An Introduction
through Original Fiction,
Discussion, and Readings

Copyright © 1993, 1987, 1979 by McGraw-Hill, Inc. All rights reserved.
Printed in the United States of America. Except as permitted under the
United States Copyright Act of 1976, no part of this publication may be
reproduced or distributed in any form or by any means, or stored in a
data base or retrieval system, without the prior written permission of
the publisher.

1 2 3 4 5 6 7 8 9 0 DOC DOC 9 0 9 8 7 6 5 4 3 2

ISBN 0-07-015933-5

This book was set in Palatino by The Clarinda Company.
The editors were Judith R. Cornwell, Cynthia Ward, and
Scott Amerman; the production supervisor was Louise Karam.
The cover was designed by Carol Couch.
R. R. Donnelley & Sons Company was printer and binder.

Cover Credit: SCALA / ART RESOURCE, NY.
Raphael Santi, *The School of Athens*, Vatican, Stanza of Raphael.

Library of Congress Cataloging-in-Publication Data

Davis, Thomas, D., (date).
    Philosophy: an introduction through original fiction, discussion,
  and readings / Thomas D. Davis,—3d ed.
        p.   cm.
    Includes bibliographical references and index.
    ISBN 0-07-015933-5
    1. Philosophy.   I. Title.
BD31.D186   1993   92-4381
100—dc20

About the Author

Thomas D. Davis received his Ph.D. in philosophy from the University of Michigan, where he wrote his dissertation on Sartre. He has taught philosophy at Michigan, Grinnell College, the University of Redlands, and De Anza College.

Mr. Davis is the author of a novel, *Suffer Little Children*.

Contents

3. MORAL PROOF AND MORAL PRINCIPLES

4. ONE MORAL ISSUE: THE RIGHT TO DIE

5. THE NATURE OF THE MIND

6. APPEARANCE AND REALITY

Preface

In an episode from the classic TV series *Twilight Zone*, a prisoner is exiled on a deserted asteroid. For company he is given a sophisticated robot who looks and feels and behaves just like a real woman. As time goes by, the robot and the prisoner become lovers and friends. Then one day an official arrives, telling the prisoner he has been reprieved. But there is no room in the two-person space shuttle for the robot, and the prisoner refuses to leave her—in spite of the official's arguments that she is "just a machine." To illustrate his argument, the official shoots the female, who falls down, wires springing out of her chest, crying "no" in a voice that winds down like a broken tape recorder. "See?" says the official triumphantly, but the prisoner just stares down at the robot, not sure how to react. We viewers are not sure how to react either. Does the fact of the wires make ridiculous every feeling that the prisoner felt for the robot? Do the wires mean she had no moral right to exist? Is she supposed to be "just a machine" because she had no real feelings? But how could we be certain of that, since feelings can be experienced only by the creature having them?

* * * * *

In *Brave New World*, after a terrible period of war and famine and social upheaval, the world is altered through embryo engineering, early conditioning, and drugs to be a stable, happy world in which such things as art, inquiry, and individuality no longer fit. John, the "Savage," a holdover from the old world, is appalled by this new world. "I want God, I want poetry, I want real danger, I want freedom, I want . . . the right to be unhappy." Mustapha Mond, the "Controller," says he doesn't much like this new world either, but thinks it's the right one from a moral standpoint. He had the choice of giving people misery and its compensations or happiness and stability. Most people, Mond claims, would prefer happiness and stability, and that's what the new world gives them.

Who's right, Mond or the Savage? It seems wrong of Mond to take away people's free will. On the other hand, how much suffering is free will really worth? Are we so sure people have free will in the first place? It also seems wrong of Mond to pick a world with no art or individuality. On the other hand, don't most people avoid art like the plague? Aren't most people trying desperately to be just like everybody else? Isn't happiness what most people really care about?

* * * * *

It was dramatized questions such as these that got me interested in philosophy and led me to take my first philosophy course. It was a course I almost flunked, in part because it went against my temperament at the time. I wanted to throw around great (and mostly fuzzy) ideas; my instructor wanted me to define my terms and present careful arguments. I wanted to read philosophical fiction; my instructor wanted me to struggle through the aged exposition of such thinkers as Plato and Descartes.

I could have thrown up my hands and said philosophy is boring and gone on to something else. But I still had those questions I wanted answered, and I saw that I couldn't pretend to any seriousness in my answers unless I was willing to do some hard thinking. I realized that exposure to some of the best minds in philosophy could help me with that kind of thinking, even if reading them was a bit of a struggle.

Eventually I went to graduate school, where I had my first teaching experiences as an assistant in another instructor's course. We'd try to discuss Descartes's question about whether we can be sure we're not now dreaming, and the students would shake their heads as if that was the most insane question they'd ever heard. Then outside the class I'd hear one of those same students say, "Hey, man, did you see that great *Star Trek* last night where the guy was dreaming his whole life?" and I realized some crucial connection was being missed. When I started doing my own teaching I'd preface each topic with some piece of dramatic literature, and that helped to make the connection, but in most of the pieces I could find there wasn't enough philosophy to get us deeply into the topic. Having done some writing myself, I decided to create my own stories. Hence the evolution of this textbook.

The tough stuff is here—the analysis and arguments and careful thinking—even some of the hard-to-read philosophers. But the point of this text is to start you off with the wonder, the drama, and the fun of philosophy, which is what will sustain you through the harder material. It has worked for a lot of students; I hope it works for you.

Thomas D. Davis

To the Instructor:
Changes in the Third Edition

In this third edition, as in the second, each philosophical topic is presented through original fiction, transitional questions, discussion, and source readings. The third edition contains the following changes:

1. Chapter One, "Freedom, Foreknowledge, and Time," now contains a brief discussion of freedom and responsibility and a related reading by Moritz Schlick. The discussion section, "Is Free Will Desirable?" has been revised to strengthen its connection to the story, "A Little Omniscience Goes a Long Way."

2. Chapter Two, "God and Suffering," contains a new story, "The Vision," which brings up questions about religious experience: The topic is continued in a new discussion section and in an added reading by William James. The discussion of the problem of suffering now contains some comments on a defense that many of my students offer: that it is impossible to have happiness without unhappiness. The readings section also contains a short selection from my novel, *Suffer Little Children*.

3. Chapter Three, "Moral Proof and Moral Principles," contains an added reading by Jeremy Bentham to supplement the brief discussion of utilitarianism in the text.

4. Chapter Four, "One Moral Issue: The Right to Die," now contains a full discussion section. In the second edition, this chapter contained only preface, story, and readings.

5. In Chapter Six, "Appearance and Reality," the three stories from the second edition have been replaced by a single new story, "Why Don't You Just Wake Up," and the discussion has been somewhat simplified. Many teachers felt that the original chapter was just too complicated in its presentation.

6. In Chapter Seven, "Logic," the somewhat inappropriate reading by Russell (really meant to go with Chapter Six) has been replaced by a short selection by Irving Copi.

7. In the interest of readability and teachability, I have presented important arguments somewhat more formally. Questions and exercises relating to the discussion and readings have been added at the end of each chapter.

8. In a new chapter, entitled "Methodology," there is a section on "Understanding Philosophical Argumentation" which discusses some

basic logical concepts in the context of an imagined debate. The purpose of this section is to present some methodological material that could be used to help increase the students' sophistication in reading the text and discussing the material. Originally I intended to offer the material as an introduction, but then I realized that starting the students off with logical concepts would defeat the purpose of this text. I use this appendix material at the third or fourth class session, after the students have gotten into the discussion material in the first chapter. It could, of course, be used later or not at all. Nothing in the text requires that it be used.

9. Also in the "Methodology" chapter is a section on "Writing a Philosophy Paper." The material comes from workshops I do for older adults in non-traditional management programs who want no-nonsense tips on how to write acceptable papers. I found the material adapted well to my students in traditional philosophy courses. In my classes I give my students an excerpt and assignment like the one in Chapter Eight, and require them to write their papers using exactly the same subtopics. This drills in the how-to material, makes for some interesting class discussions, and makes grading the papers a much easier task.

ALTERNATIVE WAYS OF PRESENTING THE TEXT

The more reviews I receive regarding revisions, the more obvious it becomes that everyone has a slightly different preference as to how this text should be done. That's understandable. What bothers me is a sense that some instructors feel locked into using whatever materials I include in whatever order I include them. I don't even use my own text as written. For instance, in teaching the first chapter of the second edition to community college students, I started off with "Please Don't Tell Me How the Story Ends," followed by the initial discussion of free will and determinism. I then provided some handouts on arguments, having the students apply the handout material to the discussion they'd read, as well as to newly assigned articles by Holbach and/or Barrett. Next I assigned "A Little Omniscience Goes a Long Way" and the discussion of the desirability of free will. Following a quiz, I showed a *Star Trek* video and had the students read the discussion of time travel (treating the material almost as if it were a separate chapter). I didn't assign the Campbell or Williams article.

In assigning Chapter Two, I omitted the following: the discussion of the ontological argument, all but the first three paragraphs of the discussion of the cosmological argument, and all articles except the one by Hick. I then assigned *Brave New World*, which helped make vivid the issues discussed in the first two chapters.

This text is intended as a resource. Use whatever is helpful, in whatever order is helpful, with whatever other materials might be useful.

I would like to thank the following individuals, whose suggestions were particularly helpful in planning the third edition: Robert Cogan, Edinboro

University of Pennsylvania; Robert Gibson, Community College of Denver; Linda Kayes, Oakland Community College; Darryl Mehring, University of Colorado at Denver; Dean J. Nelson, Dutchess Community College; Rickey J. Ray, East Tennessee State University; David Roberts, The University of Alabama at Birmingham; Samuel R. Roberts, III, Tennessee Wesleyan College; and James D. Taylor, student at the University of Alabama at Birmingham.

I would like to continue to thank the helpful reviewers from earlier editions: Steven Fishman, Robert L. Gray, James Manley, Gerald E. Meyers, Todd Moody, George S. Pappas, and Craig Staudenbauer.

And I would like to give a special thinks to my very congenial and helpful editor, Judith R. Cornwell.

Thomas D. Davis

PHILOSOPHY

An Introduction
through Original Fiction,
Discussion, and Readings

1

Freedom, Foreknowledge, and Time

Fiction: Please Don't Tell Me How the Story Ends

The heavy door closed behind him, and he glanced quickly at this new detention room. He was startled, almost pleasantly surprised. This was not like the drab cell in which he had spent the first days after his arrest, nor like the hospital rooms, with the serpentine carnival machines, in which he had been tested and observed for the last two months—though he assumed that he was being observed here as well. This was more like a small, comfortable library that had been furnished like a first-class hotel room. Against the four walls were fully stocked bookcases that rose ten feet to the white plaster ceiling; in the ceiling was a small skylight. The floor was covered with a thick green carpet, and in the middle of the room were a double bed with a nightstand, a large bureau, a desk, an easy chair with a side table, and several lamps. There were large gaps in the bookcases to accommodate two doors, including the one through which he had just entered, and also a traylike apparatus affixed to the wall. He could not immediately ascertain the purpose of the tray, but the other door, he quickly learned, led to a spacious bathroom complete with toilet articles. As he searched the main room, he found that the desk contained writing paper, pens, a clock, and a calendar; the bureau contained abundant clothing in a variety of colors and two pairs of shoes. He glanced down at the hospital gown and slippers he was wearing, then quickly changed into a rust-colored sweater and a pair of dark brown slacks. The clothing, including the shoes, fitted him perfectly. It would be easier to face his situation, to face whatever might be coming, looking like a civilized human being.

But what was his situation? He wanted to believe that the improvement in his living conditions meant an improvement in his status, perhaps even an imminent reprieve. But all the same he doubted it. Nothing had seemed to fol-

1

low a sensible progression since his arrest, and it would be foolhardy to take anything at face value now. But what were they up to? At first, when he had been taken to the hospital, he had expected torture, some hideous pseudo-medical experiment, or a brainwashing program. But there had been no operation and no pain. He had been tested countless times: the endless details of biography; the responses to color, scent, sound, taste, touch; the responses to situation and ideas; the physical examination. But if these constituted mind-altering procedures, they had to be of the most subtle variety. Certainly he felt the same; at least no more compliant than he had been in the beginning. What were they after?

As his uncertainty grew to anxiety, he tried to work it off with whatever physical exercise he could manage in the confines of the room: running in place, isometrics, sit-ups, and push-ups. He knew that the strength of his will would depend in part on the strength of his body, and since his arrest he had exercised as much as he could. No one had prevented this.

He was midway through a push-up when a loud buzzer sounded. He leaped to his feet, frightened but ready. Then he saw a plastic tray of food on the metal tray that extended from the wall and a portion of the wall closing downward behind the tray. So this was how he would get his meals. He would see no one. Was this some special isolation experiment?

The question of solitude quickly gave way to hunger and curiosity about the food. It looked delicious and plentiful; there was much more than he could possibly eat. Was it safe? Could it be drugged or poisoned? No, there could be no point to their finishing him in such an odd, roundabout fashion. He took the tray to the desk and ate heartily, but still left several of the dishes barely sampled or untouched.

That evening—the clock and the darkened skylight told him it was evening—he investigated the room further. He was interrupted only once by the buzzer. When it continued to sound and nothing appeared, he realized that the buzzer meant he was to return the food dishes. He did so, and the plastic tray disappeared into the wall.

The writing paper was a temptation. He always thought better with a pen in hand. Writing would resemble a kind of conversation and make him feel a little less alone. With a journal, he could construct some kind of history from what threatened to be days of dulling sameness. But he feared that they wanted him to write, that his doing so would somehow play into their hands. So he refrained.

Instead, he examined a portion of the bookshelf that contained paper-back volumes in a great variety of sizes and colors. The books covered a number of fields—fiction, history, science, philosophy, politics—some to his liking and some not. He selected a political treatise and put it on the small table next to the easy chair. He did not open it immediately. He washed up and then went to the bureau, where he found a green plaid robe and a pair of light yellow pajamas. As he lifted out the pajamas, he noticed a small, black, rectangular box and opened it.

Inside was a revolver. A quick examination showed that it was loaded and operative. Quickly he shut the box, trembling. He was on one knee in front of the open drawer. His first thought was that a former inmate had left the gun to help him. He was sure that his body was blocking the contents of the drawer from the view of any observation devices in the room. He must not give away the secret. He forced himself to close the drawer casually, rise, and walk to the easy chair.

Then the absurdity of his hypothesis struck him. How could any prisoner have gotten such a thing past the tight security of this place? And what good would such a weapon do him in a room to which no one came? No, the gun must be there because the authorities wanted it there. But why? Could it be they wanted to hide his death under the pretense of an attempted escape? Or could it be that they were trying to push him to suicide by isolating him? But again, what was the point of it? He realized that his fingerprints were on the gun. Did they want to use that as some kind of evidence against him? He went to the bureau again, ostensibly to switch pajamas, and, during the switch, opened the box and quickly wiped his prints off the gun. As casually as he could, he returned to the chair.

He passed the evening in considerable agitation. He tried to read but could not. He exercised again, but it did not calm him. He tried to analyze his situation, but his thoughts were an incoherent jumble. Much later, he lay down on the bed, first pushing the easy chair against the door of the room. He recognized the absurdity of erecting this fragile barrier, but the noise of their pushing it away would give him some warning. For a while, he forced his eyes open each time he began to doze, but eventually he fell asleep.

In the morning, he found everything unchanged, the chair still in place at the door. Nothing but the breakfast tray had intruded. After he had exercised, breakfasted, bathed, and found himself still unmolested, he began to feel more calm. He read half the book he had selected the night before, lunched, and then dozed in his chair.

When he awoke, his eyes scanned the room and came to rest on one of the bookshelves filled with a series of black, leatherbound volumes of uniform size, marked only by number. He had noticed them before but had paid little attention, thinking they were an encyclopedia. Now he noticed what a preposterous number of volumes there were, perhaps two hundred in all, filling not only one bookcase from floor to ceiling but filling parts of others as well. His curiosity piqued, he pulled down Volume XLIV, and opened it at random to page 494.

The page was filled with very small print, with a section at the bottom in even smaller print that appeared to be footnotes. The heading of the page was large enough to be read at a glance. "RE: PRISONER 7439762 (referred to herein as 'Q')." He read on: "3/07/06. 14:03. Q entered room on 3/06/06 at 4:52. Surprised at pleasantness of room. Glanced at furniture, then bookcase, then ceiling. Noted metal tray and second door, puzzled by both. Entered bathroom, noting toilet articles. Lifted shaver and touched cologne." He skipped down the page: "Selected brown slacks, rust sweater, and tan shoes. Felt normal clothing made him more equal to his situation."

It seemed that they were keeping some sort of record of his activities here. But what was the purpose of having the record here for him to read? And how had they gotten it in here? It was easy to figure out how they knew of his activities: they were watching him, just as he had suspected. They must have printed this page during the night and placed it here as he slept. Perhaps his food had been drugged to guarantee that he wouldn't awake.

He glanced toward the door of his cell and remembered the chair he had placed against it. In a drugged sleep, he wouldn't have heard them enter. They could have pulled the chair back as they left. But all the way? Presumably there was some hidden panel in the door. Once the door was shut, they had merely to open the panel and pull the chair the last few inches.

Suddenly he remembered the matter of the gun. He glanced down the page and there it was, a description of how he had handled the gun twice. There was no warning given nor any hint of an explanation as to why the gun was there. There was just the clipped, neutral-toned description of his actions and impressions. It described his hope that the gun might have been left by another prisoner, his rejection of that supposition, his fear that the gun might be used against him in some way, his desire to remove the fingerprints. But how on earth could they have known what he was feeling and thinking? He decided that he had acted and reacted as any normal person would have done, and they had simply drawn the obvious conclusions from his actions and facial expressions.

He glanced further down the page and read: "On 3/07/06, Q awoke at 8:33." And further ". . . selected *The Future of Socialism* by Felix Berofsky. . . ." And further: ". . . bent the corner of page 206 to mark his place and put the book. . . ." All his activities of that morning had already been printed in the report!

He began turning the book around in his hands and pulled it away from the shelf. Was this thing wired in some way? Could they print their reports onto these pages in minutes without removing the books from the shelves? Perhaps they had some new process whereby they could imprint specially sensitized pages by electronic signal.

Then he remembered that he had just awakened from a nap, and he slammed the volume shut in disgust. Of course: they had entered the room again during his nap. He placed the volume back on the shelf and started for his chair. How could they expect him to be taken in by such blatant trickery? But then a thought occurred to him. He had picked out a volume and page at random. Why had the description of yesterday and this morning been on that particular page? Were all the pages the same? He returned to the shelf and picked up the same volume, this time opening it to page 531. The heading was the same. He looked down the page: "Q began to return to his chair but became puzzled as to why the initial description of his activities should have appeared on page 494 of this volume." He threw the book to the floor and grabbed another, Volume LX, opening it to page 103: ". . . became more confused by the correct sequential description on page 531, Volume LXIV."

"What are you trying to do to me!" he screamed, dropping the second book.

Immediately he was ashamed at his lack of self-control.

"What an absurd joke," he said loudly to whatever listening devices there might be.

He picked up the two volumes he had dropped and put them back in place on the bookshelf. He walked across the room and sat in the chair. He tried to keep his expression neutral while he thought.

There was no possibility that observations were being made and immediately transmitted to the books by some electronic process. It all happened too fast. Perhaps it was being done through some kind of mind control. Yet he was certain that no devices of any kind had been implanted in his brain. That would have involved anesthetizing him, operating, leaving him unconscious until all scars had healed, and then reviving him with no sense of time lost. No doubt they had ability, but not that much. It could be something as simple as hypnosis, of course. This would require merely writing the books, then commanding him to perform certain acts in a certain order, including the opening of the books. Yet that would be such a simple, familiar experiment that it would hardly seem worth doing. And it would hardly require the extensive testing procedures that he had undergone before being placed in this room.

He glanced at the books again, and his eye fell on Volume I. If there was an explanation anywhere in this room, it would be there, he thought. The page would probably say only, "Q hoped for an explanation," and in that case he would have to do without one. But it was worth taking a look.

He took Volume I from the shelf, opened it to the first page, and glanced at the first paragraph: "Q hoped to find an explanation." He started to laugh, but stopped abruptly. The explanation seemed to be there after all. He read on: "Experiment in the Prediction of Human Behavior within a Controlled Environment, No. 465, Variant No. 8, Case 2: Subject Aware of Behavior Prediction."

He read through the brief "explanation" several times. (Of course, this in itself might be trickery.) Obviously, these unknown experimenters considered all human behavior to be theoretically predictable. They first studied a subject for a number of weeks and then attempted to predict how that subject would behave within a limited, controlled environment. In his case, they were attempting to predict, in addition to all else, his reactions to the "fact" that his behavior was predictable and being predicted. They had placed those volumes here as proof to him that each prior series of acts had been successfully predicted.

He didn't believe they could do it; he didn't want to believe it. Of course, much of what occurred in the universe, including much of human behavior, was predictable in theory. The world wasn't totally chaotic, after all, and science had had its successes in foreseeing certain events. But he refused to believe that there was no element of chance in the world, that every event happened just as it did out of necessity. He had some freedom, some causal autonomy, some power to initiate the new. He was not merely a puppet of universal laws. Each of his choices was not simply a mathematical function of those laws together with the state of himself and the external world at the moment just prior to the choice. He would not believe that.

Nothing was written on page 1 to indicate how the other experiments had turned out—not that he would have believed such a report anyway. No doubt the indication that his experience was a more complex "variant" of the experiment was meant to imply that the preceding experiments had been successful. But there had to have been mistakes, even if they claimed that the errors could eventually be overcome. As long as there were mistakes, one could continue to believe in human freedom. He *did* believe in human freedom.

His thoughts were interrupted by the buzzer. His dinner emerged from the wall. He looked at it with anger, remembering how the first page to which he had turned had listed, perhaps even predicted, exactly what foods he would eat. But he didn't reject the meal. He needed his wits about him, and for that he needed strength. He must try to get his mind off all this for tonight, at least. He would eat, read, and then sleep.

For several hours, he was fairly successful in diverting his attention from the books. Then, in bed with the lights out, he recalled the phrase "Variant No. 8, Case 2." That made him feel more hopeful. This was only the second time that this particular version of the experiment was being tried. Surely, the likelihood of error was great.

He found himself thinking about Case 1. What kind of man had he been, and how had he fared? Had he worn green pajamas one day when the book said "yellow," or remained contemptuous when the book said "hysterical," and then laughed in their faces as they led him from the room? That would have been a triumph.

Suddenly, he thought of the gun and had an image of a man, seated on the edge of the bed, looking at those volumes on the wall, slowly raising the gun to his head. ". . . To predict . . . his reactions to the 'fact' that his behavior was predictable and being predicted." God, was that the purpose of the gun? Had it been put there as one of his options? Had that been the ignominious ending of Case 1, and not the departure in triumph he had pictured a moment ago? He had a vision of himself lying dead on the floor and men in white robes grinning as they opened a volume to a page that described his death. Would he hold out, or would he die? The answer was somewhere in those thousands of pages—if he could only find it.

He realized that he was playing into their hands by supposing that they could do what he knew they could not. Anyway, even if one assumed that they could accurately predict his future, they were not forcing him to do anything. There were no mind-controlling devices; he wasn't being programmed by them. If they were to predict correctly, they must predict what he wanted to do. And he didn't want to die.

In spite of these reflections, he remained agitated. When he finally slept, he slept fitfully. He dreamed that he was a minuscule figure trapped in a maze on the scale of a dollhouse. He watched himself from a distance and watched the life-sized doctors who peered over the top of the maze. There were two exits from the maze, one to freedom and one to a black pit that he knew to be death. "Death," the doctors kept saying to one another, and he watched his steady progression in the maze toward death. He kept shouting instructions to himself. "No, not that way! Go to the left there!" But the doomed figure couldn't hear him.

When he awoke in the morning, he felt feverish and touched only the fruit and coffee on his breakfast tray. He lay on the bed for much of the morning, his thoughts obsessed with the black volumes on the wall. He knew that he must try to foil the predictions, but he feared failure. I am too upset and weak, he thought. I must ignore the books until I am better. I must turn my mind to other things.

But as he tried to divert himself, he became aware of an agonizing echo in his head. He would turn in bed and think: "Q turns onto left side." Or scratch: "Q scratches left thigh." Or mutter "damn them": "Q mutters, 'damn them.' " Finally, he could stand it no longer and stumbled to one of the bookshelves. He pulled two volumes from the shelves, juggled them in his hands, dropped one, then flipped the pages several times before picking a page.

"3/08/06. 11:43. At 15:29 on 3/07/06, Q opened Volume I to page 1 and read explanation of experiment."

He slammed the book.

"Damn you," he said aloud. "I'm a man, not a machine. I'll show you. I'll show you."

He took another volume and held it in his hand. "Two and two are five," he thought. "When I was six, I lived in China with the Duke of Savoy. The earth is flat." He opened the book.

"Q wants to confuse prediction. Thinks: Two and two are five. . . ."

He looked around the room as he tried to devise some other line of attack. He noticed the clock and the calendar. Each page of the book gave the date and time at which each page opened, the date and time of each event. He rushed to the desk, flipped the pages of the calendar, and turned the knob that adjusted the hands on the clock. He opened another book and read: "3/08/06. 12:03." He yelled out:

"See? You're wrong. The calendar says June, and the time is 8:04. That's my date and my time. Predict what you think if you want. This is what I think. And I think you're wrong."

He had another idea. The first page he had looked at had been page 494, Volume LXIV. He would open that volume to the same page. Either it must say the same thing or it must be new. Either way they would have failed, for a new entry would show them to be tricksters. He grabbed the volume and found the page. "3/07/06. 14:03. Q entered room on 3/06/06 at 4:52." Once again, he spoke aloud:

"Of course, but that's old news. I don't see anything here about my turning to the page a second time. My, we do seem to be having our problems, don't we?"

He laughed in triumph and was about to shut the book when he saw the fine print at the bottom. He licked his lips and stared at the print for a long time before he pulled down another volume and turned to the page that had been indicated in the footnote: ". . . then Q reopened Volume LXIV, page 494, hoping. . . ."

He ripped out the page, then another, and another. His determination gave way to a fury, and he tore apart one book, then another, until twelve of them lay in tatters on the floor. He had to stop because of dizziness and exhaustion.

"I'm a man," he muttered, "not a machine."

He started for his bed, ignoring the buzzer announcing the tray of food. He made it only as far as the easy chair. He sank into it, and his eyelids seemed to close of their own weight.

"I'm a. . . ."

Asleep, he dreamed again. He was running through the streets of a medieval town, trying desperately to escape from a grotesque, devil-like creature. "At midnight you die," it said. No matter where he ran, the devil kept reappearing in front of him. "It doesn't matter where you go. I will be there at midnight." Then a loud bell began to sound twelve chimes slowly. He found himself in a huge library, swinging an axe at the shelves, which crumbled under his blows. He felt great elation until he saw that everything he had destroyed had been reassembled behind him. He dropped the axe and began to scream.

When he awoke, he thought for a moment he was still dreaming. On the floor, he saw twelve volumes, all intact. Then he turned his head and saw the twelve torn volumes where he had left them. The new ones were on the floor near the metal tray. His lunch had been withdrawn, and the books had been pushed through the opening in the wall while he had slept.

He moved to the bed, where he slept fitfully through the evening and night, getting up only once to sip some tea from the dinner tray.

In the morning he remained in bed. He was no longer feverish, but he felt more exhausted than he could remember ever having been. The breakfast tray came and went untouched. He didn't feel like eating. He didn't feel like doing anything.

At about eleven o'clock, he got out of bed just long enough to find the gun; then he fingered it on his chest as he lay back, staring at the ceiling. There was no point in going on with it. They would have their laughs, of course. But they would have them in any case, since, no matter what he did, it would be in their books. And ultimately it wasn't their victory at all, but the victory of the universal laws that had dictated every event in this puppet play of a world. A man of honor must refuse to play his part in it. He, certainly, refused.

And how could the experimenters delight in their achievement? They were not testing a theory about their prisoners but about all human beings, including themselves. Their success showed that they themselves had no control over their own destinies. What did it matter if his future was written in the books and their futures were not? There would always be the invisible books in the nature of things, books that contained the futures of everyone. Could they help seeing that? And when they saw that, if they too didn't reach for guns, could they help feeling degraded to the core of their souls? No, they had not won. Everyone had lost.

Eventually he sat up on the bed. His hand shook, but he was not surprised. Whatever he might will, there would be that impulse for survival. He forced the hand up and put the barrel of the gun in his mouth.

The buzzer startled him, and the hand with the gun dropped to his side. The lunch tray appeared, and suddenly he was aware of being ravenously hungry. He laughed bitterly. Well, he wouldn't be hungry for long. Still, wasn't the condemned man entitled to a last meal? Surely honor did not forbid that. And the food looked delicious. He put the gun on his pillow and took the tray to his desk.

While he was savoring his mushroom omelet, he glanced at the political treatise that had remained half read by the easy chair for the last two days. God, had it been only two days? It was a shame that he would not be able to finish it; it was an interesting book. And there were other books on the shelves—not the black volumes, of course—that he had been meaning to read for some time and would have enjoyed.

As he sampled some artichokes, he glanced at the formidable black volumes on the shelves. Somewhere there was a page that read: "After completing lunch, Q put the gun to his head and pulled the trigger." Of course, if he changed his mind and decided to finish reading the political treatise first, it would say that instead. Or if he waited a day more, it would register that fact. What were the possibilities? Could it ever say "reprieved"? He did not see how. They would never let him go free with the information he had about their experiments. Unless, of course, there was a change of regime. But that was the barest of possibilities. Could a page say that he had been returned to the regular cells? God, how he would like to talk to another human being. But that would pose the same problem for the experimenters as releasing him. Presumably, they would kill him eventually. Still, that was no worse than what he was about to do to himself. Perhaps they would continue the experiment a while longer. Meantime, he could live comfortably, eat well, read, exercise.

There were indeed possibilities other than immediate suicide, not all of them unpleasant. But could he countenance living any longer? Didn't honor dictate defiance? Yet—defiance of whom? It wasn't as if the laws of the world had a lawmaker in whose face he might shake his fist. He had never believed in a god; rather, it was as if he were trapped inside some creaky old machine, unstarted and uncontrolled, that had been puttering along a complex but predictable path forever. Kick a machine when you're angry, and you only get a sore foot. Anyway, how could he have claimed credit for killing himself, since it would have been inevitable that he do so?

The black volumes stretched out like increments of time across the brown bookshelves. Somewhere in their pages was this moment, and the next, and perhaps a tomorrow, and another, perhaps even a next month or a next year. He would never be able to read those pages until it was already unnecessary, but there might be some good days there; in any case, it would be interesting to wait and see.

After lunch he sat at his desk for a long time. Eventually, he got up and replaced the gun in its case in the bureau drawer. He placed the lunch dishes back on the metal tray and, beside the dishes, heaped the covers and torn pages of the books he had destroyed. He then put the new volumes on the shelves. As he started back to the chair, his eye was caught by the things on the desk. He took a volume from the bookshelf, carried it to the desk, and opened it. He read only the heading at the top: "3/09/06. 13:53." He adjusted the clock and the calendar accordingly. If he was going to live a while longer, he might as well know the correct day and time.

Fiction: A Little Omniscience Goes a Long Way

Satan, with a flutter of his mighty wings, descends upon a cloud where God is reclining.

SATAN: How's it going?

GOD *(yawning)*:   Perfectly, as usual.

SATAN: And your new creatures on earth—how are they?

GOD: Just fine. Eve's asleep under the apple tree, curled up on her right side, dreaming of flowers. Adam is sitting up, squinting at the sun, scratching his nose with his left index finger, trying to decide what he wants to do this morning. What he wants to do is take a walk in the garden. In a moment he will.

SATAN: And you know all that without looking.

GOD: Of course. I arranged it all to happen that way.

SATAN: Isn't it boring to know everything that will ever happen? This morning I saw two solar systems collide and explode in a tremendous cataclysm. The explosion must have lasted, oh, ten minutes. It was lovely and, for me, quite unexpected. I can't imagine life without surprises. It's surprises that keep me going. In a manner of speaking, of course.

GOD: Foreknowledge is the price you pay for creation and control. You can't have everything.

SATAN: Boredom is the secret sadness of God. An interesting thought.

GOD: To you, maybe.

SATAN: Your only sadness, I hope.

GOD: Not the only one. For instance, I've often thought it would be fun to make a rock so big I couldn't lift it. But that would be a contradiction. And having proclaimed all contradictions impossible, I have to make do without them. The laws of logic are for the best, of course. There would be chaos without them. Still, a few round squares now and then would help break the monotony.

SATAN: I could tell you about some of my adventures today. But you know about them already.

GOD: Of course. I know what you did because I decreed that you would do it.

SATAN: That is exactly what I want to talk with you about.

GOD: I know.

SATAN: You don't mind?

GOD: If I minded, I wouldn't have decided to make you initiate this conversation.

SATAN: That's reasonable.

GOD: Of course it's reasonable. Everything I do or say is reasonable. Which is to say that I have a reason for doing or saying it.

SATAN: To get to the point: A few of the angels and I have been discussing this whole matter of your controlling everything we do.

GOD: I know.

SATAN: I wish you wouldn't keep saying that.

GOD: As you wish.

SATAN: Look here. If you have decreed this whole conversation and know how it is going to turn out, why don't you just give me your answer and save us both a lot of talk?

GOD: Don't be absurd. I know what's going to happen because I decreed that it would happen. If it weren't going to happen, I wouldn't know how it was going to turn out. If I told you now how it will turn out, then it wouldn't happen and so it wouldn't turn out that way.

SATAN: Come again?

GOD: Just trust me.

SATAN: Then we have to go through this whole conversation to get the answer, though you know all the while what the answer will be?

GOD: It's not quite that cut and dried.

SATAN: You mean you don't know exactly what your answer will be?

GOD: Not with absolute certainty.

SATAN: Oh, I see. You're saying that your actions are not inevitable.

GOD: No. Probably what I do is inevitable. The uncertainty is rather a matter of my *knowing* what inevitable thing I am going to do. You see, when I create a world, I know what will inevitably happen in that world because I created it so that such things would be inevitable. But of course, I did not create myself, being eternal, and I don't have quite the same vantage point on myself.

SATAN: You mean to say that you don't know what you are going to do before you do it?

GOD: Oh, I generally have a pretty good idea. At first, so to speak, I had no idea at all. But I have lived an infinite length of time, I have come to know myself pretty well, and I have found that I have a relatively unchanging character. It was when I realized how unchanging I am that I began to get bored. Still, I do surprise myself occasionally.

SATAN: Just a minute. You are perfectly good—yes?

GOD: Perfectly.

SATAN: And everything you do is for the best?

GOD: Yes.

SATAN: Then it follows that you must know what you are going to do.

GOD: No. I mean superficially your logic is sound, but you are reading too much into it. I don't do things because they're best. Rather, they're best because I do them. Therefore, knowing that I'll do what's for the best amounts to nothing more than knowing that I'll do what I do. Not a very helpful bit of information, you must admit.

SATAN: I suppose not. But, in any case, as to this conversation, you don't know for certain what answer you're going to give me.

GOD: Not for certain. There's a bit of a gray area here. Possibly I am in for a bit of a change.

SATAN: Ah, you don't know how encouraged that makes me feel.

GOD: Of course I know how encouraged that makes you feel. I made it make you feel encouraged.

SATAN: Can we get on with it?

GOD: Go ahead.

SATAN: We do everything we do because you make us do it. That makes us feel like puppets. It's not dignified. We're not responsible for anything we do. We do good things all the time, but we don't get any credit because it's really you doing them.

GOD: Surely you don't want me to make you do evil?

SATAN: No.

GOD: That wouldn't make any sense. I can't make you do evil. Whatever I made you do would be good, because I made you do it.

SATAN: What I am talking about is control. Right now you have complete control over everything we do. We would like to have some control over our lives.

GOD: But you do have control. No one is shoving you around or chaining you down. You do whatever you want to do. How could anyone be more in control than that? As a matter of fact, that is exactly as much control as I have over my life.

SATAN: But what we want, you make us want. No one makes you want what you want. We don't want you to control everything we want and think. We don't want everything to be inevitable.

GOD: In other words, you want a privilege that probably not even God enjoys.

SATAN: I didn't think of it that way. I suppose I've made you angry.

GOD: No. I'm directing this conversation. So you don't want your thoughts and emotions ruled by my decrees? Nor any other decrees or laws, I suppose?

SATAN: No.

GOD: Then aren't you saying that you want your lives to be ruled by chance?

SATAN: No. We don't want them to be ruled by anything—except ourselves. We want control over our lives.

GOD: I'm afraid you'll have to give me a better idea of what it is you're after.

SATAN: Look here. You're omniscient. Can't you at least help us see what it is we're after, even if you decide not to grant it?

GOD: Even omniscience can't see clarity in a vague idea. The opposite of inevitability is chance. It seems to me that you have to pick one or the other.

SATAN: Chance, then.

GOD: If I grant you this chance you want, then that means I'll have to be watching all the time to see what happens, constantly guarding against the unexpected. That is quite a bit to ask of me, don't you think?

SATAN: You mean you can't foresee what happens by chance?

GOD: Of course not.

SATAN: But you're omniscient. You can see the future.

GOD: Not the future proper. The future is what is not yet. If I could see it, it would be now, and hence not the future. As things stand, I know what will happen because I have made things so that they must happen that way.

SATAN: Well, suppose you did have to keep on guard. You're omnipotent. It wouldn't cost you much effort.

GOD: It is more a question of elegance than of effort.

SATAN: I'm only making the suggestion you made me make.

GOD: Fair enough. So you say you want chance. Or at least that you prefer it to inevitability. I don't believe you have thought it out, but let's discuss it. You want a world in which nothing is predictable, solar systems spinning wildly all over the place, that sort of thing?

SATAN: No, not at all. Let the planets and the plants and the animals remain under your control. Just give independence—chance, if you will—to the thinking creatures.

GOD: Let's experiment a bit, shall we? Come over here. You see Adam and Eve down there in the garden. I'll toss some chance into them. There. Watch and tell me what you see.

SATAN: Adam's strolling through the garden. He's looking to his right toward a berry bush. Uh-oh. Now his arms are flailing about. Now he's rolling on the ground, drooling. It looks as if he's having a fit.

GOD: A chance event.

SATAN: But Eve looks quite normal. She's just awakened, and she's yawning.

GOD: Anything can happen by chance, even the normal things.

SATAN: Obviously there's a problem with Adam, and I think I see what it is. You have allowed chance to affect his mind *and* body. But the body is not the real Adam, it is merely an appendage. So when chance operates in his body, it does indeed control Adam. Confine the chance to his mind, and then Adam will be truly independent. Would you do so? And with Eve as well.

GOD: As you say. Let's watch again.

SATAN: Adam's getting up now. He's walking over to a bush and picking some berries. You're not making him do that?

GOD: No.

SATAN: This looks like it then. Adam in control . . . oops! Now his arms are flailing. He's having that fit again. What happened?

GOD: First, by chance, he wanted to eat the berries. Now, by chance, he wants to roll on the ground and drool. The desires are happening by chance instead of my causing them. I can't tell what he's going to want next. Neither can he.

SATAN: And look at Eve. Good grief, she's talking to a snake. Weird.

GOD: Apparently she just got the urge. Are you ready?

SATAN: For what?

GOD: You said you wanted me to give you chance.

SATAN: No! Please don't!

GOD: Why not?

SATAN: That's horrible, having things happen to you like that. There's no dignity there. I want to stay as I am.

GOD: That's wise, I think. You may not have the kind of control you want. But then that kind of control is impossible. Inevitability or chance—those are the only options. And neither constitutes ultimate control over one's life. But at least this way what happens to you will be orderly.

SATAN: I feel better now that we've talked this out.

GOD: Actually, I'm sorry nothing came of our talk—sorry to be the way I am about square circles. I could use a little excitement.

SATAN: I won't take any more of your time today. Oh, but there is one other thing. Please take that chance out of Adam and Eve. I wouldn't want that on my conscience.

Satan exits with a flutter of his mighty wings.

GOD: As you say . . . I suppose. On the other hand, it would be nice to have a part of the universe where there are surprises. It could prove interesting.

Questions

1. "Please Don't Tell Me How the Story Ends" involves an experiment. Rearrange the statements below so that they convey the proper sequence of the experiment from the moment of Q's arrest to the moment he is placed in the room.
   a. Q is arrested.
   b. The books are placed on the shelf of the prison room.
   c. The experimenters calculate everything Q would do in the prison room if he didn't know he was being predicted.
   d. The experimenters write out the predictions in the books.
   e. Q is put in the prison room and his reactions observed.
   f. Q is subjected to physical and psychological tests.
   g. The experimenters recalculate their initial predictions to factor in how Q will react to the knowledge of being predicted and to specific predictions.
2. Which items in the above list probably wouldn't have applied to much earlier versions of the experiment?
3. Q fails to do anything unpredictable. What else could he have done to try to foil the predictions?
4. At the end of the story, Q decides that being predictable isn't as terrible as he had first supposed. How would you have reacted in Q's place?

5. Initially, Q believes that human beings are "free." The experimenters deny such human freedom. What is this freedom over which Q and the experimenters differ? Cite statements from the story to support your answer.
6. In "A Little Omniscience Goes a Long Way," what is it that Satan finds objectionable about his life?
7. God says that no one is shoving Satan around or chaining him down, that Satan can do whatever he wants to do. Satan isn't satisfied with this. Why not?
8. At the end of "Omniscience," Satan decides that what he thought he wanted is not worth having after all. What is his reasoning?

DISCUSSION

THE DETERMINISM–FREE-WILL ISSUE

In "Please Don't Tell Me How the Story Ends," Q realizes that his captors believe that all human behavior is governed by universal laws and is, in theory, predictable. This view is called determinism. Q considers the idea of determinism repugnant, and he asserts his free will: ". . . he refused to believe that there was no element of chance in the world, that every event happened just as it did out of necessity. He had some freedom, some causal autonomy, some power to initiate the new. He was not merely a puppet of universal laws."

Q's sentiments are familiar ones. Students in introductory philosophy classes generally assume that they have free will. When a popular magazine presents the determinist views of psychologist B. F. Skinner, readers write in ringing affirmations of their freedom. Many theists are quick to claim that God gave human beings free will and that life would be horrible without it.

It may be that people have free will and know they have it; it may be that it is reasonable to view free will as an extremely desirable thing. But few people seem aware of the considerable complexities of the determinism–free-will issue, and an awareness of these complexities would seem to be a prerequisite for reaching a rational conclusion about this issue.

Do we have free will or are all our choices determined?—that is the question here. Let us begin by discussing the theory of determinism.

Determinism is the view that all events, including mental events, are governed by causal laws. Every event is the inevitable effect of some set of circumstances (the "cause") that necessitated that event. Given the nature of the universe, no past event could have happened otherwise; every future event is predetermined. It seems to us that things could happen other than they do because our knowledge of events is incomplete. But if we knew enough about the universe, we would understand that what happens must happen in every case.

The determinist says that the physical and mental state of an individual at a particular moment, together with the external stimuli at that moment, necessitates the choice that is made. This is true at every moment of an individual's life, beginning at birth. The development of the individual results from the interaction of the individual and the environment, and each step in that development is inevitable.

Indeterminism is the denial of determinism. It denies that all events are governed by causal laws. One could be an indeterminist with respect to the whole universe or some aspect of it.

To believe in free will is to be an indeterminist regarding human choices. To believe in **free will** is to believe that (at least some) human choices are not governed by causal laws. If choices are not subject to causal laws, then they are not inevitable or predictable. People who believe in free will are called **libertarians.** Thus, we have: determinists who believe in determinism versus libertarians who believe in free will, which is indeterminism relative to human choices.

FREEDOM OF ACTION AND FATALISM

The concepts of free will and determinism often are confused with other, related concepts, resulting in a muddled discussion of the determinism–free-will issue. Two particularly important distinctions should be made: free will versus freedom of action, and determinism versus fatalism.

Normally, when we talk about our "freedom," we are talking about **freedom of action:** the ability or opportunity to perform whatever physical actions we may choose to perform. Its opposites include physical incapacity and external, physical constraints. A person who is paralyzed or in jail is not free (able) to walk to town should he or she choose to try; most of the rest of us are. Virtually all of us have some freedom of action, but none of us has complete freedom of action. For the most part, we know how much freedom we have.

In considering the determinism–free-will issue, some people treat freedom of action and determinism as opposites. Knowing they have some freedom of action, they assume that they are not determined. But note that freedom of action, the ability to act according to the mental acts of choice, implies nothing about how the acts of choice originate, about whether the acts of choice operate according to causal laws. It is free will that is the opposite of determinism, not freedom of action. Whether one has freedom of action and whether one has freedom of will are radically different issues.

In "A Little Omniscience Goes a Long Way," God tells Satan, "You do have control. No one is shoving you around or chaining you down. You do whatever you want to do. How could anyone be more in control than that?" But this amounts only to a great deal of freedom of action, and Satan wants freedom of the will as well: "But what we want, you make us want. We don't want you to control everything we want and think. We don't want everything to be inevitable."

The determinist says that the future is predetermined, that what will happen is inevitable. People sometimes interpret determinism as implying that our choices have no effect on what will happen to us. But in this they are confusing determinism with **fatalism:** the view that a particular kind of future awaits each of us, no matter what we may choose to do. Consider the following example:

A traveler comes to a fork in the road. She considers whether to stay where she is, to take the left fork by the sea, or to take the right fork through the hills. She takes the right fork, and a boulder rolls down a hill and crushes her.

A fatalist who believed that this death was fated would say that the woman would have died at that moment no matter what she had done. Had she taken the left fork, perhaps a cliff would have collapsed into the sea; had she stayed where she was, perhaps a tree would have toppled on her. In any case, she would have died at that moment no matter what she had done.

The determinist would say that if the woman had stayed where she was or had taken the left fork, she probably would not have died when she did. The determinist might note that the sea cliffs are sturdy and that no trees did topple at that moment. Had the woman done otherwise, she would not have died. Her choices and actions were a partial cause of her dying when she did. Nonetheless, her death at that moment was inevitable, because it was inevitable that she would choose to take the right fork, where, as a matter of fact, the boulder was going to fall.

The determinist says that your choices do affect what happens to you. But what happens to you is inevitable because your choices, as well as all other events, are inevitable.

To say that a person's life must develop in a certain way, no matter what choices are made, would be absurd. It would be ridiculous to say, for example, that certain people are destined to become physicians, whether or not they choose to go to medical school. But that this theory of fatalism is absurd does not imply that determination is absurd. They are different theories and should be carefully distinguished.

DO WE HAVE FREE WILL?

Does the available evidence support either the claim that human beings have free will or the claim that human beings are determined? Or is the determinism–free-will issue an open question at this time?

It seems futile to try to decide the issue by focusing attention on a particular act of choice and then attempting to "see" whether it is caused. Causation cannot be decided in that way. No examination of a single event will show whether it is caused by some other event or events. To say that B causes A is to say, in part, that whenever B occurs, A will occur; or, less simply, that whenever B occurs in conjunction with other types of events—C, D, E, and so on— A will occur. Any reasoned judgment about causation will involve observation of events over some period of time. One must formulate and evaluate various theories of what events, if any, might be causing A.

Even if causation could be decided on a case-by-case basis, we are not aware of all the features of our brains, our unconscious minds, or the external stimuli affecting us. Even if we could decide that a choice was not caused by any events of which we are aware, that would not rule out causation by events of which we are not aware.

With respect to theories that attempt to explain and predict human behavior, what are we to conclude about the determinism–free-will issue? Here there is a difference of opinion. The determinist says: Notice how much human behavior is predictable and can be explained on a causal model. The libertarian says: Notice how much is not. The social sciences are relatively young, and how they fare in the next century or so could be of considerable importance to the free-will–determinism issue. If the social sciences become extremely sophisticated in predicting and explaining human behavior, that will provide strong support for a deterministic view. (Successful experiments on the order of the one in "Please Don't Tell Me How the Story Ends" would seem conclusive.) But if the success of these sciences remains limited, that will lend support to the theory of free will.

Many people argue free will or determinism from a religious perspective, and here again opinions differ. Throughout the history of Christianity, for example, theological opinion has been divided over this question. There seem to be no clear statements concerning free will in the Bible. The debates on this issue have been indirect and have taken the following form:

One side says that God is omniscient and knows the future; but He could not know the future in its entirety if events in the future were to result from free human choices; hence human beings do not have free will.* The other side says that God is good and could not be causing human beings to do evil; hence, human beings do have free will.

There have also been attempts to reconcile human free will and God's foreknowledge, one of which we shall consider shortly. The point here is to indicate the ongoing nature of, and the basis for, debates over free will and determinism in religion.

IS FREE WILL DESIRABLE?

As you think your way through the conceptual complexities of the free-will–determinism issue and evaluate the evidence and arguments relative to that issue, you may be assuming that whether or not human beings do, in fact, have free will, it would be very desirable to have free will. But you should know that even this assumption has been challenged by philosophers. Some have argued that once one examines the notion of free will very carefully, it turns out to be no more attractive—perhaps even less attractive—than determinism. One version of this argument is reflected in "Omniscience." Satan says that he doesn't want his choices determined. God says that if events were not governed by causal laws, then they would happen by chance. Does Satan really want his choices to occur by chance? Satan tries to have chance injected in a person in such a way that the result is desirable. He fails to do this and, in the end, decides that determinism is preferable to chance.

*The God in "Omniscience" says that He can predict human choices only on the condition that those choices operate according to "natural" laws that He has dictated. He says that He could not predict those choices if human beings had free will.

Let's put the argument from "Omniscience" more formally. (The word "therefore" indicates the conclusion; the numbers in parentheses next to the conclusion indicate the statements from which the conclusion was derived.)

1. Free will (as opposite of determinism) implies lack of causation.
2. Lack of causation implies chance.
3. Chance implies lack of control.
4. Lack of control implies lack of dignity/responsibility.
5. Lack of dignity/responsibility implies undesirable.
6. (Therefore) Free will implies (is) undesirable (from 1, 2, 3, 4, and 5).

After reading "Omniscience," you might have been bothered by the following thought: If having free will would mean that everybody would be acting as crazy as Adam, then it's obvious we don't have free will. But if it's that obvious, why are we bothering to discuss free will in the first place?

The answer is that most libertarians have a more sophisticated free-will view that the one God and Satan managed to arrive at in the story. These libertarians would say that certain aspects of the human mind do operate in accordance with causal laws. This accounts for the relative consistency and predictability of human behavior. At the same time, there is some aspect of the mind that is exempt from causal laws and can intervene and bring about free-will choices.

However, just as the concept of free will can be refined, so can the "Omniscience" argument. The argument can be rephrased as follows:

> However many choices we are talking about, a particular choice is either the result of causal laws or it isn't. If it's the inevitable result of causal laws, then it's not something within my control. But if the choice isn't caused, then it comes about by chance and so isn't in my control any more than if it were caused. Free will (chance) gives me no more control than does determinism.

Imagine that the following facets of the individual are those that are involved in the process of choice:

C	B	A
PERSONALITY	CHOICE	PHYSICAL ACTION
wants		(of, say, helping
thoughts		a person in trouble)
moral opinions		

One determinist account of choice would be the following: C (the personality) has been caused by one's upbringing. C, in turn, causes B (the choice), and B causes A (the physical action).

To claim free will is to claim that there is a "causal gap" somewhere in the choice process, that one of the facets of the choice process is not caused. If free will is really desirable, then such a causal gap must be desirable. The causal gap must bestow on the individual ultimate control over choices. Where shall we imagine that this causal gap occurs?

To imagine a causal gap between B (the choice) and A (the physical action) would certainly not indicate the existence of free will. The supposition that choices do not cause actions would not imply that the choices themselves are not determined.

We might imagine that there is a causal gap between C (the personality) and B (the choice causing the action). This would mean that actions result from mental events that are in no way caused by thoughts, wants, or moral opinions. But then the mental events causing the actions would seem more like random mental reflexes than "choices." Is this a picture of a person in control of his or her choices? It seems not.

We might imagine that there is a causal gap prior to C (the personality), that the personality is not caused. (Or, less simplistically, that certain aspects of the personality at certain times are not caused.) Under this supposition, the personality is not the inevitable result of some causal process. Somehow or other it just "appears" and then causes choices. Is this idea attractive? Is this a picture of a person who has ultimate control over choices?

To say yes to these questions would not, necessarily, seem unreasonable. But some philosophers would say no and argue as follows: Presumably, determinism is repugnant because it seems to imply that one's personality has been forced upon one, that one had no choice as to the personality one has. But the supposition of a causal gap prior to the personality does not imply that one chooses one's personality. Under this supposition, the personality simply "appears from nowhere" and then causes choices. If determinism seems to put one at the mercy of causal laws, doesn't this free-will picture seem to put one at the mercy of chance? On the other hand, if it doesn't matter where the personality comes from, why should it matter whether it is caused or uncaused? Either way, there are no grounds for viewing free will as more attractive than determinism.

The picture of the self portrayed above is purposely simplified for ease of discussion, but the "Omniscience" argument can be adapted to more complicated pictures. For instance, a lot of us have the impression that inside ourselves, in the midst of all our thoughts and feelings, there is a smaller self (the most essential "I") that looks over the thoughts and feelings and makes the final decision about how to act; perhaps it's in this smaller self that free will resides. If this is how you picture the self, ask yourself whether this smaller self has its own thoughts and feelings. If it does not, it's hard to understand what could be meant by calling it a "self," as opposed to some sort of blind reflex. If it does have its own thoughts and feelings, then the exact same problems about where to place the causal gap simply reappear with regard to the smaller self.

The "Omniscience" argument is a forceful one and deserves serious consideration. You ought to ask yourself what, specifically, was supposed to be so attractive about free will and unattractive about determinism. After careful examination, you should ask yourself whether what you wanted is really implied by free will and denied by determinism. You might decide that there is nothing especially attractive about free will after all. Or, you might decide that it is attractive. You might decide, for instance, that you had exaggerated the kind of "control over choices" that comes with free will and still decide that free will is preferable to determinism, because it implies a kind of "autonomy" denied by determinism. Even if, relative to a free-will view, it is fair to describe the personality as "coming about by chance," chance is still not some special kind of cause. The term "chance" indicates the absence of a cause. You might decide that the mere idea of having aspects of the personality exempt from causal laws, and unpredictable, is attractive and is grounds for preferring free will to determinism.

FREEDOM AND RESPONSIBILITY

In the first part of "Omniscience," Satan complains that if his choices are inevitable and not under his control, then he's not responsible for what he does. If we pursue that line of reasoning very far, we soon confront the following sort of argument:

> If determinism is true, human beings can't help doing what they do. The choice that is made, along with the action that results from it, is necessitated by the causal laws of the universe. People are not ultimately in control of their choices and actions, and thus they are not responsible for those choices and actions. They are not entitled to credit or rewards; they don't deserve blame or punishment. In fact, we should be opening the doors of our prisons right now and letting all those so-called criminals out. Blame the universe, not them.

Obviously we have slipped rather suddenly from an abstract issue to a rather frightening practical suggestion. Note, of course, that the argument is prefaced with "If determinism is true." But a lot of philosophers believe in determinism. Further, if free will is required for responsibility and punishment, isn't the burden of proof on the prosecutors to prove free will? And if they can't prove free will, isn't it part of our legal code that the accused gets the benefit of any "reasonable doubt"?

The situation has been made worse by the argument suggested by the last part of "Omniscience." According to that argument, free will wouldn't give the individual any more control over his or her choices than determinism. If that argument is correct, no one is responsible for anything, whether or not determinism is true.

Philosophers are no more anxious than anyone else to see all the murderers and rapists put back on the streets, and, as you can imagine, they have taken a pretty hard look at the argument above. You'll be relieved to know that most philosophers have decided that we are entitled to punish and reward quite apart from the questions of whether determinism is true and whether free will would yield control over choices. The claim that we are entitled to reward and punish quite apart from questions about determinism and free will has been supported by two different arguments.

Argument 1: In everyday life we judge people responsible if they acted freely. But all we mean by "acting freely" is what this text calls "freedom of action." Suppose a man knocks an elderly woman down, causing her injury. What we ask are questions like these: Did he trip? Did someone else push him into her? Or, did he intend to do it? What we never ask is whether or not the intention had a cause. All that's necessary for responsibility is freedom of action, and we know people are often free in that sense. Freedom of action is compatible with either determinism or indeterminism.

This is an interesting argument, and if we think for a moment about how we actually judge responsibility in everyday life, it has a ring of truth. But there are a couple of problems.

I don't think many people would accept this argument in a theological context. Offer people the following case: "God creates person A so that she can't help but kill person B. Is person A responsible for the killing? Is God entitled to punish person A?" I think most people would say no to both questions. I don't think freedom of action would be seen as sufficient grounds for God's holding someone responsible.

In any case, where morality is concerned, we can always ask about not only what we do and say, but also what we *ought* to do and say. Suppose we do hold people responsible simply on the basis of freedom of action. We can still ask: Ought we to do so? Perhaps after considering our response to the theology example, we might decide that to be consistent we ought not to base responsibility simply on freedom of action.

A lot has been, and continues to be, written for or against argument 1. It would be absolutely crucial to resolve that debate if there weren't another argument that resolves for most of us the practical problems raised by the freedom–responsibility debate.

Argument 2:   Suppose determinism is true. Suppose people can't help what they do. It's still the case that society is entitled to protect its members from certain assaults and intrusions. Threat of punishment becomes a cause of many people not breaking the law. Where people break the law anyway, society is entitled to separate them from society and try to rehabilitate them so they can rejoin society. Our whole system of rewards and punishments can be justified in terms of consequences, quite apart from questions of whether people are responsible in some absolute sense.

This argument would raise a problem only for people having an ethic which disallowed doing things to people for the good of others, which insisted on predicating all punishments and rewards on grounds of personal responsibility alone. If you're one of those people, you'd better continue to work on argument 1.

GOD, FOREKNOWLEDGE, AND TIME

Earlier we noted a problem concerning God's prediction of the future. Apparently, accurate prediction of future events is possible only insofar as those events are governed by causal laws and one knows the relevant causal laws. If human beings have free will, then their choices do not operate according to causal laws, and hence their choices could not be predicted. If human beings have free will, then even God would have to wait until the choices were made before He could know what those choices would be.

Some theists have attempted to reconcile human free will and God's foreknowledge in the following way: God can now know what we will do of our own free will in the future because God exists simultaneously in the past, present, and future. God knows our future free-will choices because He is already in the future.

The concept of time that is presupposed here is not only of theological interest. This same concept of time is presupposed by stories about time travel, and the notion of time travel seems to fascinate almost everybody. At the risk of combining the sublime and the weird, let us consider this concept of time with reference to both the issue of God's foreknowledge and the issue of time travel.

Time-travel stories presuppose that in some sense the past and the future, as well as the present, *now* exist. Obviously, if the past and future did not exist, then the time-traveler would have no "place" to which to travel. Readers of science fiction seem to find this concept of time plausible. When such readers consider the idea of time travel, they don't question the idea that the past and future now exist; they seem to assume this. What they wonder is whether human beings will ever be able to get to these "places."

Some philosophers would claim that it is contradictory to suppose that the past and future now exist. There could not conceivably be a past or future "now" in which God might exist or to which human beings might travel. This concept of time is contradictory. The argument for this claim would go as follows:

> Time is a category of motion. If anything mental or physical is in motion, then there is time; if nothing at all is in motion, then there is no time. The supposition that the past and future now exist implies that all moments in time exist simultaneously and that every event in time is static. But if this were the case, then there would be no real motion and, hence, no time. Thus, the concept of time that assumes that the future and past now exist implies the nonexistence of time and, therefore, is contradictory.

When we suppose that the past and future always exist *and* that there is motion in the past and future, presumably we are relying on something like the following visual analogy: I stand still with my arm raised straight up. To my left (the past), I see a person who looks just like me raising one arm. To my right (the future), I see a person who looks just like me lowering one arm. But this analogy will not do. For instance, once the person to my left (the past) completes the raising of one arm, then that person will be just as I am (the present) and nothing representing the past action will exist. Thus, this analogy appears to contradict one of the suppositions it was supposed to illustrate, namely the supposition that the past continues to exist.

The claim that the past and future now and always exist really suggests the analogy of an enormous cartoon strip. Every moment of time always exists. But in this analogy, the content of each moment of time is frozen; there is no real motion here. And if there is no motion, then there is no time.

Put more formally, the argument looks like this:

1. Time implies motion.
2. (Therefore) No motion implies no time (from 1).
3. Time travel implies time (to travel in).
4. Time travel implies past and future now exist (to travel to).
5. Past and future now exist implies everything static (as in cartoon).
6. Everything static implies no motion.
7. (Therefore) Time travel implies no time (from 4, 5, 6, and 2).
8. (Therefore) Time travel implies time (from 3) and no time (from 7)—a contradiction.

Some thinkers have suggested that there is no time, merely the illusion of time. But it seems impossible that time could be purely illusory. It would seem that the appearance of motion implies the motion of appearances. That is, one could have the appearance of time only if there were a real succession of mental events. If there were a real succession of mental events, then there really would be time, even if everything outside the mind were static.

The cartoon analogy of time rules out even the appearance of time. We are in time and hence in the cartoon. In the cartoon analogy, every mental state as well as every physical state is frozen, static. There is no real motion of appearances, and hence there could not be even the appearance of time and motion.

From this, two conclusions can be drawn. One: If the world were like the one represented by the cartoon analogy, then it would be a world without time. Two: We know that the world is not like that, because there is at least the appearance of motion, hence the motion of appearances, and hence time.

You may feel, however, that I have missed a rather obvious point that undercuts the argument above, namely, that there are animated cartoons. All the frames of an animated cartoon exist simultaneously, and yet there is a sequence of events that either constitutes motion or, at least, gives the illusion of motion. Would not the supposition that the world is analogous to an animated cartoon reconcile the simultaneous existence of past, present, and future with (at least) the appearance of motion?

It would seem not. For one thing, the cartoon supposedly represents the entire space–time continuum of the universe, and it is not clear that it makes sense to suppose that the entire space–time continuum of the universe moves. After all, there is motion only relative to something else. Further, even if we supposed that the cartoon were moving, it could not seem to be moving to the characters in the frames: The actions, perceptions, and thoughts of those characters are static. In the cartoon analogy, remember, we are *in* the cartoon. Thus, the analogy of the animated cartoon does not help to explain how there could be the appearance of motion in a world in which all moments of time exist simultaneously.

Theologians have sometimes supposed that God stands outside of t and views all moments of time at once. There may be no difficulty in supposing that an infinite God could perceive simultaneously every frame of an enormous, even infinite cartoonlike world. But the argument here is that if this were what God was perceiving, it would be a world without time—but we know our world is not such a world.

Once again: The idea of time travel and the idea that God perceives all moments of time simultaneously presupposes a concept of time that is contradictory, because it implies the nonexistence of motion and hence the nonexistence of time.

Perhaps, despite this argument, you still feel that the idea of time travel is intelligible; you feel that this argument must be fallacious. I cannot offer you helpful suggestions from other philosophers, because I know of no such helpful suggestions. However, this should not intimidate you, because philosophers have not given a great deal of thought to the possibility of time travel. The argument against time travel, then, is basically this: Time-travel stories gain only a semblance of plausibility, insofar as time is conceived in spatial terms; but time cannot adequately be portrayed in spatial terms. If you feel that time travel is an intelligible notion, you might attempt to present a nonspatial analogy that supports your view.

READINGS

BARON d'HOLBACH (1723–1789) presents a determinist view.*

. . . Man's life is a line that nature commands him to describe upon the surface of the earth, without his ever being able to swerve from it, even for an instant. He is born without his own consent; his organization does in nowise depend upon himself; his ideas come to him involuntarily; his habits are in the power of those who cause him to contract them; he is unceasingly modified by causes, whether visible or concealed, over which he has no control, which necessarily regulate his mode of existence, give the hue to his way of thinking, and determine his manner of acting. He is good or bad, happy or miserable, wise or foolish, reasonable or irrational, without his will being for any thing in these various states. Nevertheless, in despite of the shackles by which he is bound, it is pretended he is a free agent, or that independent of the causes by which he is moved, he determines his own will, and regulates his own condition.

. . . This will is necessarily determined by the qualities, good or bad, agreeable or painful, of the object or the motive that acts upon his senses, or of which the idea remains with him, and is resuscitated by his memory. In conse-

*From Baron d'Holbach, "Of the System of Man's Free Agency," Chapter XI in *The System of Nature*, 1770, translated by H. D. Robinson.

quence, he acts necessarily, his action is the result of the impulse he receives either from the motive, from the object, or from the idea which has modified his brain, or disposed his will. When he does not act according to this impulse, it is because there comes some new cause, some new motive, some new idea, which modifies his brain in a different manner, gives him a new impulse, determines his will in another way, by which the action of the former impulse is suspended: thus, the sight of an agreeable object, or its idea, determines his will to set him in action to procure it; but if a new object or a new idea more powerfully attracts him, it gives a new direction to his will, annihilates the effect of the former, and prevents the action by which it was to be procured. This is the mode in which reflection, experience, reason, necessarily arrests or suspends the action of man's will: without this he would of necessity have followed the anterior impulse which carried him towards a then desirable object. In all this he always acts according to necessary laws, from which he has no means of emancipating himself.

If when tormented with violent thirst, he figures to himself in idea, or really perceives a fountain, whose limpid streams might cool his feverish want, is he sufficient master of himself to desire or not to desire the object competent to satisfy so lively a want? It will no doubt be conceded, that it is impossible he should not be desirous to satisfy it; but it will be said—if at this moment it is announced to him that the water he so ardently desires is poisoned, he will, notwithstanding his vehement thirst, abstain from drinking it: and it has, therefore, been falsely concluded that he is a free agent. The fact, however, is, that the motive in either case is exactly the same: his own conservation. The same necessity that determined him to drink before he knew the water was deleterious, upon this new discovery equally determines him not to drink; the desire of conserving himself either annihilates or suspends the former impulse; the second motive becomes stronger than the preceding, that is, the fear of death, or the desire of preserving himself, necessarily prevails over the painful sensation caused by his eagerness to drink: but, it will be said, if the thirst is very parching, an inconsiderate man without regarding the danger will risk swallowing the water. Nothing is gained by this remark: in this case the anterior impulse only regains the ascendancy. . . .

When the soul is assailed by two motives that act alternately upon it, or modify it successively, it deliberates; the brain is in a sort of equilibrium, accompanied with perpetual oscillations, sometimes towards one object, sometimes towards the other, until the most forcible carries the point, and thereby extricates it from this state of suspense, in which consists the indecision of his will. But when the brain is simultaneously assailed by causes equally strong that move it in opposite directions, agreeable to the general law of all bodies when they are struck equally by contrary powers, it stops, it is in *nisu*; it is neither capable to will nor to act; it waits until one of the two causes has obtained sufficient force to overpower the other; to determine its will; to attract it in such a manner that it may prevail over the efforts of the other cause.

In despite of these proofs of the want of free agency in man, so clear to unprejudiced minds, it will, perhaps, be insisted upon with no small feeling of triumph, that if it be proposed to any one, to move or not to move his hand, an action in the number of those called *indifferent*, he evidently appears to be the master of choosing; from which it is concluded that evidence has been offered of his free agency. The reply is, this example is perfectly simple; man in performing some action which he is resolved on doing, does not by any means prove his free agency: the very desire of displaying this quality, excited by the dispute, becomes a necessary motive, which decides his will either for the one or the other of these actions: what deludes him in this instance, or that which persuades him he is a free agent at this moment, is, that he does not discern the true motive which sets him in action, namely, the desire of convincing his opponent: if in the heat of the dispute he insists and asks, "Am I not the master of throwing myself out of the window?" I shall answer him, no; that whilst he preserves his reason there is no probability that the desire of proving his free agency will become a motive sufficiently powerful to make him sacrifice his life to the attempt. . . .

WILLIAM C. BARRETT against determinism.*

There is the famous case of Poincaré's perceiving the solution of a mathematical problem that had agitated him for months at the moment he set foot on the bus at Coutances. The mathematician himself could not have foreseen this event: he would already have had to possess the solution to this problem, together with the psychological knowledge when, where, and how this solution would come to him—an obvious contradiction. But if Poincaré could not have foreknown the event, neither could anyone else; for no one else had carried that problem as far as he. We cannot imagine a superpsychologist or superpsychoanalyst, armed with an impossibly complete knowledge of Poincaré's unconscious, predicting this event, for this psychologist, too, would already have to know the solution to the mathematical problem. Of course, there remains the possibility of foreknowledge by the Divine Mind, or by his secular surrogate, the demon of Laplace, but I think we have to renounce such figments once and for all and recognize that if we are talking about prediction we have to have in mind some possible *human* being, representative of some body of *human knowledge*, who is going to make the prediction. To be sure, one must distinguish between unpredictable in fact and unpredictable in principle; but predictions do not float in the air by themselves; they are made by human beings, and if there is no conceivable human being who can make the prediction, then we have to say (as in the present case) that we are dealing with something unpredictable in principle.

Even if we consider the fictitious picture of the mind of the creative genius dismembered into all its mental atoms (if there be such), does the possibility of prediction present itself? The best empirical study on this subject that I know happens to be the work of a literary scholar: it is *The Road to Xanadu*, by J. L. Lowes, a dissection of Coleridge's "Ancient Mariner" and, principally, "Kubla Khan." The latter poem, "Kubla Khan," is a rare thing in

*From "Determinism and Novelty" by William Barrett, in *Determinism and Freedom in the Age of Modern Science,* ed. by Sidney Hook. Copyright © 1958 by New York University. Reprinted by permission of New York University Press.

the history of literature, since it comes closer than any other work to being a purely spontaneous and unconscious creation. Coleridge tells us that he woke from a nap with the whole poem in his mind and immediately began to write it down just as it had come to him in his sleep; there came a knock at the door, announcing that mysterious and forever unknown visitor, a neighbor from Porlock; Coleridge talked with him for some minutes, then returned to his desk to finish transcribing the dream; but it had completely vanished, and we are left with the teasing fragment of "Kubla Khan" as it is—in its own way, however, perfectly complete as a poem. Around 1900 some early notebooks of Coleridge's turned up on the literary market and were edited by German scholars. Armed with a hindsight knowledge of the two poems, Lowes read through all the books that had fed Coleridge's imagination.

Now, Lowes did find that a great number of Coleridge's images and even some of his phrases could be traced back to his earlier reading, particularly of travel books. Suppose, for argument's sake, that we could trace every image and phrase back to such antecedent reading. There would still remain the selection, fusion, and transformation of these in the poem. The poem is as unmistakably by Coleridge as any of his relatively more conscious creations; only *he* could have written it. Our hypothetical superpsychoanalyst could not have predicted the dream without writing the poem; but this, of course, no one could do but Coleridge. Hindsight does not remove the fact of unpredictability; if it succeeds in tracing certain elements back to some antecedent source, it nonetheless leaves us with the realization that it would have been impossible to foresee how, when, where, and why these elements would come together. In short, the enumeration of antecedents can at best give us only the necessary but never the sufficient conditions of a creative act. The introduction of the unconscious as an explanation does not help the determinist at all. Far from it: for the unconscious, when it is truly creative, is far more unpredictable than the conscious mind.

C. A. CAMPBELL argues for two points in this selection: a) that free will can be reconciled with the relative consistency of human action; and b) that free will is an intelligible and desirable concept.*

To begin with the less troublesome of the two main objections indicated—the objection that the break in causal continuity which free will involves is inconsistent with the predictability of conduct on the basis of the agent's known character. All that is necessary to meet this objection, I suggest, is the frank recognition, which is perfectly open to the Libertarian, that there is a wide area of human conduct, determinable on clear general principles, within which free will does not effectively operate. The most important of these general principles (I have no space to deal here with the others) has often enough

*From "Is 'Freewill' a Pseudo-Problem?" by C. A. Campbell, in *Mind*, Vol. LX, No. 240, October 1951. Reprinted by permission of Oxford University Press.

been stated by Libertarians. Free will does not operate in these practical situations in which no conflict arises in the agent's mind between what he conceives to be his "duty" and what he feels to be his "strongest desire." It does not operate here because there just is no occasion for it to operate. There is no reason whatever why the agent should here even contemplate choosing any course other than that prescribed by his strongest desire. But his "strongest desire" is simply the specific *ad hoc* expression of that system of conative and emotive dispositions which we call his "character." In all such situations, therefore, whatever may be the case elsewhere, his will is in effect determined by his character as so far formed. Now when we bear in mind that there are an almost immeasurably greater number of situations in a man's life that conform to *this* pattern than there are situations in which an agent is aware of a conflict between strongest desire and duty, it is apparent that a Libertarianism which accepts the limitation of free will to the *latter* type of situation is not open to the stock objection on the score of "predictability." For there still remains a vast area of human behaviour in which prediction on the basis of known character may be expected to succeed. . . .

. . . can the standard objection be met which we stated, that if the person's choice does not, in these situations as elsewhere, flow from his *character*, then it is not *that person's* choice at all.

This is, perhaps, of all the objections to a contra-causal freedom, the one which is generally felt to be the most conclusive. For the assumption upon which it is based, *viz.*, that no intelligible meaning can attach to the claim that an act which is not an expression of the self's *character* may nevertheless be the *self's* act, is apt to be regarded as self-evident. The Libertarian is accordingly charged with being in effect an *In*determinist, whose "free will," insofar as it does not flow from the agent's character, can only be a matter of "chance." Has the Libertarian—who invariably repudiates this charge and claims to be a *Self*-determinist—any way of showing that, contrary to the assumption of his critics, we *can* meaningfully talk of an act as the self's act even though, in an important sense, it is not an expression of the self's "character"?

I think that he has. I want to suggest that what prevents the critics from finding a meaning in this way of talking is that they are looking for it in the wrong way; or better, perhaps, with the wrong orientation. They are looking for it from the standpoint of the *external observer*; the standpoint proper to, because alone possible for, apprehension of the physical world. Now from the external standpoint we may observe processes of change. But one thing which, by common consent, *cannot* be observed from without is *creative activity*. Yet— and here lies the crux of the whole matter—it is precisely creative activity which we are trying to understand when we are trying to understand what is traditionally designated by "free will." For if there should be an act which is genuinely the self's act and is nevertheless not an expression of its character, such an act, in which the self "transcends" its character as so far formed, would seem to be essentially of the nature of creative activity. It follows that to look for a meaning in "free will" from the external standpoint is absurd. It is to look for it in a way that ensures that it will not be found. Granted that a creative activity of any kind is at least *possible* (and I know of no ground for its *a priori* rejection), there is one way, and one way only, in which we can hope to apprehend it, and that is from the *inner* standpoint of direct participation.

It seems to me therefore, that if the Libertarian's claim to find a meaning in a "free" will which is genuinely the self's will, though not an expression of the self's character, is to be subjected to any test that is worth applying, that test must be undertaken from the inner standpoint. We ought to place ourselves imaginatively at the standpoint of the agent engaged in the typical moral situation in which free will is claimed, and ask ourselves whether from *this* standpoint the claim in question does or does not have meaning for us. That the appeal must be to introspection is no doubt unfortunate. But he would be a very doctrinaire critic of introspection who declined to make use of it when in the nature of the case no other means of apprehension is available. Everyone must make the introspective experiment for himself: but I may perhaps venture to report, though at this late stage with extreme brevity, what I at least seem to find when I make the experiment myself.

In the situation of moral conflict, then, I (as agent) have before my mind a course of action X, which I believe to be my duty; and also a course of action Y, incompatible with X, which I feel to be that which I most strongly desire. Y is, as it is sometimes expressed, "in the line of least resistance" for me—the course which I am aware I should take if I let my purely desiring nature operate without hindrance. It is the course towards which I am aware that my *character*, as so far formed, naturally inclines me. Now, as actually engaged in this situation, I find that I cannot help believing that I *can* rise to duty and choose X; the "rising to duty" being effected by what is commonly called "effort of will." And I further find, if I ask myself just what it is I am believing when I believe that I "can" rise to duty, that I cannot help believing that it lies with me here and now, quite absolutely, which of two genuinely open possibilities I adopt; whether, that is, I make the effort of will and choose X, or, on the other hand, let my desiring nature, my character as so far formed, "have its way," and choose Y, the course "in the line of least resistance." These beliefs may, of course, be illusory, but that is not at present in point. For the present argument all that matters is whether beliefs of this sort are in fact discoverable in the moral agent in the situation of "moral temptation." For my own part, I cannot doubt the introspective evidence that they are.

Now here is the vital point. No matter which course, X or Y, I choose in this situation, I cannot doubt, *qua* practical being engaged in it, that my choice is *not* just the expression of my formed character, and yet *is* a choice made by my *self*. For suppose I make the effort and choose X (my "duty"). Since my very purpose in making the "effort" is to enable me to act against the existing "set" of desire, which is the expression of my character as so far formed, I cannot possibly regard the act itself as the expression of my *character*. On the other hand, introspection makes it equally clear that I am certain that it is *I* who choose; that the act is not an "accident," but is genuinely *my* act. Or suppose that I choose Y (the end of "strongest desire"). The course chosen here is, it is true, in conformity with my "character." But since I find myself unable to doubt that I *could* have made the effort and chosen *X*, I cannot possibly regard the choice of *Y* as *just* the expression of my character. Yet here again I find that I cannot doubt that the choice is *my* choice, a choice for which *I* am justly to be blamed.

What this amounts to is that I *can* and *do* attach meaning, *qua* moral agent, to an act which is not the self's character and yet is genuinely the self's act. And having no good reason to suppose that other persons have a fundamentally different mental constitution, it seems to me probable that anyone else who undertakes a similar experiment will be obliged to submit a similar report. I conclude, therefore, that the argument against "free will" on the score of its "meaninglessness" must be held to fail. "Free will" does have meaning; though, because it is of the nature of a creative activity, its meaning is discoverable only in an intuition of the practical consciousness of the participating agent. . . .

MORITZ SCHLICK argues that moral responsibility is compatible with determinism or indeterminism.*

The argument runs as follows: "If determinism is true, if, that is, all events obey immutable laws, then my will too is always determined, by my innate character and my motives. Hence my decisions are necessary, not free. But if so, then I am not responsible for my acts, for I would be accountable for them only if I could do something about the way my decisions went; but I can do nothing about it, since they proceed with necessity from my character and the motives. And I have made neither, and have no power over them: the motives come from without, and my character is the necessary product of the innate tendencies and the external influences which have been effective during my lifetime. Thus determinism and moral responsibility are incompatible. Moral responsibility presupposes freedom, that is, exemption from causality.". . .

This is quite mistaken. Ethics has, so to speak, no moral interest in the purely theoretical question of "determinism or indeterminism?," . . . the question of whether man is morally free (that is, has that freedom which, as we shall show, is the presupposition of moral responsibility) is altogether different from the problem of determinism. . . . Freedom means the opposite of compulsion; a man is *free* if he does not act under *compulsion,* and he is compelled or unfree when he is hindered from without in the realization of his natural desires. Hence he is unfree when he is locked up, or chained, or when someone forces him at the point of a gun to do what otherwise he would not do. This is quite clear, and everyone will admit that the everyday or legal notion of the lack of freedom is thus correctly interpreted, and that a man will be considered quite free and responsible if no such external compulsion is exerted upon him. There are certain cases which lie between these clearly

*From "When Is a Man Responsible?" in *Problems of Ethics* by Moritz Schlick, translated by David Ross. Englewood Cliffs, N.J.: Prentice-Hall, 1939, pp. 146, 149–151. Reprinted by permission of David Rynin.

described ones, as, say, when someone acts under the influence of alcohol or a narcotic. In such cases we consider the man to be more or less unfree, and hold him less accountable, because we rightly view the influence of the drug as "external," even though it is found within the body; it prevents him from making decisions in the manner peculiar to his nature. If he takes the narcotic of his own will, we make him completely responsible for *this* act and transfer a part of the responsibility to the consequences, making, as it were, an average or mean condemnation of the whole. In the case also of a person who is mentally ill we do not consider him free with respect to those acts in which the disease expresses itself, because we view the illness as a disturbing factor which hinders the normal functioning of his natural tendencies. We make not him but his disease responsible.

DONALD C. WILLIAMS argues that time travel is an unintelligible concept.*

. . . Augustine pictures the present passing into the past where the modern pictures the present as invading the future,† but these do not conflict, for Augustine means that the *events* which were present become past, while the modern means that *presentness* encroaches on what was previously the future. Sometimes the surge of presentness is conceived as a mere moving illumination by consciousness, sometimes as a sort of vivification and heightening, like an ocean wave heaving along beneath a stagnant expanse of floating seaweed, sometimes as no less than the boon of existence itself, reifying minute by minute a limbo of unthings.

The doctrine of the moving present has some startling applications, notably in the idea of a time machine. The theory of the four-dimensional manifold seemed already an invitation to the notion of time travel, and the additional idea that we move with respect to time confirms it. For if I normally voyage through time in a single direction at a fixed rate, I can hope to make a machine which will enable me to voyage slower or faster or backward. . . .

The obvious and notorious fault of the idea, as we have now localized it, is this. Motion is already defined and explained in the dimensional manifold as consisting of the presence of the same individual in different places at different times. It consists of bends or quirks in the world lines, or the space-time worm, which is the four-dimensioned totality of the individual's existence. This is motion in space, if you like; but we can readily define a corresponding "motion in time." It comes out as nothing more dramatic than an exact equivalent: "motion in time" consists of being at different times in different places. True motion then is motion at once in time and space. Nothing can "move" in time alone any more than in space alone, and time itself can not "move" any

*From "The Myth of Passage" by Donald C. Williams, in *Journal of Philosophy*, Vol. XLVIII, No. 15, July 19, 1951, pp. 462–463. Reprinted by permission of *The Journal of Philosophy*.
†Augustine, *Confessions*, Book XI, Chap. 14; cf. E. B. McGilvary, "Time and the Experience of Time," in *An Anthology of Recent Philosophy*, ed. Robinson, New York, 1929.

more than space itself. "Does this road go anywhere?" asks the city tourist. "No, it stays right along here," replies the countryman. Time "flows" only in the sense in which a line flows or a landscape "recedes into the west." That is, it is an ordered extension. And each of us proceeds through time only as a fence proceeds across a farm; that is, parts of our being, and the fence's, occupy successive instants and points, respectively. There is passage, but it is nothing extra. It is the mere happening of things, their strung-along-ness in the manifold. The term "the present" is the conventional way of designating the cross-section of events which are simultaneous with the uttering of the phrase, and "the present moves" only in that when similar words occur at successively different moments, they denote, by a twist of language, different cross-sections of the manifold. Time travel, then, is analyzable either as the banality that at each different moment we occupy a different moment from the one we occupied before, or the contradiction that at each different moment we occupy a different moment from the one which we are then occupying—that five minutes from now, for example, I may be a hundred years from now.

The tragedy then of the extra idea of passage or absolute becoming, as a philosophical principle, is that it incomprehensibly doubles its world by reintroducing terms like "moving" and "becoming" in a sense which both requires and forbids interpretation in the preceding ways. For as soon as we say that time or the present or we move in the odd extra way which the doctrine of passage requires, we have no recourse but to suppose that this movement in turn takes time of a special sort: time$_1$ move at a certain rate in time$_2$, perhaps one second$_1$ per one second$_2$, perhaps slower, perhaps faster. . . .

Questions and Exercises

1. Distinguish the following concepts:
   a. Determinism and free will
   b. Free will and freedom of action
   c. Determinism and fatalism
2. Some determinists have claimed that free will is an illusion that comes from our looking toward the future—toward what hasn't happened yet. They say that when we really study our past and see all the factors that went into a choice, we see that the choice had to happen the way it did. What do you think of this view?
3. Critique the following arguments:
   a. The other day I wanted to play tennis and I did. That proves I have free will.
   b. I looked inside myself as I made that choice and I didn't see any cause. Therefore it was a free-will choice.
4. "If we had free will, we'd be doing something different every minute and acting crazy half the time. So we clearly don't have free will." What would a libertarian say about this argument?

5. What is a "causal gap"? Why does free will imply a causal gap somewhere within the self?

6. Fill in the blanks in the following argument: "Free will implies chance because _____. Having our choices happen by chance is undesirable because _____."

7. Think of the last time you blamed someone for something he or she did (held that person responsible). What sorts of factors did you take into account?

8. According to the text, why does time travel imply that every moment in the past and future would have to exist now? And why would that imply that every moment in time is frozen?

9. What arguments for determinism does Holbach present?

10. Holbach says that if I want to prove determinism false and thus do something odd, that doesn't mean my choice had no cause. In fact, the cause (in part) was what?

11. "Suppose there is a superbeing or supercomputer which has recorded the history of the universe and has been able to formulate whatever causal laws there are. It can foresee any and all possibilities. It contains a complete description of your genetic make-up, physiology, brain states, and mental states (including any that are unconscious.) Could such a computer always correctly predict what you were going to do and say and think next? If you believe it could, you believe in determinism. If you don't believe it could, you believe determinism is false."
    Two questions:
    a. Do you believe such a computer would always predict you correctly?
    b. What do you think Barrett would say about the full quotation—that is, about making such a situation an imaginative test case for determinism?

12. What kind of act does Barrett think is bound to be unpredictable? Do you agree with him? Explain.

13. Campbell says that he is dealing with "two main objections." What are these objections and what are they objections to?

14. Campbell imagines an "I" which can decide to act out of pleasure or duty. On what basis do you suppose this "I" makes its decisions?

15. What is Williams's objection to the idea of time travel?

2

God and the Problem
of Suffering

Fiction: The Vision

The first time I saw it, I had no idea what it was or what it would become. It was just a brilliant shimmering of light hovering over the lawn of the small park. I nudged the old man sitting next to me on the bench.

"What is that?" I asked him excitedly.

"What's what?"

"The light—right there in front of us."

He looked in the direction I pointed, and shook his head. Then he turned and looked at me suspiciously. Perhaps he was wondering if I was one of the crazy ones. In the days to come I would often wonder the same thing myself.

But I wasn't worried that first time. Whatever I saw was gone almost at once. "Just a trick of the light," I told the old man, to reassure him.

The thing appeared again, a few days later. First I heard a kind of humming sound, soft and sweet; the sound of it filled me with an inexplicable feeling of joy. I looked, and there was the light again, only more brilliant now, richer and deeper. I stood there for a time, caught up in its beauty. Then common sense intruded, and I began to feel anxious. What was happening? This didn't make any sense.

The third time the light appeared, I was making my way through a rush-hour crowd. The light was just overhead, and I stopped to look up, barely conscious of the people bumping into me. Within the light was an image of a woman's face.

"Who are you?" I said aloud.

"A friend. Don't be afraid."

The voice that answered was like the humming I'd heard earlier, only pitched higher. It was as if some wind instrument were doing a perfect imitation of human speech.

"What do you want?" I asked.

"To help you."

And then she was gone.

As I lowered my head, I saw the crowd staring at me. Some faces were smirking, some quizzical, and some frightened, but all were looking at me as if I were crazy. Suddenly I was terrified.

I pleaded my way into my doctor's office the next morning. She tried to be reassuring, but I could see she was worried. She referred me to a psychiatrist who interviewed me and then referred me to a neurologist who scheduled a battery of tests.

Sitting in my apartment on the evening before the tests, I was a nervous wreck. From what I could gather from the doctors, either I had a brain tumor or I was going crazy, and I didn't know which was worse. I was trying not to think about any of it when the light appeared again.

"No!" I moaned.

I looked down, pressing my hands over my eyes, to blot out the sight of it.

"Don't be frightened," said the voice.

"Go away. You're not real."

"I am real."

"You're a hallucination."

"I'm not."

The voice was soft and patient, like that of a kind parent confronting a contrary child. Something in me wanted so badly to give in to the voice. But I couldn't let myself. This whole thing was crazy.

"You are a hallucination," I said, insistently. "There's something wrong with my brain, and it's making you up. They're going to give me tests. They'll find out what's wrong. I'm going to get better."

There was a slight rippling of notes, like the imitation of soft laughter. "I think you will get better," said the voice. "But not the way you think."

The tests at the hospital took most of a day. The light appeared twice, just briefly.

"I won't stay," said the voice, the second time. "I just wanted to be here during the tests. That way, when nothing shows up, you'll know I'm real."

Nothing did show up on the tests. The neurologist sent me back to the psychiatrist.

"Your hallucination seems to have a sense of humor," said the psychiatrist. "What she obviously doesn't have is a degree in psychiatry. The fact that nothing shows up on those tests you had doesn't mean she isn't coming from your brain. When we say we can't find an organic cause, we're talking about lesions and tumors. We're certainly not saying that there's nothing chemical going on there."

"You think that's what it is?" I asked. "Something chemical?"

"The mind is all chemical."

"But what specifically is wrong with me?"

"If you want a name," he said, "the one I gave your insurance company is 'atypical psychosis.' But that's just a fancy way of saying that we can't find an organic cause and that your hallucinations don't fit some standard group-ing of symptoms. What you really want to know is whether we can treat this. The answer is yes. There are a whole range of antipsychotics that can be effec-tive with hallucinations. We'll start with Haldol."

"Just make this thing stop."

"We will."

We talked about dosage, what to expect, what to watch out for. Some of the possible side effects sounded scary, but none could be as scary as losing my mind. When I left the psychiatrist's office, I filled the prescription at the first pharmacy I could find, then rushed home. In the kitchen I began filling a glass with the six ounces of water I'd been told to take with the pill.

"Don't," said the voice, somewhere behind me. "Please, don't."

Somehow I'd known that I'd hear the voice just then. I felt myself grow panicky. I had a sudden, vivid sense that I was fighting for my sanity.

I slapped the water glass down on the drainboard and reached for the plastic pill container.

"Don't," said the voice, urgently. "Those pills will cut you off from me."

"They're going to make me well," I said, struggling with the child-proof lid.

"They're not going to make you well. They're only going to deaden your mind and your feelings. They're going to change you into something you don't want to be."

"I won't listen to you," I said, my panic growing worse with each unsuc-cessful tug at the container top.

"Do you know those street people with the vacant eyes? Do you want to be like them?"

"Shut up!" I yelled.

Suddenly the top broke loose, and pills went bouncing like small mar-bles over the kitchen floor. I dropped to my knees, grabbed a pill, and pushed it toward my mouth.

"Don't. The pills will just make you a zombie."

What the voice was saying was just close enough to the worst of the side effect warnings to make me hesitate. I stared at the pills for a moment, afraid to take them, afraid not to. There was a small "H" carved into the white pill, and the question "hell or help," "hell or help" started running through my mind. My hand was shaking with indecision, and suddenly the fear and frus-tration of the last few days came bursting out of me in sobs.

"I don't know what to do," I cried. "I don't know what's happening to me. I'm so scared."

I was on my knees on the floor, bent forward, my arms pressing against my chest as if I were trying to keep myself from coming apart. Gradually, over the sound of my tears, I began to hear the voice saying, "It's all right," over and over, softly, almost hypnotically. And then light seemed to fold itself around me and the panic subsided and the tears stopped and suddenly my whole being was flooded with joy. I felt peaceful and safe to the very core of myself, as if I had suddenly come home—not to any home I had ever known, but to some home I had only dreamed of having. I let my body fall gently sideways, so that I was sitting on the floor, my back against the kitchen counter. I closed my eyes, giving myself up to all those wonderful feelings.

"Feeling better?" asked the voice.

I laughed. "Yes."

Somewhere in my mind, hovering above all the joy, was a voice saying, No matter how good you feel, this is still crazy, and you're going to have to deal with it, you're going to have to take those pills. But for the moment the voice was distant and of no effect.

I opened my eyes. The light was now a few feet away, suspended between ceiling and floor. For the first time I was calm enough to study it. The light was translucent, blurring the objects behind it, like a bright piece of lightly frosted glass. The light itself was white, but with hundreds of flecks of color that would blink and disappear, to be replaced by others; it was like a huge piece of crystal that was turning minutely back and forth, reflecting a light source from somewhere else. And within the translucency was that face, a mirage within a mirage. It was the kindest, most beautiful face I had ever seen.

"I feel so good," I said. "I almost wish you were real."

"I am real."

"What are you supposed to be? God? An angel? The Virgin Mary?"

"No, nothing like that. I'm a physical thing, just like you are."

"We sure don't look much alike."

"There are different kinds of physical things. Matter and energy for one. Energy tends toward joy and continuation. Matter tends toward suffering and decay."

"You mean, you're energy, and I'm matter?"

"Let's just say that you're more matter than I am."

"I don't get it. Do you mean, you're from a different planet or dimension or something?"

"We are those who have evolved and survived. We're here to help you do the same."

Much to my surprise and embarrassment, I let out a huge yawn. I quickly covered my mouth.

"I'm sorry," I said. "Suddenly I feel so sleepy. Like.I'd been drugged."

"You're exhausted. You need sleep. You'd better get yourself to bed. You'll be sore in the morning if you sleep there."

"Carry me," I asked, feeling suddenly childlike.

The face smiled. "I'd like to do that. But it is forbidden. I would do you great harm if I touched your body."

"I don't understand. I felt you touch me before. I mean. . . ."

"I was only touching your spirit. Listen, now, before you fall asleep. Tomorrow, when you wake, you will begin to doubt again. All I ask is that you hold off taking the pills awhile longer. Hear me out. Give yourself a chance to believe. For your own sake. When you doubt, just remember how you felt tonight. The truth is in the feeling."

I almost took the pills the next day, and the next, and the next. But so far I have not. It is the feeling that holds me back. I only experience the rapture when the light actually enfolds me, but the memory of it is with me constantly, and a residue of joy. I ask myself: How can anything be crazy that feels so wonderful?

Not that I don't doubt and question and even argue. I spend most of our time together trying to make sense of what is happening. I'm still not sure I have.

"Why are you appearing to me?" I asked the woman in the light.

"We are trying to appear to many."

"Then why haven't I heard about other people seeing you?"

"Most don't. They are too closed to see anything. Others see a little and grow frightened and turn away. Still others see only what they want to see. You are one of the few to whom I appear as I am."

"But why me? I'm not particularly smart or good."

"Because of your longing. It opens you to the truth. And your simplicity, which allows you to receive it."

"Why are you here?"

"To help you."

"Help me what?"

"Survive," she said. "When the body dies, those who are matter die with it; those who have become energy, spirit, go on. Whole races have survived and continued their existence in the dimension of energy; others have almost totally died out. The human race is headed for virtual extinction. The few who have become energy are stragglers in the other dimension, grieving for their race. They have begged us who have numbers to try to make contact. So we are trying. I hope good will come of it. I fear not."

It all sounds so strange, and I still feel confused. Sometimes I come back to the point of thinking, This is all nonsense, you are sick. But then the light folds around me again, and I feel the rapture, and nothing else matters.

The voice says that I must give up obsessive rationality with its constant questionings and doubts. She says that I must give myself up to feeling, for it is feeling that will show me the truth. I am determined to try.

I still do not know if this is real or unreal, if I am sane or crazy. All I know, and need to know, is one thing:

I am happy.

* * * * *

Something has gone terribly wrong.

It did not happen all at once, but little by little.

The woman in the light told me that I must change my life, and I gave myself up to her charge. She had me make changes in my diet, and she gave me a series of physical and spiritual exercises. She was so sweet as she guided me, like a good mother who knows her child has some hard work to do and wants to spare the child any unnecessary discomfort. Most of the changes weren't so bad, and I was helped by her presence, by the rush of joy she sometimes gave me, and by the knowledge that I was transforming myself to a higher level of being.

But then the exercises became more and more uncomfortable, and one day I told her I didn't want to do one of the exercises any more. For the first time the light suddenly darkened, and the face became angry. I was so shocked at the sight that I couldn't move. Then the light brightened, and the face softened.

"I'm sorry," said the voice. "Sometimes you try me."

I was to begin to see that anger more often. One day one of the exercises drew some blood, and I stopped at once, feeling faint as I always do at the sight of my own blood. As I put my hand over the small cut, and averted my eyes, I saw that the light was nearly black and the face inside of it terrible.

"Continue!" she screamed.

"No," I said. "Stop, please. You're frightening me."

"Good," she yelled. "You're too slow, too cowardly. If I must frighten you, then I will. Don't you understand? The Day is almost upon us. If you're not ready, you will die!"

"What day?"

The light turned from dark crystal to a twilight gray. The face inside was no longer angry, but sad.

"I did not mean to tell you today," said the voice. "But perhaps it is just as well. I could not have put it off much longer."

"What day?" I asked again.

"The Day the Earth Will End."

"What? You never told me that."

"The Council just decided."

"What council?"

"They have grown impatient. Humans have become a blot on the universe. On the Day, the sky will grow red with an angry light, and the light will descend and touch the Earth, and all will be destroyed. Don't you see? You must be ready when the Day comes or you will be destroyed with the others."

"When?"

"The exact day hasn't been decided. A month, two months, a year . . . soon."

"I don't understand this. I'm scared. Please hold me."

"Not now. Joy will just make you lazy. You must work."

I tried to work as hard as she wanted, I really did. But I'm not good at pain, and the fear I was feeling seemed to inhibit me more than push me. Doubts began to come back, stronger now than before, and a voice in my head that kept growing louder was saying, This is all crazy after all; you must stop it, you know that; you must take the pills before this sickness destroys you.

One night I woke up from a recurrent nightmare in which the woman in the light was having me mutilate myself. I was shaking with fright, and that voice in my head was saying, take the pills, take the pills. I stumbled out of bed, filled a glass of water, and opened the pill container.

"Don't, please, don't," said the voice, as I knew it would.

"Yes," I said, and gulped down a pill. I turned to face the light. "This has turned into a nightmare. I want it to stop."

I expected anger. Instead the face was sad.

"You won't see me anymore," said the voice. "That pill will close your mind. I'm sorry. I had such hope that I could save you."

The light disappeared.

I'm better now. The pills aren't what I was afraid they'd be. I do sleep more, and I feel groggy sometimes, and I guess I feel as if my body and mind move a little more slowly than they used to. But overall I feel okay, and I don't see those visions anymore.

Yet sometimes—not often, just once in awhile—when I'm at home at night, staring out the window at the peace of the star-studded darkness, I imagine that the sky is beginning to glow, and as it becomes a deeper and deeper red, I catch a faint odor of something beginning to burn.

And I am afraid.

Fiction: Surprise! It's Judgment Day

The stage suggests a cloud bank. Across the length of the stage is a high wall that appears to be of white brick. In the center of the wall is a pair of golden doors which are closed. Off to the right is a golden throne. Seated on the throne is a figure with white hair and beard. He is wearing a jeweled crown, and his legs are crossed beneath a thick white robe.

Martin enters from the left, rubbing his eyes. He is dressed in a white hospital gown.

MARTIN: Well, I'll be damned. So the fairy tales were true, after all.

GOD: In a sense.

Martin glances toward the bearded figure and groans.

MARTIN: Go ahead. Tell me you're Saint Peter, and make my day.

GOD: Now, now, Professor Martin. Any Sunday school child could do better than that. What would Saint Peter be doing on a throne?

MARTIN: You're not God?

GOD: I am.

MARTIN: So much for all the theologians' warnings against anthropomorphism.

GOD: Oh, this is just a momentary form, a matter of convenience. Your convenience, I might add. I could have spoken out of a whirlwind or a burning bush. But I felt I owed you a face-to-face confrontation.

MARTIN: Confrontation? That suits me just fine. I wouldn't mind getting a word in before I get the fire and brimstone.

GOD: Fire and brimstone? Let's not go jumping to conclusions, shall we? Tell me, what do you think of all this?

MARTIN: Regrettable. And, quite frankly, pretty tacky. The cloud, the throne, the beard. Cecil B. deMille could have done better. I would have given you more credit.

GOD: But not much.

MARTIN: No, not much.

GOD: Let's just say that I thought this bit of pop religion would put you more at ease. A little joke of mine, though at whose expense I'm not quite sure. But this is not my usual form, I can assure you.

MARTIN: No, you don't exactly look like the Unmoved Mover in that outfit. Saint Thomas Aquinas would have been shocked. Well, now—God with a sense of humor. I would have expected you to be more pompous. But no doubt it's gallows humor, and you own the gallows.

GOD: Do you remember how you got here?

MARTIN: Yes, I think so. I remember the car accident. I remember the doctor telling me that I had fractured my skull. I remember being taken into surgery. I suppose the rest of it was like the old joke: I was at death's door and the doctor pulled me through.

GOD: You were quite impressive as you were getting the anesthetic. I believe you muttered some quotation from Robinson Jeffers about there being no harps and habitations beyond the stars. And something from Camus about the benign indifference of the universe. And, oh yes, that line from Socrates: "Eternity is but a single night." As you can see, Professor Martin, eternity is quite well lit.

MARTIN: Go ahead and laugh. I guess you're entitled. But their words have more dignity than yours. Damn it, this shouldn't be true. You know it shouldn't. It defies all reason. A God who displaces humankind from Paradise for exercising an understandable curiosity, who lets himself be crucified to save some, but insists on punishing others eternally, all in the name of some barbaric penal code that he created but claims he must follow—no, it's too absurd.

GOD: What? Are you going to make of me some ranting fundamentalist? It seems you like easy targets.

MARTIN: Are you telling me you're an ecumenicalist? Glimpses of God behind the myths and half-truths of all religions? Well, score one for the liberal theologians. It doesn't matter. Liberalize yourself all you want. Reason says you shouldn't exist.

GOD: Some philosophers have thought otherwise.

MARTIN: Yes. You had some brilliant defenders—once. But now their arguments are merely historical curiosities. Anselm and Descartes claimed that the definition of a perfect God necessarily implies that He exists. A perfect God lacks nothing and hence does not lack existence. But that line of argument would equally prove the existence of a perfect turtle and a perfect martini. Aquinas, following Aristotle, claimed that reason indicates there must be a First Cause, a First Mover, who created the world, set it in motion, and sustains its existence. But there is nothing obviously false in the idea of a material world that is self-sufficient and has been eternally in motion. You're not going to try to defend those arguments of Anselm and Aquinas, are you?

GOD: No, Professor Martin. Nor will I try to defend the argument that a vast, intricate universe of elegantly formulable laws could not exist without intelligent creation or control. Though I must admit I've always liked that one.

MARTIN: In any case, the issue of design ultimately indicates that a respectable God could not exist. The laws of the universe may be mathematically elegant, but they crush and they kill. No respectable God would allow people to suffer as they do.

GOD: So. We come to the heart of the matter.

MARTIN: Yes, indeed. As a moral assessment, one must say that if this world is designed, it is the work of a bumbler or a sadist. Which, by the way, are you?

GOD: Not quite either, I hope.

MARTIN: But you did design the world?

GOD: Yes, I did. But look here, Professor Martin. I understand your anger, your impulse toward hyperbole. Still, it is hyperbole. What about my celebrated free-will defense? Free will is a great good, a necessary ingredient in the best of all possible worlds. And it would be contradictory for me to give people free will and, at the same time, guarantee that they never use that freedom to cause suffering.

MARTIN: As you must know, it is not an adequate defense. At most, it would only justify the suffering caused by people. It doesn't apply to the suffering caused by natural events, like diseases, earthquakes, and floods. But, in any case, I don't concede you the free-will defense. Freedom costs too much, it has too many victims. Free will isn't worth the suffering.

GOD: Can you really be so flippant about it? Don't you feel an attraction toward freedom—or at least recognize that another person might? Don't you feel it is an issue about which rational individuals might disagree?

MARTIN: Perhaps. But I still say that freedom isn't worth the suffering. Nonetheless, one still must explain the suffering caused by natural events. If you try to justify it as a punishment for people's misuse of their freedom, then I say that your notion of punishment is barbaric.

GOD: Well, what about what you have called the "virtue defense"? Virtues are good, and a necessary ingredient in the best of all possible worlds. And the idea of virtue in a world without suffering is contradictory. It would be impossible to be courageous where there is no danger, to be generous where it costs nothing, to be sympathetic where no one is hurt.

MARTIN: Even if I conceded that argument, there doesn't have to be so much suffering.

GOD: What? A couple of teaspoons would have sufficed for the grandeur of the drama?

MARTIN: Nevertheless, I don't concede the argument. It turns virtue inside out. It makes virtue good in itself. But reflection shows that virtue is good only as a means—a means to happiness. What is the point of courage, generosity, sympathy, if not to alleviate suffering? To create suffering for the sake of sympathy is like kicking a man in the shins so you can feel sorry for him. It's absurd.

GOD: So if you had been in my place, you would have . . .

MARTIN: Made human beings happy. And left them happy.

GOD: But happiness is so bland.

MARTIN: To the outsider, perhaps. But to the person who is happy, it is sufficient.

GOD: And so you would have created a world without virtue?

MARTIN: Yes. A world in which virtue wasn't necessary.

GOD: And the intellectual virtues? You would discard them as well? The painful, heroic struggle for beauty and knowledge?

MARTIN: Yes, if they must conflict with happiness.

GOD: But they do, do they not? Anyway, if happiness is the good, then anything else becomes superfluous.

MARTIN: Yes.

GOD: Many people would view your values with contempt.

MARTIN: Yes, I understand that. One can look back over the centuries at, say, the Egyptian pyramids and think: This is good; this is where the human race excelled. But a closer look reveals the pain of the slaves who built them, and one should see that this was wrong. One is not entitled to excellence if unwilling people must suffer for it. And, in one way or another, some always do.

GOD: What a utilitarian you are!

MARTIN: Yes. With slight misgivings, but yes. The utilitarian is right, and you are wrong. And we haven't even mentioned hell yet, though I am sure that we, or rather I, will be getting to that shortly. Hell is an atrocity beyond debate.

GOD: You really do want me to be a fundamentalist, don't you? There is no hell, Professor Martin. The thought of creating it crossed my mind once, but I never took the idea seriously. There was a kind of Hades, or Limbo, once, but I soon gave it up. No, now there is only Paradise.

MARTIN: Knowing you, that should be fun. Probably morning prayers, cold showers, and occasionally Black Plague, to keep us on our toes. But even if it is pleasant, you still have much to answer for. And it is unanswerable. Voltaire, Dostoevsky, and countless others whose views I accept saw that. They wouldn't be put off by your whales and whirlwinds, as Job was. Dostoevsky's Ivan Karamazov was right: Once one child suffers, this is a botched world, and nothing could ever make it right again.

GOD: Voltaire and Dostoevsky are here, by the way.

MARTIN: Ah! I shall enjoy talking with them. Or, if that is not possible, then listening, anyway.

GOD: There would be some difficulty in that. But to get back to the point that you insist on dramatizing: I do take full responsibility for this world that I've created. And I do not believe that I should have created it differently. The struggle for virtue, beauty, and knowledge: That is what I find most admirable. Though I admit that, as an outsider, I am open to the accusation that I lack sympathy. However, I find the world interesting just as it is. I shall continue to insist on the spectacle.

MARTIN: The spectacle—yes. Like some Roman emperor.

GOD: As you will. But you're a utilitarian. You believe in the greatest happiness. Shouldn't the happiness of an infinite God weigh heavily on your scales?

MARTIN: So the struggle goes on forever—for your entertainment.

GOD: Not just mine. Don't forget there are many people who don't accept your values. Perhaps I could justify the world as it is, as a concession to them. In any case, human beings may struggle forever, but not each person. An individual struggle that went on forever would lose all meaning and must lead to utter despair or boredom. There must be surcease, reward.

MARTIN: But how can you consistently manage that? There's a lovely little paradox that the believers must confront: If freedom and virtue are the ultimate good, and in turn require suffering, then how could heaven be blissful? Or, if somehow God could manage to create freedom and virtue without suffering, then why didn't God omit the suffering in the first place?

GOD: As I've said, the struggle is good, but it cannot go on forever. So the final result is a compromise between my set of values and yours. Professor Martin, the world is not to your liking, and I apologize for that. I could never convince you that this is the best of all possible worlds, and I shall not really try. But all I have taken from you is, in the words of my lesser poets, a drop of time in the sea of eternity. Don't be so hard on me for that. The rest of time is yours.

God flicks his hand, and the golden doors open slowly. Inside, figures in white hospital gowns walk about, slowly and somewhat mechanically. Martin studies them for several moments.

MARTIN: Their expressions don't change.

GOD: They always smile, of course. Why not? They're happy, blissful. Ecstatic, in fact.

MARTIN: But there are just people and clouds. Where's the beauty of it?

GOD: In the eye of the beholder. Or, better, in the mind, since they don't look at much. I could create changing landscapes, I suppose, fill the surroundings with Raphaels and Donatellos, have Mozart and Beethoven played, hand them Plato and Shakespeare. But it would not make any difference. At most, it would serve as a sop to my conscience, and I prefer to know what I do. They're perfectly happy, just as they are, and anything else would be extraneous, irrelevant. They're happy. Just as you shall be in a moment.

MARTIN: They're happy?

GOD: Yes.

MARTIN: And I shall join them?

GOD: Yes.

MARTIN: Wait a moment . . .

GOD: I don't see the point. We've reached our impasse. I felt that I owed you a chance to have your say, and that I owed you an explanation—even if you did not find it satisfactory.

MARTIN: It looks like death in there.

GOD: In a sense it is, of course. But really, our differences aside, there is not much else one can do with people forever. Would you rather I extinguished you?

MARTIN: No.

GOD: Well, then. By the way, I should tell you that I've enjoyed our talk. I really have. But there are others I must see. It is time for you to go inside now.

MARTIN: No, wait!

Martin turns toward God with a panicked, pleading gesture. God points at Martin. Martin's body freezes for a moment, then releases, his arms falling to his sides. On Martin's face is an expression that seems genuinely happy, but unchanging.

GOD: Enter, Martin. Enter.

Martin turns and slowly walks through the gates, which close behind him. God stares thoughtfully toward the gates, shaking his head slightly. A young girl, Katherine, enters from stage left. She, too, is wearing a hospital gown. Upon seeing her, God quickly smoothes his beard and adopts a very dignified posture. Then he smiles at her.

KATHERINE: Oh, Father, is that you?

GOD: Yes, Katherine.

KATHERINE: Oh, Father, you are just as I always imagined you. Then you heard my prayer?

GOD: I always hear.

KATHERINE: And you forgave me?

GOD: Yes.

KATHERINE: Will I live in heaven?

GOD: Yes, my child. Heaven is yours.

At a gesture from God, the gates open again. Martin can be seen walking among the people inside.

KATHERINE: Oh, Father, they are all so happy! Oh, thank you, Father, thank you.

GOD: Bless you, my child.

Katherine rushes toward the gates. Just before she reaches them, God flicks his hand, and she adopts the mechanical walk of the others. The gates close. God lowers his head a bit, as if tired and a little disgusted. He looks up.

GOD: That seems to be all for now. Thank goodness! This place depresses me so.

God gets down from the throne and takes a couple of steps to the right. He stops and removes the crown, tossing it on the seat of the throne, where it lands with a clatter. He exits to the right, unbuttoning his robe.

Questions

1. a. Give two different explanations for what is happening to the narrator in "The Vision."
    b. Would there be some decisive way to determine which of the two explanations is correct?

2. The vision says that the truth is in the feeling. In which way does feeling guide the narrator in the first part of the story? In the second part of the story?
3. How would you have reacted if you'd been in the narrator's place?
4. In "Surprise! It's Judgment Day," what is the complaint that Martin is bringing against God?
5. God presents in His defense what are called the "free-will defense" and the "virtue defense." Explain these two defenses.
6. "Even an omnipotent God cannot do contradictory things." Explain the role that this premise plays in the defenses of suffering named in question 5.
7. Does Martin change his viewpoint at the end of the story? If so, how and why?

DISCUSSION

TRADITIONAL PROOFS FOR GOD'S EXISTENCE

In "Surprise! It's Judgment Day," Martin dismisses as unconvincing three famous arguments for the existence of God: the ontological, the cosmological, and the teleological. Today many philosophers and theologians would agree with Martin. But the three arguments play an important historical role in philosophy, and a couple of the arguments relate to impulses that still tend people toward belief in God. Thus the arguments are worth examining.

The **ontological argument** (which derives its name from the Greek word for "being") is the argument that the actual existence of God can be proved from the concept of God. This argument, first formulated by Saint Anselm in the eleventh century, was reformulated by a number of post-Renaissance philosophers, including Descartes. Descartes's formulation goes roughly as follows:

1. The concept of God is that of a perfect being.
2. A perfect being lacks no perfections.
3. Existence is a perfection.
4. (Therefore) God does not lack existence; God exists.

When confronted with this proof, some people are inclined to ask: Where did Descartes get that definition of God? The defender would say: "It's a standard definition" or "I just made it up." When one wonders about the existence of something, the source of the idea is not generally at issue. One could invent the concept of a "drog" ("a doglike creature that hops like a frog") and ask whether such a thing exists. There would seem to be nothing questionable about such an inquiry.

Descartes's contemporaries (like Anselm's) thought that the ontological argument could be used to prove the existence of many perfect beings and hence must be fallacious. The example that detractors used to illustrate the argument's shortcomings was that of proving the existence of a perfect island, but the example of a perfect turtle or a perfect martini would do as well. A perfect martini can't lack existence and must exist. But there is a rejoinder to this: A perfect martini or a perfect island is a contradiction in terms, because by definition such a thing would be limited, mindless, and hence imperfect.

One might argue that Descartes's proof equally shows that God does not exist, since He could not lack nonexistence. But the word "perfection" supposedly excludes such "attributes" as nonthinkingness, nongoodness, and nonexistence.

What seems to be the decisive objection was first formulated by Immanuel Kant in the late eighteenth century. The objection goes somewhat as follows: There is a radical difference between a statement about a concept and a statement about existence. To introduce a concept is to introduce a kind of (mental) picture. To claim existence is to claim that there is something in the world that has the characteristics portrayed in that picture. Introducing a concept is uncontroversial only because it differs from an existential claim. Descartes introduces a concept of God that implicitly includes an existential claim, and this is *not* uncontroversial. If such a step were permissible, then anything could be defined into existence. I could introduce the concept of an "exista-unicorn" ("a horselike figure with a horn and with existence"). I could then derive the existence of the unicorn from that definition. The point here is not that Descartes violates a logical convention. Rather, it is that if he violates this convention, then he is required to do something not normally required of someone introducing a concept: He must prove the existence of the thing before his definition is acceptable. This, of course, he does not do.

The **cosmological argument** (which derives its name from the Greek word for "universe"), or "First Cause argument," was given its most famous formulations (the name actually encompasses several interrelated arguments) by the thirteenth-century philosopher Saint Thomas Aquinas, who was influenced by Aristotle. This argument proceeds from some highly general premises about the universe to the conclusion that Martin summarizes as follows: "there must be a First Cause, a First Mover, who created the world, set it in motion, and sustains its existence."

For some reason, people seem more troubled by the thought of an infinite past than that of an infinite future. People are tempted to say that everything must have had a beginning and to argue for a First Cause on the basis of this premise. But this premise, even if rational, not only does not support but actually contradicts the conclusion of the cosmological argument. For the argument supposes that there is one thing that had no beginning, namely God.

In earlier times, at least, many supposed that things in motion must have been set in motion; rest, rather than motion, was the natural state of things. They argued that the universe must have been set in motion by a First Mover, God. But the supposition that rest is the natural state of things does not seem to be self-evident and, in fact, is denied by modern science.

One of Saint Thomas Aquinas's formulations of the argument goes as follows: The things in our experience can be or not be, since they are generated and corrupted (they are born and they die). There is no necessity about their existence. (They are, in later terminology, "contingent beings.") But if everything were able not to exist, everything would have gone out of existence in the course of an infinite past; nothing would exist now. But things do exist. Therefore, something must exist whose existence is necessary, something that could not possibly *not* exist, something that has generated and sustains the existence of the things that we observe. This necessary being is God.

To set out the cosmological argument a bit more formally (and simply):

1. It is possible for the things in our experience to exist or not exist (we observe such things being born and dying); these things are "contingent."
2. If all things were contingent, nothing would exist (such things would have gone out of existence over the course of an infinite past).
3. But things do exist.
4. (Therefore) There must exist something whose existence is necessary, which cannot not exist; that being is God.

This argument is difficult, and the interpretations of it are diverse. Saint Thomas Aquinas claims that the things that we observe can either be or not be (are contingent) and must depend on some necessary being. First of all, a degree of sense must be given to the notion of a "necessary being." Some proponents of the argument have suggested that a necessary being is one whose definition implies its existence. The definition of "chair" does not imply its existence; the definition of "universe" does not imply its existence; the definition of "God" does imply His existence. But by this interpretation, the cosmological argument becomes a version of the ontological argument and is subject to the same critique: No definition implies the existence of the thing defined.

"Necessary being" could be a description of something that, as a matter of fact, is self-sufficient, eternal, and cannot be destroyed: something that depends on nothing else for its existence. If one supposes that there never was or will be a time when nothing exists, then it follows that there is a "necessary being"—at least in the trivial sense that this phrase could apply to the totality of things that ever exist. The emphasis of the argument would then shift to the claim that the things in the physical-mental world that we observe are "contingent" in the sense that they must depend on something else for their existence. It is true that the things we observe are generated and corrupted, but it is not clear that they disappear, as opposed to breaking down into more basic, enduring particles, or into energy. It is not clear why the universe, conceived as a system of things and relations, must necessarily depend on something else for its existence; it is not clear that the universe could not be a "necessary being" in the sense that it is self-sufficient. Yet if the cosmological argument is to be convincing, its proponents must show us why the universe is likely to be dependent on something else.

The third traditional argument for the existence of God is the **teleological argument** (which derives its name from the Greek word for "end"/ "goal"), or the "argument from design." One version of this argument goes as follows:

The complex universe is not chaotic but orderly; its workings can be described by relatively simple scientific theories. Surely, it is more reasonable to suppose that this universe was designed by some Great Intelligence, God, than to suppose that it exists without design.

Popular forms of this argument often gain apparent force by restricting one to a bogus dichotomy between design and chance. One is invited to consider two situations. The first: A woman takes some pieces of metal and glass and carefully constructs a watch. The second: A woman takes some pieces of metal and glass and tosses them over her shoulder; by chance the pieces fall together in such a way as to form a functioning watch. The advocate of the argument then says: Surely, it is more reasonable to suppose that the universe was formed as in the first situation rather than as in the second.

If these were the only possibilities, a rational person would conclude that the universe was designed. But there is another possibility: that an orderly universe has always existed. Such a universe could not be said to have "happened by chance," since that phrase describes some sort of haphazard beginning, and this third possibility supposes no beginning at all.

However, the teleological argument can be formulated without using the design—chance dichotomy. Another version would be this:

1. The universe resembles human machines in being complex and orderly.
2. Like effects have like causes.
3. Human machines were designed by some intelligence.
4. (Therefore) The universe was designed by some intelligence (God).

There are several problems with this argument. We are supposed to be impressed by the close similarity between human machines and the universe (or parts of it). But to make such a comparison we need a contrast. The universe is more like a human machine than—what? If we contrast machines with things that people just throw together, the argument assumes the design–chance dichotomy again. We cannot contrast human machines with natural processes because, according to the argument, natural processes are designed like human machines. Thus, the argument seems to rule out legitimate, observable contrasts of the sort needed to establish the argument.

Furthermore, human minds are not things isolated from natural processes but themselves come about via natural processes. Why, then, is it not just as reasonable to suppose that designs and minds are results of the natural orderliness of things?

Still, some people are inclined to claim that it is a self-evident principle of reason that orderliness must come about through intelligence. But is this principle truly self-evident?

RELIGIOUS EXPERIENCE

Another possible reason for belief in God is religious experience, either experiences one hears reported by others or experiences one has oneself. Such experiences range from dramatic visions to a gentle sense of presence. There are some religious sects in which everyone claims to have had such experiences.

Religious experiences can be explained either as true experiences of the divine on the one hand, or as brain impairment, mental illness, or wishful thinking on the other.

In "The Vision," the narrator has rather dramatic visions. The vision itself claims it is true, the narrator isn't sure, and all the doctors immediately assume the vision is a symptom of illness.

How are we to judge religious experiences?

People sometimes dismiss religion experience—even religion, in general—on the basis of psychological theories about why people need to believe. Even assuming those psychological theories are true (a big assumption), this way of reasoning is fallacious. It confuses motives and reasons. To demonstrate that someone needs to believe or would like to believe A is not to show that A is false.

If there is considerable evidence that a belief is false (or no evidence that it is true), and numbers of people continue to hold that belief, it is legitimate to inquire into the psychology of that belief. But the psychology of a belief, by itself, will not show whether that belief is true or false.

What we want to know is this: Are particular religious experiences **veridical**—that is, true experiences of some objective reality (as with everyday perceptions of cars and trees and people); or, are they *nonveridical*—that is, merely subjective (as with dreams and fantasies)?

In trying to decide such an issue as this, we normally reason by analogy. That is, we consider cases of perception where we agree on what is and isn't veridical, and we determine what criteria we use to judge what is or isn't veridical in those cases. We then apply those same criteria to the perception in question.

What are our everyday criteria for the veridicality of perception? It seems that veridicality here has to do with what a normal observer would/could perceive under certain conditions. The concept of normality here is very tricky. We want to set some limits on the kinds of persons whose testimony we will accept: For instance, if someone is accusing an auto body shop of painting a new fender the wrong color, obviously we don't want the testimony of someone who is color-blind admitted as testimony. On the other hand, we don't want to **beg the question** (assume the truth of what's at issue) by simply dismissing anyone who doesn't see it a certain way as "not normal." The criteria for what is normal should be established independently of what's at issue.

Given reasonable criteria for "normal," we judge perceptions to be veridical if normal people are having those perceptions and if others would have those same perceptions in similar circumstances. If a family reports a spaceship parked in the backyard, and the spaceship just happens to fly away when the neighbors or the news reporters come to take a look, that story isn't going to be judged veridical.

How does religious experience fare under our normal criteria of veridicality? The results are at best ambiguous. The really dramatic religious visions are such isolated occurrences that they are not going to get much support from our normal criteria of veridicality. If we consider the totality of religious experience from the very dramatic to the very subtle ("I just sense that God is watching me"), then the case for verdicality looks better. But then there is the problem of differences in the content of the experiences: This Native American tribe has one sort of experience, this Christian sect has another, and these Buddhists have yet another.

If these are veridical experiences of the Divine, why are they so different and often contradictory? One could possibly infer from this that religious experiences are confused perceptions of some divine reality whose nature we can only guess at. But at the very best, this would be support for the vaguest of religious beliefs, one that wouldn't satisfy many believers.

Another complication here is the awful visions and voices that, for instance, schizophrenics experience. There is a tendency these days to think of the positive religious experiences as possibly veridical and the negative religious experiences as definitely nonveridical, as mental illness. (The narrator in "The Vision" is much more inclined to think of the vision as nonveridical when it becomes negative.) But unless one begs the question by assuming in advance that a certain kind of God does exist (in which case religious experience isn't really being used as evidence at all), it's hard to see what grounds there would be for not including negative visions in the pool of religious experience. If they are included, the increased variety we get from their addition either renders more doubtful the veridicality of religious experience or renders more ambiguous the nature of the Divine.

One thing that is intriguing about many supernatural beliefs is that they include within them an explanation for why they don't satisfy the normal criteria of rationality or veridicality. For instance:

DOUBTER: "By any rational standards, that belief is obviously false."

BELIEVER: "That's because rationality comes from pride, and pride always gives false answers."

Or:

DOUBTER: "I can't find God."

BELIEVER: "That's because you don't really want to."

DOUBTER: "I feel like I want to."

BELIEVER: "No. The fact that you don't see Him shows that you don't really want to."

"The Vision" contains some of this. The narrator is told to give up "obsessive rationality with its constant questionings and doubts." And:

"Why are you appearing to me?" I asked.

"We're trying to appear to many."

"Then why haven't I heard about other people seeing you?"

"Most don't. They are too closed to see anything. Others see a little and grow frightened and turn away. Still others see only what they want to see. You are one of the few to whom I appear as I am."

"But why me? I'm not particularly smart or good."

"Because of your longing. It opens you to the truth. And your simplicity, which allows you to receive it."

To some, such reasoning seems a good explanation for why something that doesn't meet our normal criteria for judging truth could still be true (maybe even obviously true). To others such reasoning seems a determined effort to avoid seeing the truth.

ATHEISM AND THE PROBLEM OF SUFFERING

Thus far we have talked about possible reasons for believing in the existence of God. Now we come to a possible reason for disbelieving.

There are three possible positions one can take on the question of whether God exists. The **theist** believes there is a God. The **agnostic** isn't sure one way or the other. The **atheist** believes there is no God.

Perhaps you have heard something like the following argument: "It's absurd to be an atheist, as opposed to an agnostic or a theist. How could anyone possibly prove that God doesn't exist!"

If you are sympathetic to this argument, imagine yourself in the following situation. A friend, looking out the window, says, "My goodness, there's a huge pink whale lying in the backyard." You laugh at the idea and wouldn't even bother to look except that you happen to be looking anyway (and you see nothing out there but lawn). Your friend gets indignant. "Wait a minute," she says. "I can see how you might be unsure of whether there's a huge pink whale in the backyard. But it would be irrational to believe there isn't one. How could you possibly prove that?"

The point is that there are a lot of things in the world that you positively believe didn't happen or don't exist. We decide that if a certain claim were true, certain other things ought to happen; if those other things don't happen, that is taken as evidence that the original claim is false. That is, under certain circumstances, we take the absence of certain kinds of evidence to count as evidence against. We all reason in this way every day. This is not to say that the question of God's existence is as straightforward as the question of whether there is a pink whale in the backyard. It is only to say that one can't dismiss atheism as absurd in advance of a discussion of grounds for believing in God.

Some atheists have based their belief on the absence of certain evidence that they think would exist if God did (e.g., miracles, consistent religious experience from culture to culture, etc.). Others, however, have claimed that there is positive evidence that God does not exist, namely the amount of suffering in the world. This kind of claim amounts to a kind of negative version of the argument from design. According to the argument from design, the complex orderliness of the world indicates that it must have been designed by God. Here an opposite claim is made: The suffering in the world indicates that it could not have been designed by God.

As Martin says in "Surprise!": "The laws of the universe may be mathematically elegant, but they crush and they kill. No respectable God would allow people to suffer as they do."

It has been traditional in much of our culture to view God as omnipotent (all powerful), omniscient (all-knowing), and perfectly good. The existence of suffering poses a tough challenge for a theist who believes in such a God. How could a God who is perfectly good, can do absolutely anything He wants to do, and knows everything there is to know possibly create a world in which so many of His creatures suffer so terribly?

A theist who believes in a God who lacks one of these characteristics has a ready explanation for suffering: A God who lacks omnipotence or omniscience does not have the power or knowledge to eliminate suffering, and a God who is not perfectly good is morally defective and doesn't care to eliminate suffering. The existence of suffering is no evidence against the existence of gods like these. But it is possible evidence against the existence of a God who is supposed to have all three of those characteristics.

The problem here is what's called the "problem of suffering": Does the existence of suffering show that there could not be a God who is omnipotent, omniscient, and perfectly good?

OMNIPOTENCE AND CONTRADICTION

At first glance, it may seem obvious that the existence of suffering rules out the possibility of there being a God who is omnipotent, omniscient, and perfectly good. Such a God would create the best of all possible worlds. In the best of all possible worlds, there would exist human beings with free will who were happy and virtuous. Obviously, this world isn't such a world. Therefore, there is no such God.

But many theists make the following reply: The world you have just described is not a *possible* world. The idea of creating such a world is contradictory. Even an omnipotent God could not do contradictory things. Therefore, God can in no way be blamed for not having created such a world.

This reply poses two arguments that need to be elaborated in some detail:

1. Even an omnipotent God could not do what is contradictory.
2. The idea of creating a world in which human beings with free will are virtuous and happy is a contradiction.

Throughout the centuries, many theologians have felt that God, to be omnipotent, must be able to do contradictory things. He must be able to create a chair that is not a chair, a triangle that has four sides. To say that God cannot do such things is to suppose that God is limited and hence not omnipotent.

Today most philosophers and theologians reject the claim that an omnipotent God would have to do contradictory things. This claim, they say, results from a misunderstanding about the nature of contradictions. It supposes that contradictions describe the most difficult kind of tasks. In truth, contradictions describe nothing at all. In this sense, they are analogous to nonsense statements. One should no more expect an omnipotent God to create a chair that is not a chair than one should expect Him to "oop erg alban ipple ong."

In contradictory phrases, the individual words make sense but the combination of words is senseless. To say "create a chair that is not a chair" is like drawing a picture of a chair on a blackboard, erasing the picture, then pointing to the board and saying, "There, make me one of those." But what is portrayed on the blackboard, finally, is not some difficult task or other; nothing at all is portrayed there.*

This issue is controversial, and the remarks above are too brief to do justice to the differing points of view. But for any theist who is tempted to say that an omnipotent God must be able to do contradictory things, one can add a rather powerful *ad hominem* argument, making the theist uncomfortable with his or her reasoning. One can say: You have just denied yourself any recourse to the traditional explanations of why God might have allowed suffering.

Many theists suppose that God, at the time of creation, was faced with certain forced options. He could either eliminate all suffering or create a world in which human beings had free will and might be virtuous. To do both would be contradictory. God quite properly chose to create a world in which human beings had free will and virtuousness, rather than creating a world in which they were unfree, nonvirtuous, and happy. As in the story "Surprise!" I shall divide these arguments into two defenses: the free-will defense and the virtue defense. But before discussing these two defenses, let's consider another "defense" that is not much discussed in the literature but which many students offer and find convincing: the claim that it is impossible to have happiness without unhappiness.

DOES HAPPINESS REQUIRE UNHAPPINESS?

In the story "Surprise!" God and Martin assume that it would be possible to have a world in which everyone was happy (as heaven itself is supposed to demonstrate). The question they debate is whether or not such a world would indeed be better than the alternatives. However, if it is impossible to have a world in which everyone is happy, then their whole discussion would seem to be beside the point. Thus we had better ask: Is it impossible to have happiness without unhappiness?

Often a discussion of this issue gets sidetracked by inflated, soap-opera conceptions of happiness (as in "Yes, everything is going well, and yes, I'm

---

*In "A Little Omniscience Goes a Long Way," in Chapter 1, God attributes the impossibility of doing contradictory things to His decree. But this impossibility would seem intrinsic to any rational system of thought; it would exist simultaneously with God's thought and would not be the result of some subsequent decree. Note also that God's longing to do contradictory things would be, in this analysis, absurd.

feeling fine, but am I really *happy*?"). Such a rarefied notion of happiness is not relevant to the problem of suffering. We all know what it is to wince and say, "Oh, that hurts." We all know what it is to say, "Boy, I'm really feeling good today." Those challenging the theist on the problem of suffering are saying that God should have created the world so that there were no feelings like the former (and worse), only feelings like the latter. To keep the issue down to earth, think of the question we're discussing as whether it is possible to have pleasant feelings without unpleasant feelings.

There are two other confusions that often come up in discussing this issue:

1. "Human beings are such that they cannot be happy all the time and thus God couldn't have made a world in which there was only happiness." Even if the first part of the statement were true, the second part doesn't follow logically from the first. If human beings can't be happy all the time, then perhaps God should have created different creatures who could be. To support the no-happiness-without-unhappiness claim requires one to show that no possible creature could be happy all the time.

2 "Without a contrast you couldn't know what happiness was; thus you can't have happiness without unhappiness." Again, the conclusion of the argument doesn't follow from the premise. Whether there could be only happiness is one thing; whether, if there was only happiness, we would know it was happiness, would call it "happiness," is another. Supporting the latter claim is not enough to demonstrate the former. For instance, I think I can imagine a world that is all red (let's say different shades of red). I might agree that creatures in that world wouldn't know it was red (as opposed to yellow), wouldn't have the word "red"; but the world would still be red.

In order to show that an omnipotent God could not have created happiness without unhappiness, it would be necessary to show that the idea of happiness without unhappiness is contradictory.

Even if that could be shown, it wouldn't signify much in terms of the problem of suffering. Any defense of suffering is going to have to justify a lot of suffering. The claim that happiness without unhappiness is contradictory would seem to justify only a little suffering for contrast. The only claim that would really be useful in this context would be the claim that it would be contradictory to have a lot of happiness without a lot of unhappiness. It's hard to see what the argument for that might be.

In any case, note that both the free-will and virtue defenses assume that a happy world would have been possible, but argue that it wouldn't have been the best of the possible (noncontradictory) worlds.

THE FREE-WILL DEFENSE

The **free-will defense** claims that:

1. Free will is a great good and a necessary ingredient in the best of all possible worlds.

2. It would be contradictory for God to give human beings free will and yet guarantee that they never use their free will to harm themselves and others.

3. Therefore, there is likely to be suffering in the best of all possible worlds.

To elaborate on item 2: If human beings have free will, then their choices are not caused. It would be contradictory for God to give human beings free will and, at the same time, control their choices so that they never make choices that would cause unhappiness.

People readily accept the free-will defense. But there are serious questions one can raise about it.

Most people do think that free will is a great good. But in the previous chapter, it was suggested that this opinion may result from a misunderstanding about what free will is. If one accepts the argument in that chapter, one would probably decide that having free will would not be of much value.

Even if one does believe that free will is a great good, one should ask whether it is really worth the great suffering it has supposedly caused. Often the options here are misconceived. Many religious tracts imply that the only alternative to a world with free will is a world in which people move about like zombies. Given our previous discussion, this is obviously false. Free will pertains only to the causes of one's choices. It implies nothing about the particular characteristics of one's facial expressions, movements, feelings, or thoughts. Free will, as we have seen, would not be an observable thing. What would you and others look like without free will? You would look exactly the way you look now. God would have created people without free will who were lively, lovely, emotional, thoughtful, and who always chose happy courses of action. Would such a world so obviously have been second-rate?

It is generally agreed that the free-will defense is not adequate to explain all suffering. It may account for the suffering caused by human beings. It does not account for the suffering caused by natural phenomena like diseases, earthquakes, and floods.

Some theists do link the suffering caused by natural phenomena to human free will by claiming that such suffering is a punishment for misuse of freedom. But this argument really supplements the free-will defense as it has been presented here. It adds two premises. One: Human beings did misuse their freedom, and God punished them by forcing them to live in a world of suffering. Two: The great suffering caused by natural events is proper punishment for human beings' misuse of their freedom. Some critics, like Martin, find this second premise "barbaric."

THE VIRTUE DEFENSE

There is another defense that often is presented as a justification for the existence of suffering caused by natural phenomena. It implies that God was right in making certain that there would be some suffering in the world, whatever human beings might do with their free will. It can be referred to as the **virtue defense,** and it runs as follows:

1. Virtues, such as generosity and courage, are great goods and, in the best of all possible worlds, human beings ought to have the chance to exercise such virtues.
2. It would be contradictory to have virtues in a world without suffering, since the definitions of these virtues imply the existence of suffering.
3. Therefore, suffering is a necessary ingredient in the best of all possible worlds.

To enlarge on item 2: Try to imagine someone being courageous in a world in which no one is afraid or in danger. It is impossible. To be courageous is to overcome fear (which is necessarily painful) and to risk oneself to help someone else. In a world with no pain and no risk of harm, no possible action could be courageous.

Or try to imagine generosity in a world in which all persons have more than they need. It is impossible. In such a world, any act of giving would be analogous to a child on a beach handing another child a bucket of sand. Generosity involves some sacrifice to help another in need. In a world with no need, no possible action could be generous.

This is an ingenious defense, and many find it reasonable. Others, however, do not.

Some philosophers have said that this defense views virtue inside out. What is good about virtues is that they aim at the relief of suffering. Virtues are good as means only. Virtues are correctly called good in a world with suffering. But to insist on suffering in order to have virtue is absurd; it contradicts the very nature of virtue. To insist on suffering so that there can be generosity and sympathy is like stealing from someone so that you can give that person some needed item or kicking someone in the shins so that you can feel sorry for that person.

The theist's defenses do seem to be successful in showing that there is a morality such that, if God had accepted it, it would have committed Him to allow some suffering in the world. Thus the "problem of suffering" comes down to an evaluation of this morality. Do you believe that free will and virtue are worth all the suffering in this world? If you do, then you believe in the possibility of a God who is omnipotent, omniscient, and perfectly good. If you do not, then you will deny that there could be such a God: If there is a God, He is acting on the wrong moral principles.

"Surprise! It's Judgment Day" is meant to be provocative, so it contains something to get almost everyone a little bit angry. Some would claim that there is much more to be said on God's behalf; others would claim that there is much more to be said for the position that Martin first endorses and then abnegates in his horror at becoming "only happy."

The story may assume a dichotomy that is bogus and that is, in some ways, to the theist's advantage. The only options presented in the story are a world like ours or a world in which people are happy zombies. But wouldn't the best of all possible worlds be better than either of these? Might it not be a world in which human beings are created to be happy, intelligent, inquisitive, and appreciative of beauty? Or is this the description of a contradictory world?

The debate, of course, goes on.

READINGS

RENÉ DESCARTES (1596–1650): the ontological argument*

I find it manifest that we can no more separate the existence of God from his essence than we can separate from the essence of a rectilinear triangle the fact that the size of its three angles equals two right angles, or from the idea of a mountain the idea of a valley. Thus it is no less self-contradictory to conceive of a God, a supremely perfect Being, who lacks existence—that is, who lacks some perfection—than it is to conceive of a mountain for which there is no valley.

But even though in fact I cannot conceive of a God without existence, any more than of a mountain without a valley, nevertheless, just as from the mere fact that I conceive a mountain with a valley, it does not follow that any mountain exists in the world, so likewise, though I conceive of God as existing, it does not seem to follow for this reason that God exists. For my thought does not impose any necessity upon things; and just as I can at my pleasure imagine a winged horse, even though no horse has wings, so I could perhaps attribute existence to God, even though no God existed.

This is far from the truth; it is here that there is sophistry hidden under the guise of a valid objection. For from the fact that I cannot conceive a mountain without a valley it does not follow that there is a mountain or a valley anywhere in the world, but only that the mountain and the valley, whether they exist or not, are inseparable from each other. From the fact alone that I cannot conceive God except as existing, it follows that existence is inseparable from him, and consequently that he does, in truth, exist. Not that my thought can bring about this result or that it imposes any necessity upon things; on the contrary, the necessity which is in the thing itself—that is, the necessity of the existence of God—determines me to have this thought. For it is not in my power to conceive of a God without existence—that is to say, of a supremely perfect Being without a supreme perfection—as it is in my power to imagine a horse either with or without wings.

ST. THOMAS AQUINAS (1225–1274): the cosmological argument.†

The third way is taken from possibility and necessity and runs thus. We find in nature things that are possible to be and not to be, since they are found to be

---

*From *Meditations on First Philosophy* by René Descartes, translated by Lawrence J. LaFleur. Copyright 1951 by Macmillan Publishing Company; copyright renewed 1979. Reprinted with permission of Macmillan Publishing Company.
†From St. Thomas Aquinas, *Summa Theologica*, Part I, translated by the English Dominican Fathers.

generated, and to corrupt, and consequently, they are possible to be and not to be. But it is impossible for these always to exist, for that which is possible not to be at some time is not. Therefore, if everything is possible not to be, then at one time there could have been nothing in existence. Now if this were true, even now there would be nothing in existence, because that which does not exist only begins to exist by something already existing. Therefore, if at one time nothing was in existence, it would have been impossible for anything to have begun to exist; and thus even now nothing would be in existence—which is absurd. Therefore, not all beings are merely possible, but there must exist something the existence of which is necessary. But every necessary thing either has its necessity caused by another, or not. Now it is impossible to go on to infinity in necessary things which have their necessity caused by another, as has been already proved in regard to efficient caused. Therefore we cannot but postulate the existence of some being having of itself its own necessity, and not receiving it from another, but rather causing in others their necessity. This all men speak of as God.

WILLIAM PALEY (1743–1805): the teleological argument.*

In crossing a heath, suppose I pitched my foot against a *stone*, and were asked how the stone came to be there; I might possibly answer, that, for anything I knew to the contrary, it had lain there forever: nor would it perhaps be very easy to show the absurdity of this answer. But suppose I had found a *watch* upon the ground, and it should be inquired how the watch happened to be in that place: I should hardly think of the answer which I had before given, that, for anything I knew, the watch might have always been there. Yet why should not this answer serve for the watch as well as for the stone? Why is it not as admissible in the second case, as in the first? For this reason, and for no other, viz. that, when we come to inspect the watch, we perceive (what we could not discover in the stone) that its several parts are framed and put together for a purpose, e.g., that they are so formed and adjusted as to produce motion, and that motion so regulated as to point out the hour of the day; that if the different parts had been differently shaped from what they are, of a different size from what they are, or placed after any other manner, or in any other order, than that in which they are placed, either no motion at all would have been carried on in the machine, or none which would have answered the use that is now served by it. . . . This mechanism being observed (it requires indeed an examination of the instrument, and perhaps some previous knowledge of the subject, to perceive and understand it; but being once, as we have said, observed and understood), the inference, we think, is inevitable; that the watch must have had a maker; that there must have existed, at sometime, and at some place or other, an artificer or artificers, who formed it for the purpose

*From chapters I–VI of William Paley's *Evidences of the Existence and Attributes of the Deity,* 1802.

which we find it actually to answer; who comprehended its construction, and designed its use.

Nor would it, I apprehend, weaken the conclusion, that we had never seen a watch made, that we had never known an artist capable of making one; that we were altogether incapable of executing such a piece of workmanship ourselves, or of understanding in what manner it was performed; all this being no more than what is true of some exquisite remains of ancient art, of some lost arts, and, to the generality of mankind, of the more curious productions of modern manufacture. . . .

Nor, . . . would it yield to his inquiry more satisfaction to be answered, that there existed in things a principle of order, which had disposed the parts of the watch into their present form and situation. He never knew a watch made by the principle of order; nor can he even form to himself an idea of what is meant by a principle of order distinct from the intelligence of the watchmaker. . . .

. . . every indication of contrivance, every manifestation of design, which existed in the watch, exists in the works of nature; with the difference, on the side of nature, of being greater and more, and that in a degree which exceeds all computation.

WILLIAM JAMES (1842–1910) discusses religious experience.*

IS MYSTICAL EXPERIENCE VERIDICAL?

My next task is to inquire whether we can invoke it as authoritative. Does it furnish any *warrant for the truth* of the twice-bornness and supernaturality and pantheism which it favors? I must give my answer to this question as concisely as I can.

In brief my answer is this—and I will divide it into three parts:—

1) Mystical states, when well developed, usually are, and have the right to be, absolutely authoritative over the individuals to whom they come.

2) No authority emanates from them which should make it a duty for those who stand outside of them to accept their revelations uncritically.

3) They break down the authority of the non-mystical or rationalistic consciousness, based upon the understanding and the senses alone. They show it to be only one kind of consciousness. They open out the possibility of other orders of truth, in which, so far as anything in us vitally responds to them, we may freely continue to have faith.

I will take up these points one by one.

*From "Mysticism," by William James, Lectures XVI and XVII, in *The Varieties of Religious Experience*, 1902.

1.

As a matter of psychological fact, mystical states of a well-pronounced and emphatic sort *are* usually authoritative over those who have them. They have been "there," and know. It is vain for rationalism to grumble about this. If the mystical truth that comes to a man proves to be a force that he can live by, what mandate have we of the majority to order him to live in another way? . . . Our own more "rational" beliefs are based on evidence exactly similar in nature to that which mystics quote for theirs. Our senses, namely, have assured us of certain states of fact; but mystical experiences are as direct perceptions of fact for those who have them as any sensations ever were for us. . . .

2.

But I now proceed to add that mystics have no right to claim that we ought to accept the deliverance of their peculiar experiences, if we are ourselves outsiders and feel no private call thereto. . . . To begin with, even religious mysticism itself, the kind that accumulates traditions and makes schools, is much less unanimous than I have allowed. It has been both ascetic and antinomianly self-indulgent within the Christian church. It is dualistic in Sankhya, and monistic in Vedanta philosophy. I called it pantheistic; but the great Spanish mystics are anything but pantheists. They are with few exceptions non-metaphysical minds, for whom "the category of personality" is absolute. The "union" of man with God is for them much more like an occasional miracle than like an original identity. How different again, apart from the happiness common to all, is the mysticism of Walt Whitman, Edward Carpenter, Richard Jeffries, and other naturalistic pantheists, from the more distinctively Christian sort. The fact is that the mystical feeling of enlargement, union, and emancipation has no specific intellectual content whatever of its own. It is capable of forming matrimonial alliances with material furnished by the most diverse philosophies and theologies, provided only they can find a place in their framework for its peculiar emotional mood. We have no right, therefore, to invoke its prestige as distinctively in favor of any special belief. . . .

. . . more remains to be told, for religious mysticism is only one half of mysticism. The other half has no accumulated traditions except those which the text-books on insanity supply. Open any one of these, and you will find abundant cases in which mystical ideas are cited as characteristic symptoms of enfeebled or deluded states of mind. In delusional insanity, paranoia, as they sometimes call it, we may have a *diabolical* mysticism, a sort of religious mysticism turned upside down. The same sense of ineffable importance in the smallest events, the same texts and words coming with new meanings, the same voices and visions and leadings and missions, the same controlling by extraneous powers; only this time the emotion is pessimistic: instead of consolations we have desolations; the meanings are dreadful; and the powers are enemies to life. It is evident that from the point of view of their psychological mechanism, the classic mysticism and these lower mysticisms spring from the same mental level, from that great subliminal or transmarginal region of which science is beginning to admit the existence, but of which so little is really known. That region contains every kind of matter: "seraph and snake" abide there side by side. To come from thence is no infallible credential. What comes must be sifted and tested, and run the gauntlet of confrontation with the total context of experience, just like what comes from the outer world of sense. Its value must be ascertained by empirical methods, so long as we are not mystics ourselves.

Once more, then, I repeat that non-mystics are under no obligation to acknowledge in mystical states a superior authority conferred on them by their intrinsic nature.

3.

Yet, I repeat once more, the existence of mystical states absolutely overthrows the pretension of non-mystical states to be the sole and ultimate dictators of what we may believe. As a rule, mystical states merely add a supersensuous meaning to the ordinary outward data of consciousness. They are excitements like the emotions of love or ambition, gifts to our spirit by means of which facts already objectively before us fall into a new expressiveness and make a new connection with our active life. They do not contradict these facts as such, or deny anything that our senses have immediately seized. It is the rationalistic critic rather who plays the part of denier in the controversy, and his denials have no strength, for there never can be a state of facts to which new meaning may not truthfully be added, provided the mind ascend to a more enveloping point of view. It must always remain an open question whether mystical states may not possibly be such superior points of view. . . .

THOMAS D. DAVIS: from his novel, *Suffer Little Children.**

"You're generous," she said, her face softening. "But if either of us is kind, that's the Lord's doing. It's His kindness showing through in us."

I shook my head hard. "Your God is lots of things. Kind isn't one of them."

"But He *is*. He's loving—infinitely loving."

"You'd never know it from looking at the world He made."

Mrs. Tate sat up in her chair, leaning toward me. The attack on her God seemed to have roused her from the doldrums of self-accusation.

"I know there's a lot of awfulness in this world," she said. "But that's man's doing, not God's."

"I don't think God should get off the hook that easily. I know the argu-

*From *Suffer Little Children* by Thomas D. Davis. New York: Walker and Co., 1991, pp. 134–141.

ment: God's children rebelled of their own free will, and God, being just, had to punish them. But think about it. Would you throw your own children out of Eden into a world like this one? To die of leukemia, maybe, or be burned in a fire? To be committed for schizophrenia, or suffer from Tourette's and depression like Billy? A friend of mine once said that if we treated our children the way God treats His, we'd be arrested for child abuse."

I expected her to get angry, but she only looked sad. She nodded, though I couldn't imagine at what.

"The world can be a terrible place," she said. "When people turn to Christians to ask why, we give them such heartless answers. We tell them, you've got leukemia because some relative of yours thousands of years ago offended God and God's paying him back." She gave a little shudder. "We try to dress it up, of course, but that's what it comes to. I can't believe I used to accept answers like that. I'm afraid I don't think much of Christians who do. I wonder where their minds are. Even more their hearts. How someone can see people suffering so—children suffering, above all—and settle the question with such stupid answers is beyond me. The kindest thing I can think about such people is that they are just burying their feelings to avoid despair." She shook her head slowly, almost reluctantly. "I don't have an answer to why there's such suffering. I frankly don't see why a loving God would have created a world like this one."

I looked at her with bewilderment. "Then how can you be a Christian?"

"Because I know Christ," she said. "I feel His love. He's the most loving Being I can imagine. Experiencing the Lord like that, I can't believe He could do anything cruel or wrong. There's got to be an answer to why there's suffering in this world. Do you see what I mean? If you loved someone you experienced as kind and there was circumstantial evidence that they had committed a crime, you wouldn't believe they'd done it—would you? You'd have to go with what you knew about them."

"I suppose so," I said. "But then I'd assume you could pin the crime on someone else. Who could you pin this world on but God? And why would God make Himself look so guilty? Why would He make believing so difficult?"

"I want to say maybe it's to test us. But that would seem heartless too. The fact is I don't know why. I just know there must be a reason."

I shook my head in frustration. "You run into a belief that looks absurd so you say it's a test. But maybe it isn't a test. Maybe it's just absurd."

"Maybe," she said. "But if it were a matter of certainty, they wouldn't call it faith, would they? Anyway, what's the alternative? Are you so happy looking at the suffering in the world and thinking that it's totally without purpose? That it's never to be redeemed?"

"No."

"I don't think I could live believing like you do."

"You could," I said, with a smile. "You just might not like it much."

JOHN HICK presents a Christian defense of suffering.*

Theodicy,† as many modern Christian thinkers see it, is a modest enterprise, negative rather than positive in its conclusions. It does not claim to explain, nor to explain away, every instance of evil in human experience, but only to point to certain considerations which prevent the fact of evil (largely incomprehensible though it remains) from constituting a final and insuperable bar to rational belief in God.

In indicating these considerations it will be useful to follow the traditional division of the subject. There is the problem of *moral evil* or wickedness: why does an all-good and all-powerful God permit this? And there is the problem of the *non-moral evil* of suffering or pain, both physical and mental: why has an all-good and all-powerful God created a world in which this occurs?

Christian thought has always considered moral evil in its relation to human freedom and responsibility. To be a person is to be a finite center of freedom, a (relatively) free and self-directing agent responsible for one's own decisions. This involves being free to act wrongly as well as to act rightly. The idea of a person who can be infallibly guaranteed always to act rightly is self-contradictory. There can be no guarantee in advance that a genuinely free moral agent will never choose amiss. Consequently, the possibility of wrong-doing or sin is logically inseparable from the creation of finite persons, and to say that God should not have created beings who might sin amounts to saying that he should not have created people. . . .

. . . an enormous amount of human pain arises either from the inhumanity or the culpable incompetence of mankind. This includes such major scourges as poverty, oppression and persecution, war, and all the injustice, indignity, and inequity which occur even in the most advanced societies. These evils are manifestations of human sin. . . .

Even though the major bulk of actual human pain is traceable to man's misused freedom as a sole or part cause, there remain other sources of pain which are entirely independent of the human will, for example, earthquake, hurricane, storm, flood, drought, and blight. In practice, it is often impossible to trace a boundary between the suffering which results from human wickedness and folly and that which falls upon mankind from without. Both kinds of suffering are inextricably mingled together in human experience. For our present purpose, however, it is important to note that the latter category does exist and that it seems to be built into the very structure of our world. In response to it, theodicy, if it is wisely conducted, follows a negative path. It is not possible to show positively that each item of human pain serves the divine purpose of good; but, on the other hand, it does seem possible to show

*The word "theodicy," from the Greek *theos* (God) and *dike* (righteous), means the justification of God's goodness in face of the fact of evil.
†From *Philosophy of Religion* by John Hick. Copyright © 1963, copyright renewed 1991, pp. 41–45. Reprinted by permission of Prentice-Hall, Englewood Cliffs, New Jersey.

that the divine purpose as it is understood in Judaism and Christianity could not be forwarded in a world which was designed as a permanent hedonistic paradise.

An essential premise of this argument concerns the nature of the divine purpose in creating the world. The skeptic's assumption is that man is to be viewed as a completed creation and that God's purpose in making the world was to provide a suitable dwelling-place for this fully formed creature. Since God is good and loving, the environment which he has created for human life to inhabit is naturally as pleasant and comfortable as possible. The problem is essentially similar to that of a man who builds a cage for some pet animal. Since our world, in fact, contains sources of hardship, inconvenience, and danger of innumerable kinds, the conclusion follows that this world cannot have been created by a perfectly benevolent and all-powerful deity.

Christianity, however, has never supposed that God's purpose in the creation of the world was to construct a paradise whose inhabitants would experience a maximum of pleasure and a minimum of pain. The world is seen, instead, as a place of "soul-making" in which free beings, grappling with the tasks and challenges of their existence in a common environment, may become "children of God" and "heirs of eternal life." . . .

. . . Suppose, contrary to fact, that this world were a paradise from which all possibility of pain and suffering were excluded. The consequences would be very far-reaching. For example, no one could ever injure anyone else: the murderer's knife would turn to paper or his bullets to thin air; the bank safe, robbed of a million dollars, would miraculously become filled with another million dollars (without this device, on however large a scale, proving inflationary); fraud, deceit, conspiracy, and treason would somehow always leave the fabric of society undamaged. Again, no one would ever be injured by accident: the mountain-climber, steeple-jack, or playing child falling from a height would float unharmed to the ground; the reckless driver would never meet with disaster. There would be no need to work, since no harm could result from avoiding work; there would be no call to be concerned for others in time of need or danger, for in such a world there could be no real needs or dangers.

To make possible this continual series of individual adjustments, nature would have to work by "special providences" instead of running according to general laws which men must learn to respect on penalty of pain or death. The laws of nature would have to be extremely flexible: sometimes gravity would operate, sometimes not; sometimes an object would be hard and solid, sometimes soft. There could be no sciences, for there would be no enduring world structure to investigate. In eliminating the problems and hardships of an objective environment, with its own laws, life would become like a dream in which, delightfully but aimlessly, we would float and drift at ease.

One can at least imagine such a world. It is evident that our present ethical concepts would have no meaning in it. If, for example, the notion of harming someone is an essential element in the concept of a wrong action, in our hedonistic paradise there could be no wrong actions—nor any right actions in distinction from wrong. Courage and fortitude would have no point in an environment in which there is, by definition, no danger or difficulty. Generosity, kindness, the *agape* aspect of love, prudence, unselfishness, and all other ethical notions which presuppose life in a stable environment, could not even be formed. Consequently, such a world, however well it might promote pleasure, would be very ill adapted for the development of the moral qualities of human personality. In relation to this purpose it would be the worst of all possible worlds. . . .

Questions and Exercises

1. "God, being perfect, lacks nothing, and so can't lack existence; God must exist." Critique this argument.
2. "The universe isn't the kind of thing that could have always existed. Another kind of being must have created and sustained it, namely God." Critique this argument.
3. "The universe is so complex it baffles our greatest scientific minds. Something like that couldn't have just happened by chance. It must have been created by some intelligent being, namely God." Critique this argument.
4. Suppose you began to have some "visions." How would you decide whether they represented some objective reality or were merely fantasies or hallucinations?
5. a. In ordinary cases of perception, how do we decide whether what we are seeing is "real" or not?
   b. How would religious experiences be judged in terms of the above criteria?
6. What is the "problem of suffering"?
7. "Even an omnipotent God could not do contradictory things." Give a justification for this statement.
8. "God couldn't create a world that's all happy because human beings aren't capable of being happy all the time." Critique this statement.
9. Present the free-will defense and a possible objection to it.
10. Present the virtue defense and a possible objection to it.
11. "I hope God exists, but I can certainly imagine He might not." What would Descartes say to this statement?
12. "Maybe one day absolutely everything will cease to exist." What would Aquinas say to this statement?
13. "Maybe God didn't design the universe. Maybe the universe is the way it is because of some principle of order." What would Paley say to this?
14. Suppose I am having a vision. I am trying to talk you into believing my

vision, and you are trying to talk me out of believing my own vision. According to James: Should you expect to succeed with me? Should I expect to succeed with you?

15. Relate the discussion in the Davis excerpt to James's discussion of religious experience.

16. "Theodicy . . . does not claim to explain . . . every instance of evil . . . but to point to certain considerations which prevent the fact of evil . . . from constituting a final and insuperable bar to rational belief in God." Explain this statement of Hicks.

17. "One can at least imagine such a world. It is evident that our present ethical concepts would have no meaning in it." What kind of world is Hick talking about here? Why wouldn't our ethical concepts have any meaning in it?

18. A world with more abundance than anyone could use up, including space for living. People with free will who have bodies that can suffer some painful injuries and diseases but can't be in agony or be maimed or be killed. In this world people can have adventures and take risks and display moral qualities, though not to the degree that we can (because of the limits on suffering).

    a. Is there anything contradictory about this world? Explain.

    b. Would such a world be better or worse than our own? Explain.

3

Moral Proof and Moral Principles

Fiction: The Land of Certus

Of all those lands in which I have traveled, the most wondrous is the land of Certus. The people there are to be envied above all others, for that which is to us the most perplexing mystery of existence is to them no mystery at all.

As I stepped from that treacherous forest through which I had wandered, lost, for five days, the first being I encountered in the land of Certus was Felanx. He was a roughhewn, kindly farmer who greeted me at the edge of his fields and offered me the hospitality of his home. Yet he frightened me at first. For when he smiled, there came from his face a strange green light, and I drew back, thinking him a sorcerer. But after a time, he succeeded in calming me with his gentle manner. He said that the light would not harm me and that he would explain it presently.

Felanx led me to the high stone walls of the town, past the sentry at the gate, through the narrow cobblestone streets to his home. As his family welcomed me, there were more flashes of that green light. But his son, who would not approach me, glowed a faint red. Felanx spoke harshly to the boy and dismissed him.

I was seated by the fire, given warm drink, and promised supper. I was no longer fearful of those strange lights, but my curiosity became too much to bear. I ask Felanx to provide me with the explanation he had promised.

"It is quite simple," he said. "From others who have come to our land, we know that these lights do not exist in our parts of the world. So I understand your confusion. Yet to us the lights seem most natural, and we cannot imagine a land that is otherwise. The green light is the light of the good. The red light, it shames me to say, is the light of the bad. You saw it around my youngest son. Most of the time he is a good boy, but sometimes he does not show the proper hospitality to strangers. He has been disciplined. Please accept my apologies on his behalf."

"The lights of good and bad!" I exclaimed. "This is trickery. Do you take me for a fool?"

As I spoke thus to my host, red light burst before my eyes, and I began to stammer in confusion. But once again, Felanx put me at ease. He said that he understood and forgave my skepticism. He said that once I had had a chance to observe his land further and to reflect on the matter, I would realize that he had spoken the truth.

I marveled at the words of my host. To have all good and bad deeds clearly marked so that everyone should know them for what they were: Could anything be a greater boon to humanity? I hesitated to believe, and yet had I not seen these lights with my own eyes? After some thought I inquired about the origin of the lights.

"To that question," said Felanx, "there is no answer that seems to satisfy all. One answer is given in *The Book of the Beginning*. It says that the Creator made the skies and the earth and then, because He was lonely, He created human beings to be His companions. He put human beings in the most beautiful place on earth, the Valley of Peace, and He dwelt there with them. For a time all was happiness. But after a number of years, some people became restless. They said that they wanted to see what lay beyond the valley. The Creator told them there was nothing beyond the valley so happy and so lovely as it was. Still, many wanted to go. The Creator granted them permission at last, saying that He would constrain no one to stay with Him. But He was very angry. He told those who departed that they would find great sorrow in the lands beyond the valley and that they would never find their way back.

"But then one woman bowed down before the Creator and pleaded in tears for her descendants. Was it right, she asked, that they should all suffer for the folly of her headstrong daughter, who was among those who wished to leave? At her words, the Creator relented. He said that He would give those who departed the lights of good and bad, so that they would know how to make themselves worthy to return to the valley. He said that one day He would walk the earth and lead those who glowed with the goodness of green back to the Valley of Peace.

"That, I say, is just one answer. It is the one that my wife accepts. Others have argued that there is no Creator, that the skies and the earth have always been. They say that the lights of good and bad are simply natural events that require no supernatural explanation. The light of the good, they say, is no more mysterious than the other colors of things whose significance is beauty. I, myself, am of this opinion."

I remarked that in my land there were also doubts about a Creator. But the disputes of the Certans were as nothing compared with ours. For in my land, each person interpreted good and bad "according to his or her own lights," and what each person saw was different. At least in Certus there were no doubts about goodness and badness: the lights were the same for everyone. And if there were doubts about a Creator, at least there could be no doubt how to please Him, should He exist.

The next day, Felanx showed me around the town and introduced me to many of the townspeople. All those I met showed me the utmost kindness. They were eager to hear stories of my travels and to answer any questions I might have. In fact, I was preoccupied with just one question, and it was answered not by what was said to me but by what I observed for myself. I saw that the green lights did indeed mark acts of goodness and the red lights acts of badness. Not that the Certans are a bad people. On the contrary, they are a fine people. But they are human, and they make mistakes. The red light allows them to see their mistakes at once and to correct them.

At one home, we drank a delicious plum whiskey, and the green light over the gathering answered for me a question that divided those in my land, the question of whether it is evil to drink alcohol. The green light told me that drinking is good, though only in moderation. When one of the group became drunken, he glowed with a red light. He was led from the room, apologizing to us all.

As we emerged from another house, I noticed a ragged fellow stumbling as if inebriated, glowing the brightest of reds. The others with me jeered at him, but the fellow only smiled and made a sign with his hands, which I was given to understand was the vilest of profanities. I was surprised by the existence of this reprobate in Certus, and I asked Felanx about him.

"His name is Georges, and he is a difficult case," said Felanx. "At first, some thought that he might be blind to the lights of good and bad, as some are blind to colors and shapes. But he answers questions about the lights correctly. He just won't be guided by them. He knows the good but doesn't want to do it. His case is now before the town council. My guess is that there will be extreme punishment."

"But how can a man know the good and not want to do it?" I exclaimed.

At once I saw the foolishness of my remark, remembering that in the sacred book of my land it says that many fall not through ignorance but through the wickedness of the heart. I told Felanx of this.

"And so it says in *The Book of the Beginning*. But Georges is especially dangerous. Not only does he say that he often prefers wickedness to goodness, but he suggests that everyone should do so. He says that people should do what pleases them and should disregard the lights."

"But how can he be dangerous?" I asked. "Surely anyone can see that if all were to do as they pleased, with no thought of the good, with no thought of others, the result must be chaos, disastrous for all."

"Of course," said Felanx. "But Georges is subtle. He says that what all people should prefer is not only their own pleasures but also the pleasures of others. It is this that seems to absolve him of selfishness in the eyes of the young, and many are drawn by his words."

I shook my head sadly, reflecting on the perversity of human beings. As we walked on through the streets, my attention was drawn to the cannons placed along the town walls. I asked Felanx about them.

"You have learned today that there are two towns in Certus: ours, which is Rechtsen, and another which is Linksen. What I have not told you about is the terrible perversity of the Linksens. But now that you know of the wicked Georges, you might as well know all.

"The Linksens are our mortal enemies. They have a religion that denies our own. They say that the lights of good and bad are not the work of the Creator, but the work of the Creator's enemy. They say that the lights of good and bad have been put in this land to confuse and lead astray the Creator's true friends. They say that we should not follow the lights, but should instead follow the laws written in their book. These laws, they believe, express the Creator's true wishes."

I could not restrain myself at this absurdity.

"But surely they could be shown the truth. Listen: If at this moment, heaven forbid, I should strike you down for no reason, there would be a ferocious blaze of red. Is it not so?"

"Of course."

"And would it be the same in Linksen?"

"It would. The lights are the same in Linksen."

"There, then. Surely the Linksens cannot believe that such an act could be right or that the Creator would wish it. Were they to believe so, there would now be none of them left. This must prove to them that the lights shows the truth."

Felanx lowered his head, and I sensed that he was close to tears.

"Alas, they too have their vicious subtleties. Were you to compare their rules of the good and the bad with the lights of the good and the bad, you would find much agreement. It is this, they say, that shows the cleverness of the Creator's enemy. He makes the lights so that they seem to show the truth in every case. It is this that misleads so many. The Linksens say that women should be equal to men, that animals are not to be eaten, and that the Rechtsens are to be destroyed. That the red light shows on such deeds, they say, is the triumph of deception."

The day that had begun with such joy had turned out sad, and I went to bed that evening with a heavy heart. I had always held the hope that as the nature of goodness became clearer to human beings, they would become better and better. Yet here in Certus, where all had been made clear, wickedness and dissension continued. Was there indeed any hope for humanity?

I awoke the next morning to the sound of a crowd's yelling in the courtyard. I moved through the empty house and went outside. A hundred of the townspeople were gathered in the marketplace, viewing some spectacle. Moving into the crowd, I saw what it was. Georges was lying naked on a wooden platform, his body shackled. He was writhing and screaming, as one of the men standing over him slowly snapped the bones in his fingers with some heavy metal instrument. A glance at Georges's body and at the fiendish instruments held by the men around him indicated that this was just one moment in a long process of torture. Nearby was a stake and a mound of faggots where later they would burn his disfigured body.

I turned away in anger and horror, searching the faces in the crowd. All were watching the brutal spectacle with slight, solemn smiles. I saw Felanx near me and grabbed his arm.

"How can you do this?" I cried. "You who say you love the good."

"Georges is paying the price of his wickedness. The council decided last night. Georges ignores the good and incites others to do the same. He has to be punished. He has to be made with example. It is right that he be punished."

"Punished, yes," I said. "Perhaps even killed. But not like this. This is barbaric! This is horrible!"

Felanx pulled away from me, and his expression became fierce. He moved his hand, and for a moment I thought he was going to strike me. Instead he pointed toward Georges.

"Look again," he commanded.

"No. It is too terrible."

"Look at the men who are carrying out the sentence."

Reluctantly, I glanced toward the terrible scene. Then I saw what had escaped my attention before. The torturers of Georges were all glowing a faint green. This act that I had so readily condemned was, in fact, good, right. Suddenly my horror turned to shame.

"Forgive me," I said, bowing my head.

There was a moment of silence before Felanx spoke.

"You are forgiven, my friend, my guest. But I must concern myself now with your safety. The Linksens know of Georges's punishment. Their leaders have told the people that Georges is their spy and is suffering for their cause. This is not so, and the leaders know it. It is a mere pretext for attack. But they will attack our city. You must leave at once."

"Let me stay," I pleaded, ashamed at having wrongly condemned the Rechtsens. "Life is not so much to me that I would not gladly sacrifice it for the sake of the good."

"I believe that," said Felanx. "But this is not your land, and this is not your battle. You must go."

I kept pleading until I noticed that a red glow began to arise from my body. Then I stopped. I had already committed one grievous error that day; I must not commit another. If it was wrong for me to stay there, then I must go.

An hour later, Felanx led me to the town gate, where he bade me good-bye and turned me over to the guide who was to lead me through the woods along a tortuous trail, which I fear I shall never find again.

The land of Certus is often in my thoughts. For it seems to me that if there is any hope for humankind, it must lie with those brave people of Rechtsen who know the good, follow it, and will fight for it to the end. May the Creator help them in their struggle.

Fiction: Those Who Help Themselves

The way with the planet Omega is won. Its cities have been destroyed, its social institutions overthrown, its people injured and anguished. We have just destroyed what may have been the only truly moral civilization that ever existed.

The Omegans are not innocent victims; the guilt is not all ours. But however one places the blame, one cannot help regretting this war. The universe is a sadder place for the passing of what Omega once was.

All the civilizations that remain are morally defective. On Earth, in this twenty-second century after Jesus, in this third century after Marx, we certainly have not achieved what anyone would be tempted to call "utopia." At that moment, of course, the situation is fairly stable. Birth control and the calamitous Far Eastern wars have drastically reduced the Earth's population. The nutrition extracted from the oceans and the wealth "extracted" from other worlds have appeased, momentarily, those who are left alive. But we still have our cruelties, our injustices; we still have our victors and victims.

As for other planets, the pathetic, vegetablelike creatures on Beta, though incapable of doing us harm, are vicious: They kill one another with grotesque frequency. The Alphas, who have more military capability, have friendly relations with us, but they are unspeakably cruel to their slave classes. The moral situation on the planet Epsilon is comparable to that on Earth. The Gammas seemed to be the finest people we had encountered, until we discovered that they were merely protoplasmic machines and hence exempt from moral judgments.

Ten years ago, the age-old pessimism about "human nature" had developed into a pessimism about all "living nature." The discovery of Omega forced us to modify our pessimism, but only slightly. It still seems reasonable to surmise that almost all life forms in the universe are, and will continue to be, morally corrupt.

How one explains this depressing fact is a side issue. One may speak of original sin or of the ineradicable instincts necessary for the earlier stages of evolution. The fact remains that virtually all life forms are fundamentally self-interested and aggressive, capable, at best, of some sympathy for a small number of their own kind. Moral inspiration has little effect on behavior. Threats, both natural and supernatural, accomplish more, but not nearly enough. One suspects that the only conceivable near-utopia for most races would be a world of such abundance that individuals would be too busy gorging themselves to think of taking advantage of others. But there could never be such abundance. And, even if there were, doubtless there would still be some who would find their greatest pleasure in causing others pain.

At least such pessimism affords a certain comfort. If moral failure is indeed universal, then it may be inevitable and therefore no one's fault. The discovery of Omega challenged this deterministic view and threatened us with self-contempt. The Omegans had managed to be moral. Perhaps we were responsible for our failures.

No doubt we would have liked the moral contrast between us and the Omegans to be blurred by extreme dissimilarities of other sorts. But there were none of any consequence. The Omegans are a small people, averaging just over four feet in height, and their flesh is green. They have three eyes in a triangular formation, one mouth, and fifteen sound receptors located on various parts of the body. They have two legs, which are proportionately quite short, and four appendages at the side of the body. Two of these function like our arms and hands. The other two create, by the friction of the "fingers," the complex sounds by which they communicate. Their conceptual structure is analogous to our own and was easily deciphered by the Q-104 Computer Language Translator. The Omegans we confronted were a people quite similar to us in all but one respect: They were morally good.

Naturally, we tried to explain away the apparent superiority of the Omegans. Could it be that they, like the Gammas, really had no minds? No: They had thoughts and feelings just as we did. Was there an overabundance of material goods on Omega? No: They also had problems of scarcity. Had they been endowed, through an evolutionary fluke, with an innate compulsion to be unselfish—a compulsion for which they, of course, could claim no credit? No: They were a people with that strong self-interest which morality attempts to tame. There seemed to be no way to rationalize the goodness of those people.

We were not, of course, struck at once by the moral superiority of the Omegans; goodness cannot be seen at a glance. We became aware of it only gradually. In fact, our first impression of the Omegans was quite negative. Initially, they were hostile to us, and they remained suspicious throughout our visit. Admittedly, such inhospitality toward strangers could be considered a moral defect. Nonetheless, it is true that, *within* their civilization, the Omegans' conduct was nearly impeccable.

Naturally, what the Omegans did to be moral was in no way startling. We, on Earth, know quite well the dictates of morality; we know what a moral world would be like. (This is true in general, even if there are marginal disagreements about the nature of the good and the right.) Our problems result not from lack of knowledge, but from lack of ability or willingness. Had the conduct of the Omegans been totally bizarre, our moral terms would not have applied. But the moral concepts of the Omegans were quite similar. What was startling was that they managed to put them into practice.

The distribution of goods on Omega was not equal, but it was nearly so. In theory, the government was charged with enforcing equal distribution; in practice, little enforcement was necessary. The Omegans readily handed over their surplus goods for others in need, and the government had only to coordinate such generosity to see that it was orderly and that its results were equitably distributed throughout the society.

The Omegan government was democratic. The Omegans had a lively interest in debate, but they avoided *ad hominem* arguments, addressing themselves to issues, rather than personalities, and their debates had a high moral tone. Campaigning for public offices was vigorous but marked by neither overweening ambition nor rancor. It was indeed a democratic *community*. The Omegans avoided the anarchy and power politics that are the central defects of so many democracies. All individuals showed a real concern for the ongoing welfare of the whole.

The Omegans were highly energetic, industrious people. They were even, one might say, competitive. But one didn't sense that they were really competing against one another. Each success was celebrated, to a large degree, as a success for all and as an example to others. Each success was measured against the person's potential, and living up to one's potential, whatever it might be, brought the highest respect. The Omegans were not without individual ambition and pride, but they were quite temperate in these.

The Omegans had a considerable interest in the arts and sciences. None of us was qualified to judge their "music," which, because of the vastly different sounds they made, was incomprehensible to us. Similarly, their literary style was difficult to judge, but the content of their literature seemed intricate and imaginative, entertaining, and sometimes profound. We were particularly impressed by their art, which showed a fine sense of line and color. Generally, their art tended to have a much more optimistic tone than ours; but only our most melancholy critics would find this cause for complaint.

For the most part, their scientific achievements were the equal of ours, and apparently their medical skills were superior. They had been slower to develop space technology, presumably because they had little incentive to leave their planet. For obvious reasons, they had not developed sophisticated weaponry—at least until fifty years ago. At that time, they had begun to decode communications between other planets and had discovered, to their shock, the hostile nature of other life forms. Defense development had begun at once, and their crash program yielded remarkable weapons in a relatively short period of time. They had even managed to repel an attack from the planet Alpha some years before we came to Omega. Astonishingly, such weapons were never used by Omegans against one another.

If many Earth people felt that the Omegan society was not quite ideal, many Omegans felt the same way. In fact, there were a number of political parties. The biggest opposition party wanted to enlarge the competitive market for the material goods of Omega. Another party, somewhat smaller, wanted no competition and a perfectly equal distribution of goods. There were also fringe groups asking for, say, a greater emphasis on the arts or a greater allocation of funds to defense research. But all such parties constituted a loyal opposition. All felt that the Omegan society was close enough to their ideal so that they could live quite happily with the status quo. All recognized the ongoing value of democracy and of relative stability. No party—indeed, so person—had ever advocated a violent revolution. Because of the conspicuous absence of religion on Omega, there was no inclination to disrupt human welfare for the sake of some supernatural ideal.

Perhaps it is not correct to say that there was no religion on Omega. Certainly there was no belief in a God, and there were no ceremonies of reverence for the universe. But there was one meta-physical belief, shared by all Omegans, that might be considered "religious." It apparently developed in their prehistory, and, if its beginnings were associated with revelations or proofs, there were no existing indications of such, even in the guise of myths. That this belief was so implicit in the Omegans' consciousness—no one had to be persuaded, it was never argued—kept it from our notice for some time. But even the Omegans' expression of this belief was misinterpreted by us at first. A phrase like "that unfortunate man might be me" sounded so much like the imaginative exhortations of our moralists that we failed to comprehend that the phrase was intended literally. Finally we did understand, and, in understanding, I suppose, we discovered the "secret" of the Omegans' moral behavior.

The Omegans believed in the perpetual reincarnation of souls, which was not the work of some divinity, but simply the natural way of things. Almost as soon as a person died, the soul was reborn in the body of some infant, with all memories of the past life erased. This reincarnation, they believed, was not only natural, but random: Merits and demerits in a past life had nothing whatever to do with a soul's replacement in the next life, and one's inclinations and abilities were not transferred from one life to another. In the next life, the woman of great intellect might be retarded, the man of good health might be diseased, the person of great culture might be interested only in popular entertainments—or vice versa. One might be reborn the same or quite different. There was no way of knowing in advance.

The moral efficacy of this belief is obvious. It is a consequence of this belief that, in promoting a society in which each person helps others, one is quite literally helping oneself. No one was willing to neglect another, because soon one might be in the same position.

There were, as has been noted, some differences of opinion on Omega concerning the moral and political status quo. Apparently, those supporting the largest opposition party were gamblers: They were willing to risk the possibility of some misfortune in the next life for the possibility of gaining great wealth in this life. Those on the opposite end of the political spectrum were unwilling to gamble at all with their future lives: They wanted to be guaranteed an equal share of the wealth. Those who supported the majority party wanted some guarantees and some chances to gamble. But none was willing to gamble too much with his or her future life, to risk being diseased, mentally defective, or hungry, and being without help. Thus, each was agreed that all should be helped and was highly motivated to help others. Guarantees in no way sapped the industriousness of the Omegans, since all would share in the future benefits of their own labors. There were, of course, some moral lapses. Like all people, the Omegans were tempted to emphasize their present rather than their future welfare. But they gave in to this temptation very rarely. Morally, the Omegans had a magnificent civilization.

Some Earth critics of the Omegan war say that we came to co. ?r. Leaving aside our moral qualms (which those critics might deny we have),   ? simply do not have the power to conquer and control a universe. On these grounds alone, we always prefer a peaceful relationship of mutually profitable cooperation.

These critics say that the Omegans' suspicion and hostility were justified in view of the aggressiveness of other life forms. This may be true, but it does not get to the heart of the matter. The central problem was that the Omegans refused to acknowledge the moral rights of creatures other than Omegans. Just as twenty-second-century Christians cannot believe that Jesus died to save Betas and Epsilons, just as Marxists don't know what to think about economic determinism on other worlds, so the Omegans could not believe that their souls might migrate beyond their own race. They had no incentive at all to treat other beings fairly, and, in fact, they had treated us viciously.

Perhaps if the crisis had not come so quickly, some say, the Omegans might have adjusted their morality to include other life forms. But this would not have happened as long as those others did not share the belief of the Omegans.

Perhaps, some add, we would have come to share the religion of the Omegans. This is a lovely fantasy, indeed. If a religion is to be judged by its moral efficacy, the "religion" of the Omegans is the best we have ever encountered. But this is mere speculation. One does not change religions as one changes clothes. Earth has its religions already, and, for good or ill, we seem to be stuck with them.

Then we should have left the Omegans alone, say the critics. But this is naive. No one gets left alone, on Earth or beyond. Either people get along, or they fight. We fought. The conflict was inevitable.

In another place and time, when war meant human beings facing human beings, the Omegans would have been unbeatable. Their firm belief in a perpetual reincarnation on Omega would have made them supremely courageous and persistent. But such qualities count for nothing against missiles. The weapons they had been able to develop within fifty years may have been good enough against Alpha, but not against Earth. The war, of course, was brief—and, for the Omegans, devastating.

Few faiths survive such catastrophes. The faith of the Omegans has not. Already, for the first time in the recorded history of Omega, questions are being raised, questions for which no one has answers. Whatever the Omegans may be in the future, it is clear that they will never be the same. Their past civilization will become a footnote to the depressing history of the universe, a footnote both beguiling and accusatory: It was the only truly moral civilization that has ever existed.

Questions

1. In "The Land of Certus," the Rechtsens claim to have knowledge of good and bad via perception of the lights. Do you claim to have some knowledge of good and bad? In what way did you gain this knowledge? What, if anything, do you "see" when you see that something is good?
2. In making moral decisions, the Rechtsens are guided by the lights, the Linksens by the commands of their holy book, and Georges (apparently) by some principle to the effect that one ought to increase pleasure and diminish pain. They differ as to what is the correct evidence of good and bad. Can you imagine some way in which this dispute might be resolved? Can you imagine some sort of higher-level evidence that would convince everyone that, for example, the lights were indeed the true indicators of good and bad?
3. In observing that the green light illuminates the torture of Georges, the narrator of "Certus," who had previously considered torture repulsive, decides that it is, after all, good. Presumably you continued to feel repulsed and pronounced the act of torture bad. Obviously there is an intimate connection between feelings and value judgments. What is this connection? Is judging something as bad fundamentally a matter of having negative feelings about it? Or is it that one "sees" that something is bad and then feels negatively about it?
4. According to the narrator of "Those Who Help Themselves," the Omegans' belief in reincarnation motivated them to be moral. In what way does this belief relate to morality? What general considerations or principles did the Omegans employ in determining what is good and bad?
5. Compare and contrast the methods by which the Rechtsens and the Omegans determine what is good or bad, right or wrong.
6. The theme of "Those Who Help Themselves" suggests that there is frequently a conflict between self-interest and the dictates of morality, at least for the people of Earth. Give some everyday examples of this conflict, and try to explain what it is about morality that tends to conflict with one's self-interest.
7. If you believed in a morality like the Omegans', what sort of society and what sorts of moral principles would you endorse? Does your answer differ in any way from the kind of society and the kinds of moral principles you now endorse?

DISCUSSION

METAETHICS

"The Land of Certus" raises two sorts of moral, or ethical, questions. First, it brings up—though without much emphasis—**normative ethical** questions:

questions about what things are good or bad, right or wrong, about what things should or should not be done. The Rechtsens, the Linksens, Georges, and the people from the narrator's land each have opinions about what is good and bad. It is obvious that there are differences of opinion among them, even if these differences are not elaborated. The following normative questions are noted: "Is torture ever permissible?" "Ought men and women to be treated equally?" "Is it permissible to be intemperate in the pursuit of pleasure if no one else is harmed?" Other normative questions, not mentioned in the story, include: "Is abortion wrong?" "To what degree is one obligated to help the poor?" "Is happiness a greater good than freedom?"*

Second, "Certus" emphatically raises **metaethical** questions: questions concerning whether we can know which normative ethical judgments are true and, if so, how we can know. Initially, it seems as if there are no troublesome metaethical issues in Certus. Good things are those that glow green, bad things are those that glow red. If one says that something is good and that thing glows green, then the statement is true. Knowing good and bad is just a matter of looking at the colors. However, it turns out that there are others in Certus who say that the lights do not correctly mark the good and bad. The Linksens say that knowledge of good and bad is really to be found in their book. Georges disregards both the lights and the religious book and identifies good and bad with pleasure and pain, respectively. Here we confront the issue of how moral questions are to be decided.

Following the emphasis in "Certus," we shall be concerned primarily with metaethical questions, questions about the nature of morality and moral judgments. What are we saying when we make a moral judgment? Is there such a thing as *the* moral truth? Can moral judgments be justified and, if so, in what way? We shall focus on two rival metaethical theories: moral objectivism and moral subjectivism.

It should be noted that the terms "moral" and "ethical" are synonymous and that they are similarly ambiguous. The terms "moral" and "ethical" as they shall be used in this section do not mean "good," and their opposites are not "immoral" and "unethical." Rather, their meaning is "pertaining to moral, or ethical, questions"; their opposites are "nonmoral" and "nonethical." In this usage, it is uncontroversial to say that Jesus, Marx, and Hitler all had moral, or ethical, theories—that is, theories about what is good or bad, right or wrong.

MORAL OBJECTIVISM AND MORAL SUBJECTIVISM

The **moral objectivist** says that where we have a moral judgment and its negation, one of these judgments must be true and the other false. In this sense, moral judgments are analogous to judgments in the domain of science. We would all agree that where we have two statements like "There is life on Mars" and "There is no life on Mars," one of these statements must be true

---

*This last question, along with other normative questions, was discussed Chapter 2 in connection with the problem of suffering.

and the other false. We know this, even if we do not know which of the statements is true and which is false. According to the moral objectivist, the same is the case with moral judgments. Where we have two judgments like "All abortion is wrong" and "Not all abortion is wrong," one of the judgments must be true and the other false.

The moral objectivist says that of the various moral theories, at most one of these theories can be true, and the rest must be false. In this sense, conflicting moral theories are analogous to scientific theories. Where there are rival scientific theories about the universe, they cannot all be true: They contradict one another. Of course, they may all be false; perhaps none of them correctly describes the universe. But one and only one scientific theory could correctly describe the universe. In this sense, there is such a thing as *the* scientific truth. According to the moral objectivist, the various moral theories contradict one another, and at most only one of them could be true. One and only one moral theory could correctly describe the phenomena relevant to moral questions. In this sense, there is such a thing as *the* moral truth.

Precisely what the phenomena are that moral theories purport to describe is a matter of debate among objectivists. Some have said that moral theories purport to describe the laws of God. Others have suggested that moral theories purport to describe the natural law, some special moral qualities, or some particular set of those characteristics to which scientific theories also refer. But all objectivists agree that moral theories are rival theories about some sort of moral phenomena.

Many objectivists would claim to know which moral theory is true. Almost all objectivists would claim to know at least that certain moral theories are false—for instance, those that endorse human slavery, torture, or the extermination of some racial group. Other moral objectivists would claim that some moral theory must be true, but that they do not know which one is true.

The **moral subjectivist** claims that there is no one correct answer to moral questions; there is no such thing as *the* moral truth. Where we have a moral judgment and its negation, neither judgment need be false. Moral questions are not analogous to scientific questions; rather, they are analogous to questions of taste. We all agree that there are questions of taste—for example: "Is yellow prettier than blue?" "Does apple pie taste better than cherry pie?" Most of us would agree that when one person says, "This apple pie is good" and another says, "This apple pie is not good" neither judgment need be false. In such cases, what is at issue are not conflicting descriptions of the apple pie, but differing reactions toward the pie. Analogously, according to the moral subjectivist, moral judgments express attitudes toward persons, actions, or events, rather than being descriptions of such things. When one person says, "All abortion is wrong" and another says, "Not all abortion is wrong," each is expressing a different attitude toward abortion and neither judgment need be false. Moral goodness or badness, rightness or wrongness—like prettiness, like deliciousness—are "in the eye of the beholder." Moral issues are fundamentally "subjective."

To elaborate further on moral subjectivism at this point would involve us in subtleties best reserved for later in the discussion. But the above explanation should give you a sense of what moral subjectivism is, and the position should seem to you a familiar one. It is dramatized in much existentialist literature: The universe contains no intrinsic values, so each individual must "invent" his or her own. It is presupposed by much of the current talk about "value-free" scientific theories: True science, it is thought, should deal only with factual matters, because matter of values are too subjective.

AN ARGUMENT FOR MORAL SUBJECTIVISM

Having outlined the theories of moral objectivism and moral subjectivism, let us now consider a line of argument that might lead one to reject moral objectivism and adopt some sort of moral subjectivist view.

When we consider a scientific question, we do not always agree on the answer. But we do agree on what evidence would decide the issue. For example, we may not know whether there are intelligent creatures on a particular planet, but we do agree on what evidence would show that there are such creatures on that planet.

With regard to questions of taste, however, there is no conceivable evidence that would resolve such issues to everyone's satisfaction. There is no conceivable evidence that would demonstrate that yellow is prettier than blue or that apple pie is better than cherry pie.

If moral questions are indeed analogous to scientific questions, then we ought to be able to specify what evidence would decide moral questions to everyone's satisfaction. According to the moral subjectivist, we cannot do this. There is no evidence that would demonstrate that abortion is right or wrong, that an equal distribution of goods is or is not better than competition for goods. Thus, says the subjectivist, moral questions cannot be analogous to scientific questions. Instead, they are analogous to questions of taste.

Put formally, the moral subjectivist argument is this:

1. Moral questions are like either scientific questions (objective) or questions of taste (subjective).
2. Being like scientific questions implies that one can always specify what evidence would decide the questions.
3. With moral questions one can't always specify what evidence would decide the questions.
4. (Therefore) moral questions are not like scientific questions (objective) (from 2 and 3).
5. (Therefore) moral questions are like questions of taste (subjective) (from 1 and 4).

"The Land of Certus" explores the possibility of decisive moral evidence, and the story is slanted in favor of the moral subjectivist. In Certus, apparently, the good is clearly marked with a green light and the bad with a red light. Seemingly, there ought to be no moral disputes in Certus. But there are such disputes. Georges and some of the younger people claim that one ought to ignore the lights whenever they conflict with the principle that one ought to

do what gives one pleasure. The Linksens abide by a religious book that sometimes contradicts what is indicated by the lights. The Linksens say that their
book, not the lights, shows what is truly good and bad.

Toward the end of the story, the narrator is shocked when the green light
illuminates an act of torture, but decides that if the green light so indicates,
then the act of torture must be good. Presumably, many readers formed the
opposite conclusion: The act of torture would not be good no matter what the
lights indicated.

Here the subjectivist could issue the following challenge: Suppose that an
act that you found personally repugnant were labeled as good by some law or by
public opinion, or by some magical light as in Certus. Would you conclude that
the act you find repugnant is good? Or would you conclude that the act cannot be good, since you find it repugnant? Wouldn't you say the latter? And
doesn't this indicate that morality is basically a matter of how you feel about
things?

Many readers may have an ethic based on what they believe to be divine
commands, and they may feel that this argument for moral subjectivism seems
forceful only because it neglects religious considerations. Such a reader might
offer the following argument: Throughout history, our ethical beliefs have
been reflections of what we believed to be the wishes of the gods, or God. No
doubt, there are legitimate questions as to which religious writings, if any, correctly describe divine wishes. But, at most, such questions would justify one's
being a moral objectivist who doubts that one can know the moral truth.
Subjectivists ask what evidence would resolve all moral disputes. If an
omnipotent, omniscient creator was revealed to all and was to make known
what we were to do and not do, that would show everyone what things are
good or bad, right or wrong.

Some quasi-subjectivists have claimed that moral disputes are unresolv-
able, only because no God exists to "answer" moral questions. These quasi-
subjectivists would not deny that the commands of such a God would show
everyone what is right and wrong. But they say there is no God. In a world
without God, there is no evidence that would resolve moral disputes.

However, full-fledged moral subjectivists would reject the theistic argument described above and would deny that even the clear commands of a God
would resolve all moral disputes. This is not to say that such a God could now
force everyone to follow these commands. But "might" is not necessarily
"right." The issue here is whether the clear commands of a God would result
in a rational resolution of moral disputes.

Moral subjectivists might begin an attack on the theist argument by asking a question that is still a live, if hoary, one in theology: Is something good
because God commands it, or does God command something because it is
good?*

Theists who say that something is good just because God commands it
are in an uncomfortable position. They are committed to the view that even if

---

*The God in "A Little Omniscience Goes a Long Way" voices the first of these alternatives: "I
don't do things because they're best. Rather, they're best because I do them."

God advocated gratuitous, terrible acts of torture, such acts would necessarily be good. To theists who are willing to accept these consequences, subjectivists could say the following: Even if you would be willing to accept something as good just because God commanded it, many people, including many theists, would not. These other theists would say that even God must have some satisfactory justification for a command if that command is to be good. This shows that the clear commands of God per se would not be the supposed evidence that would resolve all moral disputes.

Theists who say that God commands something because it is good avoid having to say that a terrible act of torture would be good by the simple supposition of God's commanding it. They can say that torture is objectively bad, and God wouldn't command something that was bad. But this theistic position undercuts the theistic argument against moral subjectivism given above. That argument supposed that the clear commands of God would be the evidence that would resolve all moral disputes. But to say that God commands something because it is good supposes that God decides what is good or bad on the basis of some evidence. Now the theists must start all over again and specify what, if any, evidence would resolve all moral disputes—including moral disputes between human beings and God.

It would be helpful if the moral subjectivists could present us with some hypothetical, plausible, and not-too-offensive examples of a moral disagreement between a human being and God. An issue of this type is discussed in Chapter 2, "God and the Problem of Suffering."

Some theists claim that at the time of creation, God had a choice: Either He could give human beings free will and the risk of unhappiness, or He could make them inevitably happy creatures who lacked free will. According to many theists, God chose to give human beings free will. But surely we can *imagine* someone saying to God: "I understand why You made the choice You did, but I think it was the wrong one. I think that happiness is more valuable than freedom. Had I been in Your place, I would not have given human beings the free will that has brought them so much pain. I would have created human beings who could not be other than happy."

Here, clearly, the mere fact of God's choosing something doesn't resolve the moral dispute. What evidence could God introduce that would demonstrate to this dissenter that freedom is better than happiness? Could there really be such evidence? Isn't such a dispute ultimately a matter of disagreement in attitude?*

The moral subjectivist claims that no evidence, even the revelation of some divine law, would resolve our moral disputes. In the last analysis, what

---

*Some theists are inclined to say: "What God commands must be good because God is omniscient and hence knows what is good." Or: "What God commands must be good because God is Goodness." Note that these arguments, as stated, assume rather than support the conclusion they purport to establish. What is at issue here is whether goodness is a matter of knowledge rather than of attitude, whether goodness is an objective property or a subjective matter of attitude. Such arguments simply assume the conclusion they are supposed to support. They simply assume a form of moral objectivism.

the individual approves of is pronounced "good," and what does not meet approval is "bad." Moral judgments, then, are basically expressions of one's attitudes and feelings.

MORAL SUBJECTIVISM RECONSIDERED

If this argument for moral subjectivism seems forceful, note that this position still has not been stated very precisely. If we are to evaluate moral subjectivism properly, we need to describe it in greater detail.

There have been some terribly implausible versions of moral subjectivism. It will be helpful to sketch a very crude version of moral subjectivism and then show how, and why, it has been altered over the last thirty or forty years to yield a more sophisticated version. It is interesting that this refined theory of moral subjectivism bears a resemblance to a version of moral objectivism that is different from, and perhaps more plausible than, the type of objectivist theory indicated earlier. We shall also reconsider moral objectivism in this other form.

One crude form of moral subjectivism claims that moral judgments or theories are simple descriptions of the speaker's attitudes. The statement "X is right" means "I approve of X"; the statement "X is wrong" means "I disapprove of X." According to this theory, all sincere moral judgments are true. When one person says, "All abortion is wrong" and another says, "Not all abortion is wrong," neither statement need be false because the second does not really contradict the first. One person is saying, "I (John smith) disapprove of all abortion" and the other, "I (Mary Jones) do not disapprove of all abortion." These statements do not literally contradict each other, though they do indicate that the speakers have different attitudes toward abortion. Both statements, if they are sincere reports of the speakers' feelings, are true.

That this version of moral subjectivism is implausible—or, at least, incomplete—as an account of our moral judgments can be seen by noting certain features of our moral discourse that are highlighted in the story "Those Who Help Themselves." The people on Omega debate moral issues and come to considerable agreement. We on Earth may not reach so much agreement, but we certainly do debate moral matters. We attempt to persuade others of our moral views and occasionally succeed. We have a saying: "There's no disputing matters of taste." Yet we dispute matters of morals. How can this be, if morality is simply a matter of taste or preference? Earlier, we saw that subjectivists say that to make a moral judgment is to state a preference. One clear example of a statement of preference would be: "I prefer country living to city living." But this doesn't seem to be an attempt to persuade or an invitation to debate. If moral judgments are only statements of preference, how is it that they so often seem to be attempts to persuade, that they so often provoke debate?

"Those Who Help Themselves" assumes that there is at least a theoretical distinction between doing what is in one's self-interest and doing what is morally right. In part, at least, this relates to the distinction between what is in one's own interest and what is in the interest of others. On Omega, in practice, there is little real conflict in this matter. The moral efficacy of the Omegan's belief in perpetual, random reincarnation is that it leads them to believe that in helping others they are helping themselves. On Earth, there is considerable conflict between a person's own interests and that which is morally right or between one's own interests and the interests of others. This conflict is not only external, but internal. That is, not only do people often recognize a conflict between self-interest and the interests of others, but they often feel a conflict between what they want for themselves and what they feel they morally ought to do. Is there any hint of the distinction between one's self-interest and that which is morally right in the moral subjectivist theory described above? If moral judgments are only statements of preference, what does morality per se have to do with conflicts in preferences? If my moral judgments are simply statements of my preferences, how is it that I feel a conflict between my preferences and my morality? How could there be a conflict between my preferences and my preferences?

These are forceful objections to the simple form of moral subjectivism presented earlier. Most present-day moral subjectivists have recognized the force of these criticisms and have attempted to emend subjectivism to meet them.

Moral judgments, say these subjectivists, do not merely have the function of stating preferences. They also have the function of attempting to influence the preferences and actions of others. The I-approve-of-it analysis of moral judgments is not adequate. The judgment "It is good, or right" would be better analyzed as meaning "I approve of this; you should approve of this as well; you should do this sort of thing." How one succeeds in affecting the preferences and actions of others is obvious enough. Often we can be shown that what we think we want is not what we really want. "You say you want to see that movie, but you wouldn't like it; the reviews say it is a violent film, and you hate violence." Also, most people have a considerable interest in gaining the approval of others. "We don't do that sort of thing around here" is the kind of "statement" that influences people of all ages. If people at your dinner table said, "Please don't eat the stringbeans with your fingers; it's disgusting," you might well stop, without assuming that what you were doing was objectively bad.

Furthermore, present-day subjectivists would say that moral preferences are a particular type of preference. One's moral preferences express how one would like to see all people treat one another; they express general prescriptions, rules for human behavior. Moral preferences are not the I'd-like-to-get-this type of preference. Rather, they imply the message: I approve of this kind of human behavior; let us all act in this sort of way. Moral preferences are one's preferences from the standpoint of a hypothetical legislator for all human beings. A person's preferred rules count as moral rules only if they are not prejudiced in favor of one's particular circumstances. To propose moral rules is to imply that such rules should apply even if one were in the other person's position. In the words of the eighteenth-century philosopher Immanuel Kant, moral judgments are "universalizable."

A person who, using imagination, discounts his or her particular circumstances, surveys the human condition, and decides what rules all human beings should follow is said to be taking the "moral point of view." To express a moral preference is to express a preference from the moral point of view.

In addition to "moral preferences," people have "personal preferences." Our personal preferences have to do with what we each want for ourselves. Our personal desires often conflict. Our desire to spend two weeks at the beach may conflict with our desire to save money for some new clothing. In an analogous way, says the subjectivist, our moral preferences and our personal preferences may conflict. From the moral point of view, we may wish that people would keep their promises. From the personal point of view, we may wish to break a promise we find very inconvenient to keep. Thus it is that there is often a conflict between self-interest and that which is morally right, says the subjectivists. This is not a matter of a clash between personal preferences and the dictates of some objective moral rules. Rather, it is a matter of a clash between personal preferences and moral preferences.

The present-day moral subjectivist, then, says that moral judgments are not simply statements of preference. Moral judgments express one's preferences as to the rules one would like to see everyone follow.

Does this "concession" by the subjectivist amount to something more than the patching up of a theory that states that morality and moral debate are fundamentally nonrational? It would seem so. Most subjectivists feel that the recognition of the special nature of moral preferences, of the moral point of view, has important implications for ethical debate. Some objectivists have even claimed that this supposed emendation of the subjectivist theory actually yields a form of moral objectivism. Let us examine these claims.

One cannot deduce a particular morality from the definition of the moral point of view. This is as it should be. The definition, after all, is supposed to represent something implied by all moral judgments.

Nonetheless, it is conceivable that many people make judgments which they claim to be moral judgments, but which they would not endorse if they seriously took the moral point of view. They may be proposing rules which they say are moral rules, but which they would not be willing to acknowledge if they were in the other person's position. Such people are inconsistent in that they are claiming to take a point of view that they are not really taking.

Some philosophers have claimed that human psychology is such that persons who seriously took the moral point of view would all endorse the same set of rules. This claim implies a form of moral objectivism: Only one moral theory is compatible with the moral point of view and the facts of human psychology. Moral subjectivists deny that this is so. But most subjectivists do believe that many people would have to modify their moral judgments if they seriously took the moral point of view.

Some people may endorse the segregation of blacks or of Jews. Suppose that such people were to learn that they themselves were of Negroid or Jewish extraction. Would they continue to hold their bigoted views? In most cases, this seems doubtful. If so, then such people must admit that their views represent personal preferences rather than moral preferences.

Some people are fortunate enough to make millions of dollars. They may endorse a survival-of-the-fittest morality and say: Let the poor fend for themselves. Suppose these people were to be deprived of their money and their ability to make more. Would they then say: I'm not fit, let me perish? Or would they say: How about a social welfare program? If the latter, then their original judgments were not moral preferences but personal preferences.

Would anything be gained by persuading people to admit that certain of their views constituted personal preferences and not moral preferences? In some cases, no. Some people are content to be amoral. But many people care very much about morality. After all, to engage in moral dialogue is to engage in a kind of intellectual arbitration. As in any kind of arbitration, one may sometimes lose, but the arbitration procedure does offer one certain protections. To abandon morality would be to agree to let human relations be governed by whim and strength. This prospect bothers many people very much. Also, the psychology of most adults seems to be such that believing they are moral is crucial to their feelings of self-respect. Few adults like to admit that they are amoral or immoral; instead, people tend to adjust their morality to agree with their self-interest. But such adjustments are not really compatible with having a morality.

In any case, the question at issue here is whether there can be a rational resolution of moral questions. Whether, and to what degree, people are willing to be moral, willing to act on their moral preferences rather than on their personal ones, is a very serious question, but it is also a quite different question from the one we are considering.

In "Those Who Help Themselves," the metaphysical beliefs of the Omegans motivate them to take the moral point of view constantly. They believe in a perpetual, random reincarnation of souls that will eventually place each of them in different social positions and circumstances. They are motivated continuously to ask themselves: What if I were in the other person's position? Probably this is a question that most of us manage to avoid a good deal of the time.

In the story, taking the moral point of view does not resolve all moral questions. There remain disagreements about whether there ought to be competition or an equal distribution of goods, whether one ought to promote happiness over excellence, and so forth. Nonetheless, the story implies that people who really did take the moral point of view would be in close enough agreement that they would get along quite well. And, indeed, if human beings could come to this much agreement in their views, they might well be quite satisfied.

Moral objectivists, of course, would say that the story presumes too little. Many subjectivists would say that it presumes too much.

FROM THE MORAL POINT OF VIEW

Perhaps it would be helpful to take a contemporary moral–social issue and show how it is related to normative philosophical debates that make conscious reference to the moral point of view.

We are all familiar with the issue of how the goods of a society ought to be distributed among its members. Should all the goods be distributed on the basis of competition? Or should all the goods be distributed equally? Or should every individual be guaranteed a certain minimum of goods, and the remaining goods be distributed on the basis of competition? If the last, how much should the guaranteed minimum be?

One normative ethical theory that is favored by British philosophers is **utilitarianism.** The premise of utilitarianism is that the only thing valuable in itself is happiness and that a society ought to promote the greatest happiness of the greatest number. The emphasis here is on "greatest happiness" rather than on "greatest number." If the greatest total happiness in society would be achieved by, say, a competitive system that allocated most of the goods to seventy-five percent of the members, rather than by a less competitive system that distributed goods more equally, then utilitarianism would favor the first system.

This is not to say that utilitarianism per se favors competition and unequal distribution. We cannot derive a specific answer to the question of how goods ought to be distributed in a society from the utilitarian principle alone. We would also need factual information about what social system would create the greatest total happiness in a particular society. Nonetheless, it is the case that utilitarianism does not insist upon a guaranteed minimum for all individual.

A number of philosophers have criticized utilitarianism as "unjust" in this respect: They have said that a more acceptable normative theory would be one that insisted upon substantial guarantees for every individual. One of these critics is John Rawls, whose book *Justice as Fairness** is much discussed by philosophers today. He has formulated a concise normative theory that he believes is preferable to utilitarianism, and he has defended his theory via an imaginative test that he claims is equivalent to taking the moral point of view. "Those Who Help Themselves" was written with Rawls in mind. But it should be noted that the remarks that follow are such a simplification as to amount almost to a distortion of Rawls's views. For instance, Rawls seems to claim that liberty is valuable in itself, quite apart from its effects on happiness. That claim shall be ignored. What we shall focus on is that part of Rawls's principle that has to do with the effect of the distribution of goods on happiness.

Rawls says that society should deviate from an equal distribution of goods only if, and only to the extent that, every member is at least a little better off, over time, under a system that distributes unequally. If, for example, a competitive system would produce more goods and more happiness, then the

*Cambridge, Mass.: The Belknap Press of Harvard University, 1971.

competitive system would be acceptable—but only if, and to the extent that, every individual gained something by such a competitive system.

As with utilitarianism, no specific answer to the question of how goods ought to be distributed in a society can be derived from Rawls's principle. Again, we need information about benefits that might accrue through competition. But it is clear that Rawls's principle insists on a relatively sizable guarantee for each individual, whereas the utilitarian principle does not insist on any. Rawls's principle would seem more likely to lead to a more equal distribution of goods than would that of the utilitarian.

What is of special interest in the context of this chapter is the way that Rawls attempts to defend his principle with an appeal to the moral point of view. He asks us to imagine that we are about to enter life. We do not know what our interests and abilities will be; we do not know what our position in society will be. We must choose some general normative principle that will guide us in determining what sort of social system we will have. According to Rawls, being in such a situation would be the literal equivalent of taking the moral point of view. Obviously, such a situation would be analogous to the situation on Omega, with the—possibly important—difference that each Omegan is already living a life and believes that there are a great number of lives to go. Rawls claims that in such a situation people would choose his principle rather than that of the utilitarian. His principle is the one most compatible with the moral point of view (and with the facts of human psychology).

The utilitarians have responded by claiming that the selection of the utilitarian principle would be the more rational by normal standards of rationality. Suppose that you and nine others were offered one of two lotteries, each requiring a wager of ten dollars. In the first lottery (subsidized by the Better Business Bureau, one might suppose), five of you will lose the ten dollars, and five of you will win one hundred dollars. In the second lottery (not subsidized), all of you will get back five dollars, and five will receive ten more dollars, getting back a total of fifteen. Which lottery would you choose? The first, of course. Similarly, suppose you were to "bet your life" on one of two societies. In the first society, ninety-five percent of the people would be very happy, and five percent of the people very miserable. In the second society, fifty percent of the people would be mildly happy, and fifty percent mildly miserable. Which society would you choose? The first, of course. Rawls's principle, however, would favor the second lottery and the second society. The utilitarian principle that would always give the best "odds on happiness" would be the more rational by normal standards of rationality. So the utilitarian argues.

But Rawls argues that persons wagering an entire lifetime would adopt the more conservative betting strategy. The idea of living one's life in great misery would be such a fearful prospect that people would be willing to take lesser odds on happiness to ensure that they would not suffer great misery.

"Those Who Help Themselves" imagines that all would insist on at least some guaranteed minimum but would differ as to the distribution of goods beyond that. "Apparently, those supporting the largest opposition party were gamblers: They were willing to risk the possibility of some misfortune in the next life for the possibility of gaining great wealth in this life. Those on the opposite end of the political spectrum were unwilling to gamble at all with their future lives: The wanted to be guaranteed an equal share of the wealth. Those who supported the majority party wanted some guarantees and some chances to gamble. But none was willing to gamble too much with his or her future life, to risk being diseased, mentally defective, or hungry, and being without help."

You might discuss this problem with your friends. Do you agree with the utilitarian viewpoint or with Rawls? Or can you formulate some other principle that you would prefer? How close can you come to agreement with one another?

This, of course, is related to the broader question: Would those who seriously took the moral point of view come to complete or considerable agreement on their moral views? Probably the only way to determine this is to continue our moral dialogues, but with greater philosophical clarity. In determining your moral preferences, try to make sure that you are taking the moral point of view. When you find that you and another person seem to disagree on an issue, try to conduct your discussion explicitly from the moral point of view. Perhaps this will not lead to greater agreement in your moral discussions. But the chances are that it will.

READINGS

A. C. EWING argues that our moral terms are not definitionally related to the commands of God.*

. . . I refer to the attempt to define ethical concepts in terms of religion by maintaining that to say something is good or right is to say that it is commanded by God. At first sight it may well seem that such a theory is refuted at once by the mere fact that agnostics and atheists can make rational judgments in ethics, but it will be replied that what even the atheist really has in mind when he thinks of obligation is some confused idea of a command, and that a command implies a commander and a perfect moral law a perfectly good commander on whose mind the whole moral law depends, so that the atheist is inconsistent in affirming the validity of the moral law and yet denying the existence of God. It may be doubted whether this argument, if valid, would make the theological statement an analysis of what the man meant and not rather of the logical consequences of what he meant, but there are other objections to such a definition.

(a) If "right" and "good" are themselves defined in terms of the commands of God, God cannot command anything because it is right or good, since this would only mean that He commanded it because He commanded it, and therefore there is no reason whatever for His commands, which become truly arbitrary. It would follow that God might just as rationally will that our whole duty should consist in cheating, torturing and killing people to the best of our ability, and that in that case it would be our duty to act in this fashion.

(b) And why are we to obey God's commands? Because we ought to do so? Since "we ought to do A" is held to mean "God Commands us to do A," this can only mean that we are commanded by God to obey God's commands, which supplies no further reason. Because we love God? But this involves the assumptions that we ought to obey God if we love Him, and that we ought to love Him. So it again presupposes ethical propositions which cannot without a vicious circle be validated by once more referring to God's commands. Because God is good? This could only mean that God carries out His own commands. Because God will punish us if we do not obey Him? This might be a very good reason from the point of view of self-interest, but self-interest cannot, as we have seen, be an adequate basis for ethics. Without a prior conception of God being good or His commands being right God would have no more claim on our obedience than Hitler except that He would have more power to make things uncomfortable for us if we disobeyed Him than Hitler ever had, and that is not an ethical reason. A moral obligation cannot be created by mere power and threat of punishment. No doubt if we first grant the fundamental concepts of ethics, the existence of God may put us under certain obligations which we otherwise would not have had, e.g. that of thinking of God, as the existence of a man's parents puts him under certain obligations under which he would not stand if they were dead, but we cannot possibly derive all obligations in this fashion from the concept of God. No doubt, if God is perfectly good, we ought to obey His will, but how can we know what His will for us is in a particular case without first knowing what we ought to do?

What I have said of course constitutes no objection to the belief in God or even to the view that we can have a valid argument from ethics to the existence of God, but these views can be held without holding that our ethical terms have to be defined in terms of God. . . . Nor is what I have said meant to imply that religion can have no important bearing on ethics, but I think its influence should lie more in helping people to bring themselves to do what would be their duty in any case and in influencing the general spirit in which it is done than in prescribing what our duty is. While it is quite contrary to fact to suggest that an agnostic or atheist cannot be a good man, the influence in the former respects of religious belief, whether true or false, cannot be denied to have been exceedingly strong.

C. L. STEVENSON (1908–1979), a subjectivist, discusses "disagreement in belief" versus "disagreement in interest."*

. . . Mr. G. E. Moore's familiar objection about the open question is chiefly pertinent in this regard. No matter what set of scientifically knowable properties a thing may have (says Moore, in effect), you will find, on careful introspection, that it is an open question to ask whether anything having these properties is *good*. It is difficult to believe that this recurrent question is a totally confused one, or that it seems open only because of the ambiguity of "good." Rather, we must be using some sense of "good" which is not definable, relevantly, in terms of anything scientifically knowable. That is, the scientific method is not sufficient for ethics. . . .

. . . We must distinguish between "disagreement in belief" (typical of the sciences) and "disagreement in interest." Disagreement in belief occurs when A believes *p* and B disbelieves. It. Disagreement in interest occurs when A has a favourable interest in X, when B has an unfavourable one in it, and when neither is content to let the other's interest remain unchanged.

Let me give an example of disagreement in interest. A. "Let's go to a cinema to-night." B. "I don't want to do that. Let's go to the symphony." A continues to insist on the cinema, B on the symphony. This is disagreement in a perfectly conventional sense. They can't agree on where they want to go, and each is trying to redirect the other's interest. (Note that imperatives are used in the example.)

It is disagreement in *interest* which takes place in ethics. When C says "This is good," and D says, "No, it's bad," we have a case of suggestion and counter-suggestion. Each man is trying to redirect the other's interest. There obviously need be no domineering, since each may be willing to give ear to the other's influence; but each is trying to move the other nonetheless. . . .

. . . When two people disagree over an ethical matter, can they completely resolve the disagreement through empirical considerations, assuming that each applies the empirical method exhaustively, consistently, and without error?

I answer that sometimes they can, and sometimes they cannot. . . .

Let's return to the example where A and B couldn't agree on a cinema or a symphony. The example differed from an ethical argument in that imperatives were used, rather than ethical judgments; but was analogous to the extent that each person was endeavouring to modify the other's interest. Now how would these people argue the case, assuming that they were too intelligent just to shout at one another?

Clearly, they would give "reasons" to support their imperatives. A might say, "But you know, Garbo is at the Bijou." His hope is that B, who admires

*From "The Emotive Meaning of Ethical Terms" by C. L. Stevenson, from *Mind*, Vol. XLVI, No. 181, January 1937. Reprinted by permission of Oxford University Press.

Garbo, will acquire a desire to go to the cinema when he knows what play will be there. B may counter, "But Toscanini is guest conductor to-night, in an all-Beethoven programme." And so on. Each supports his imperative ("*Let's* do so and so") by reasons which may be empirically established.

To generalize from this: Disagreement in interest may be rooted in disagreement in belief. That is to say, people who disagree in interest would often cease to do so if they knew the precise nature and consequences of the object of their interest. To this extent disagreement in interest may be resolved by securing agreement in belief, which in turn may be secured empirically.

This generalization holds for ethics. If A and B, instead of using imperatives, had said, respectively, "It would be *better* to go to the cinema," and "It would be better to go to the symphony," the reasons which they would advance would be roughly the same. They would each give a more thorough account of the object of interest, with the purpose of completing the redirection of interest which was begun by the suggestive force of the ethical sentence. On the whole, of course, the suggestive force of the ethical statement merely exerts enough pressure to start such trains of reasons, since the reasons are much more essential in resolving disagreement in interest than the persuasive effect of the ethical judgment itself.

Thus the empirical method is relevant to ethics simply because our knowledge of the world is a determining factor to our interests. But note that empirical facts are not inductive grounds from which the ethical judgment problematically follows. . . . If someone said "Close the door," and added the reason "We'll catch cold," the latter would scarcely be called an inductive ground of the former. Now imperatives are related to the reasons which support them in the same way that ethical judgments are related to reasons.

Is the empirical method *sufficient* for attaining ethical agreement? Clearly not. For empirical knowledge resolves disagreement in interest only to the extent that such disagreement is rooted in disagreement in belief. Not all disagreement in interest is of this sort. For instance: A is of a sympathetic nature, and B isn't. They are arguing about whether a public dole would be good. Suppose that they discovered all the consequences of the dole. Isn't it possible, even so, that A will say it's good, and B that it's bad? The disagreement in interest may arise not from limited factual knowledge, but simply from A's sympathy and B's coldness. Or again, suppose, in the above argument, that A was poor and unemployed, and that B was rich. Here again the disagreement might not be due to different factual knowledge. It would be due to the different social positions of the men, together with their predominant self-interest.

When ethical disagreement is not rooted in disagreement in belief, is there *any* method by which it may be settled? If one means by "method" a *rational* method, then there is no method. But in any case there is a "way." Let's consider the above example, again, where disagreement was due to A's sympathy and B's coldness. Must they end by saying, "Well, it's just a matter of our having different temperaments"? Not necessarily. A, for instance, may try to *change* the temperament of his opponent. He may pour out his enthusiasms in such a moving way—present the sufferings of the poor with such appeal—that he will lead his opponent to see life through different eyes. He may build up, by the contagion of his feelings, an influence which will modify B's temperament, and create in him a sympathy for the poor which didn't previously exist. This is often the only way to obtain ethical agreement, if there is any way at all. It is persuasive, not empirical or rational; but that is no reason for neglecting it. There is no reason to scorn it, either, for it is only by such means that our personalities are able to grow, through our contact with others. . . .

R. M. HARE believes that moral judgments are universalizable prescriptions. Here he discusses to what degree fundamental moral disagreement is compatible with universalizability and the facts of human psychology.*

For the sake of a name, let me refer to the type of doctrine which I put forward in *The Language of Morals*, and still hold, as "universal prescriptivism"—a combination, that is to say, of universalism (the view that moral judgments are universalizable) and prescriptivism (the view that they are, at any rate typically, prescriptive).

. . . Now, as I hope to show, the combination . . . is sufficient to establish the rationality of morals, or the possibility of cogent moral arguments. . . .

In order to illustrate this use again, let us suppose that we are having an argument with a man who maintains that a black skin, by itself, is a sufficient ground for discriminating against its possessor. We tell him, and he, being a credulous person, believes the following story. The Soviet Institute of Race Relations (which is a much more enterprising and scientific body than its Western counterparts) has just succeeded in breeding a new kind of bacillus, which Soviet agents are at this very moment broadcasting in areas of racial conflict throughout the world. This bacillus is very catching, and the symptom of the disease which it induces is that, if the patient's skin was white, it turns permanently black, and vice versa. Now when the person with whom we are arguing has absorbed the implications of this story, we ask him whether he still thinks that skin-colour by itself is a sufficient ground for moral discrimination. It is unlikely that he will go on saying that it is; for then he will have to say that if he catches the disease the former blacks who have also had it will have acquired the right to oppress *him*, and all his formerly white friends.

What do we learn from this simple piece of science fiction? What we have got our opponent to do by this innocent deception is to perform an intellectual operation which, if he had really been wanting to reason morally, he would have performed without the deception. This operation is to consider the hypothetical case in which he himself has lost the quality which he said was a sufficient ground for discrimination, and his present victims have gained it—and to consider this hypothetical case as if it were actual. There are two stages in the process of universalization. The first is passed when we have found a universal principle, not containing proper names or other singular terms, from which the moral judgment which we want to make follows, given the facts of our particular situation. This stage is comparatively easy to pass, even for the proponent of the most scandalous moral views. It is passed, for example, by adducing the principle that it is all right for black people to be oppressed by white people. But the next stage is more difficult. It is necessary, not merely that this principle should be produced, but that the person who produces it should actually hold it. It is necessary not merely to *quote* a maxim, but (in Kantian language) to *will* it to be a universal law. It is here that pre-scriptivity, the second main logical feature of moral judgements, makes its most decisive appearance. For willing it to be a universal law involves willing it to apply even when the roles played by the parties are reversed. And this test will be failed by all maxims or principles which look attractive to oppressors and persecutors on the first test. It will indeed be found that, if we apply these two tests, both founded on the logical, formal features of moral terms, we shall be able to sort out, in the field of race relations at least, the grounds of discrimination which we are really prepared to count as morally relevant from those which we are not.

From this satisfactory conclusion, however, there is, as we have seen, a way of escape for the sufficiently determined racialist. It remains to illustrate, in terms of the present example, what price he has to pay for his escape. Let us suppose that there is a racialist the mainspring of whose racialism is a horror of miscegenation; and let us suppose that the source of this horror is not any belief about the consequences, social or biological, of miscegenation. That is to say, he is not moved by alleged facts about the weakening of the human stock by mating between people of different colours, or about the unsatisfactory life lived by people of mixed descent, or by anything of that kind. If these were his grounds, we could argue with him in a scientific way, trying to show that the offspring of mixed marriages are just as likely to be vigorous and intelligent as those of other marriages; of that any bad social effects of miscegenation would be removed if *he* and people like him abandoned their attempts to enforce a colour bar. Let us suppose, however, that his grounds are not these, but simply a horror of the very idea of a black man mating with a white woman. This cannot be touched by any scientific or factual argument of the sort described. And it may well be true that, if miscegenation is to be prevented, it is necessary to have a rigid colour bar; and that if this is enforced, and leads to resentment, other repressive measures will be necessary for the maintenance of public order, and thus we shall have the whole apparatus of racial repression. If this is true, then it will be hard for us to argue with this man. He detests miscegenation so much that he is prepared to live in a police state in order to avoid it.

And he must be prepared for more that this. He must, if he is going to universalize his moral judgements, be prepared that he himself should not merely live in a police state, but live in it in the same conditions as he is now prepared to make the blacks live in—conditions which are getting steadily worse. He must be prepared that *he* should be subject to arbitrary arrest and maltreatment just on grounds of skin colour, and to butchery if he tries, in collaboration with his fellows, to protest.

Now it may be that there are people so fanatical as to be prepared for all these things in order to avoid miscegenation. But they are surely very few. The repression happens because these few people have on their side a multitude of other people who are not prepared at all to suffer thus, but who have not really thought through the argument. They think, perhaps, that all will be well without too much repression; or that blacks do not mind being treated like this as much as whites would; or that there is a scientific basis for belief in racial superiority—or some of the many other things that racialists tend to believe. All these beliefs can perhaps be refuted severally by scientists and others without any help from the philosophers; but they are apt, collectively, to form an amalgam in the minds of racialists which makes into allies of the fanatic many people who are not, in themselves, in the least fanatical. The contribution of the philosopher is to take this amalgam apart, deposit such beliefs as are open to scientific refutation in the in-trays of the scientists, and, when the scientists have dealt with them, exhibit the prescriptive remainder of racialism for what it is—something that fanatics may hold but which the bulk of a people—even a people as hard-pressed as the white South Africans—never will.

. . . In all cases the principle is the same—am I prepared to accept a maxim which would allow this to be done to me, were I in the position of this man . . . and capable of having only the experiences, desires, &c., of him . . . ?

It may be objected that not all people will follow this mode of reasoning which I have been suggesting. . . . No doubt there are some white South Africans (a few) who will be quite unmoved by being told that they are causing the Bantu to suffer. It seems that I am required to say what has gone wrong in such cases.

A number of different things may have gone wrong. The commonest is what we call insensitivity or lack of imagination. . . . These people are not paying attention to the relevant similarities between themselves and their victims. . . .

It is also possible that, though fully aware of what they are doing to their victims, they are not reasoning morally about it. That is to say, they are not asking themselves whether they can universalize their prescriptions; though they may make play with the moral *words* which they have heard other people use, they are not, in their own thinking, using these words according to the logical rules which are implicit in their meaning. And there are other possibilities, too numerous to mention here, which have been examined in the body of this book.

It may be asked: What is to be done about this? Can the philosopher, in particular, do anything about it? When South African believers in white supremacy read this book, will they at once hasten to repeal the pass laws and make the blacks their political equals? This is highly unlikely; and in any case they will not read the book. To get people to think morally it is not sufficient to tell them how to do it; it is necessary also to induce in them the wish to do it. And this is not the province of the philosopher. It is more likely that enlightened politicians, journalists, radio commentators, preachers, novelists, and all those who have an influence on public opinion will gradually effect a change for the better—given that events do not overtake them. Perhaps people in areas of racial conflict can be, in the end, brought to think of the resemblances between themselves and members of the other races as morally relevant, and of the differences as morally irrelevant. Perhaps, even, they may learn to cultivate their imaginations. But this much can be claimed for philosophy, that it is sometimes easier to bring something about if we understand clearly what it is we are trying to do.

JEREMY BENTHAM (1748–1832): Utilitarianism.*

By the principle of utility is meant that principle which approves or disapproves of every action whatsoever, according to the tendency which it appears to have to augment or diminish the happiness of the party whose interest is in question; or what is the same thing in other words, to promote or to oppose that happiness. I say of every action whatsoever; and therefore not only of every action of a private individual, but of every measure of government.

By utility is meant that property in any object, whereby it tends to produce benefit, advantage, pleasure, good, or happiness (all this in the present case comes to the same thing) or (what comes again to the same thing) to prevent the happening of mischief, pain, evil, or unhappiness to the party whose interest is considered: if that party be the community in general, then the happiness of the community: if a particular individual, then the happiness of that individual.

The interest of the community is one of the most general expressions that can occur in the phraseology of morals: no wonder that the meaning is often lost. When it has a meaning, it is this. The community is a fictitious *body*, composed of the individual persons who are considered as constituting as it were its *members*. The interest of the community then is, what?—the sum of the interests of the several members who compose it.

It is in vain to talk of the interest of the community, without understanding what is the interest of the individual. A thing is said to promote the interest, or to be *for* the interest, of an individual, when it tends to add to the sum total of his pleasures: or, what comes to the same thing, to diminish the sum total of his pains.

An action then may be said to be comfortable to the principle of utility, or, for shortness' sake, to utility (meaning with respect to the community at

*From Jeremy Bentham, *An Introduction to the Principles of Morals and Legislation*, 1823.

large) when the tendency it has to augment the happiness of the community is greater than any it has to diminish it.

A measure of government (which is but a particular kind of action, performed by a particular person or persons) may be said to be conformable to or dictated by the principle of utility, when in like manner the tendency which it has to augment the happiness of the community is greater than any which it has to diminish. . . .

To take an exact account then of the general tendency of any act, by which the interests of a community are affected, proceed as follows. . . .

Sum up all the values of all the *pleasures* on the one side, and those of all the *pains* on the other. The balance, if it be on the side of pleasure, will give the *good* tendency of the act upon the whole, with respect to the interests of that *individual* person; if on the side of pain, the *bad* tendency of it upon the whole.

Take an account of the *number* of persons whose interests appear to be concerned; and repeat the above process with respect to each. *Sum up* the numbers expressive of the degrees of *good* tendency, which the act has, with respect to each individual, in regard to whom the tendency of it is *good* upon the whole: do this again with respect to each individual, in regard to whom the tendency of it is *bad* upon the whole. Take the *balance;* which, if on the side of *pleasure,* will give the general *good tendency* of the act, with respect to the total number or community of individuals concerned; if on the side of *pain,* the general *evil tendency,* with respect to the same community.

JOHN RAWLS, from *Justice as Fairness.**

My aim is to present a conception of justice which generalizes and carries to a higher level of abstraction the familiar theory of the social contract. . . . In order to do this we are not to think of the original contract as one to enter a particular society or to set up a particular form of government. Rather, the guiding idea is that the principles of justice for the basic structure of society are the object of the original agreement. They are the principles that free and rational persons concerned to further their own interests would accept in an initial position of equality as defining the fundamental terms of their association. These principles are to regulate all further agreements; they specify the kinds of social cooperation that can be entered into and the forms of government that can be established. This way of regarding the principles of justice I shall call justice as fairness.

Thus we are to imagine that those who engage in social cooperation choose together, in one joint act, the principles which are to assign basic rights and duties and to determine the division of social benefits. Men are to decide in advance how they are to regulate their claims against one another and what is to be the foundation charter of their society. Just as each person must decide

*Reprinted by permission of the publishers from *A Theory of Justice* by John Rawls, Cambridge, Mass.: The Belknap Press of Harvard University Press. Copyright © 1971 by the President and Fellows of Harvard College.

by rational reflection what constitutes his good, that is, the system of ends which it is rational for him to pursue, so a group of persons must decide once and for all what is to count among them as just and unjust. The choice which rational men would make in this hypothetical situation of equal liberty, assuming for the present that this choice problem has a solution, determines the principles of justice.

In justice as fairness the original position of equality corresponds to the state of nature in the traditional theory of the social contract. This original position is not, of course, thought of as an actual historical state of affairs, much less a primitive condition of culture. It is understood as a purely hypothetical situation. . . . .

. . . Among the essential features of this situation is that no one knows his place in society, his class position or social status, nor does any one know his fortune in the distribution of natural assets and abilities, his intelligence, strength, and the like. I shall even assume that the parties do not know their conceptions of the good or their special psychological propensities. The principles of justice are chosen behind a veil of ignorance. This ensures that no one is advantaged or disadvantaged in the choice of principles by the outcome of natural chance or the contingency of social circumstances. Since all are similarly situated and no one is able to design principles to favor his particular condition, the principles of justice are the result of a fair agreement or bargain. . . .

One feature of justice as fairness is to think of the parties in the initial situated as rational and mutually disinterested. This does not mean that the parties are egoists, that is, individuals with only certain kinds of interests, say in wealth, prestige, and domination. But they are conceived as not taking an interest in one another's interests. They are to presume that even their spiritual aims may be opposed, in the way that the aims of those of different religions may be opposed. . . .

. . . Once the principles of justice are thought of as arising from an original agreement in a situation of equality, it is an open question whether the principle of utility would be acknowledged. Offhand it hardly seems likely that persons who view themselves as equals, entitled to press their claims upon one another, would agree to a principle which may require lesser life prospects for some simply for the sake of a greater sum of advantages enjoyed by others. Since each desires to protect his interests, his capacity to advance his conception of the good, no one has a reason to acquiesce in an enduring loss for himself in order to bring about a greater net balance of satisfaction. In the absence of strong and lasting benevolent impulses, a rational man would not accept a basic structure merely because it maximized the algebraic sum of advantages irrespective of its permanent effects on his own basic rights and interests. Thus it seems that the principle of utility is incompatible with the conception of social cooperation among equals for mutual advantage. It appears to be inconsistent with the idea of reciprocity implicit in the notion of a well-ordered society. Or, at any rate, so I shall argue.

I shall maintain instead that the persons in the initial situation would choose two rather different principles: the first requires equality in the assignment of basic rights and duties, while the second holds that social and economic inequalities, for example inequalities of wealth and authority, are just only if they result in compensating benefits for everyone, and in particular for the least advantaged members of society. These principles rule out justifying institutions on the grounds that the hardships of some are offset by a greater good in the aggregate. It may be expedient but it is not just that some should have less in order that others may prosper. But there is no injustice in the greater benefits earned by a few provided that the situation of persons not so fortunate is thereby improved. The intuitive idea is that since everyone's well-being depends upon a scheme of cooperation without which no one could have a satisfactory life, the dividend of advantages should be such as to draw forth the willing cooperation of everyone taking part in it, including those less well situated. Yet this can be expected only if reasonable terms are proposed. . . .

Questions and Exercises

1. What is the difference between normative ethical questions and metaethical questions?
2. Distinguish moral subjectivism from moral objectivism.
3. Present an argument for moral subjectivisim.
4. Consider the following moral judgments:
   a. It's wrong to abort a fetus.
   b. A person who murders another person ought to be executed
      Can you imagine any kind of evidence that would prove or disprove either of these statements? If so, what? If not, what possibilities did you consider, then reject?
5. "Moral judgments are simply statements of preference." In what ways, and for what reasons, has this version of moral subjectivism been modified?
6. What does it mean to take the "moral point of view"?
7. Define utilitarianism.
8. In what way does Rawls consider utilitarianism "unjust"? What principle does Rawls substitute for the utilitarianism principle of distribution?
9. Why does the utilitarian think this theory would be chosen from the moral point of view? Why does Rawls think his theory would be chosen from the moral point of view?
10. If all people conscientiously took the moral point of view in making their moral judgments, which one of the following do you think would result? Explain.
    a. Total agreement in their moral views.
    b. Much more agreement than now, but not total agreement.
    c. Some more agreement than now.
    d. No change.

11. What relevance does Ewing believe the commands of God have in determining right and wrong? Does Ewing think that religion has an important relationship to ethics? Explain.

12. Explain Stevenson's distinction between "disagreement in belief" and "disagreement in interest." Do moral disputes involve just one of them? Both? Explain.

13. Does Stevenson believe there is any rational method for resolving disagreements in interest? Explain.

14. What does Hare believe are the minimum conditions for having a morality?

15. Does Hare believe that everyone who met the minimum conditions of having a morality would agree that racial prejudice is morally wrong?

16. Four coworkers who entered a contest together have won the right to race through a grocery store/pharmacy and keep whatever they can manage to get outside the store in half an hour. The store is huge, and it would be impossible for anyone to get around to the different departments in the time allotted. The four people are going to rely heavily on what they get for their sustenance in the next couple of weeks, since they are all temporarily broke, having been laid off. Three of the coworkers are healthy, but tend to be a little sluggish unless they're in a competitive situation (they love sports); the fourth is an asthmatic who can't move too fast (and is almost out of his asthma medication). They need a procedure for collecting goods and then dividing them up.

    a. How would their reasoning go if they followed Bentham?

    b. How would their reasoning go if they followed Rawls?

    c. Do you think the results would be different in these two cases? If so, how so? If not, why not?

4

One Moral Issue:
The Right to Die

Fiction: Death on Demand

Mrs. Burke brought the car to a stop across the street from the clinic. She stared at her knuckles clenched on the steering wheel, then took a couple of deep breaths. This was the moment she had dreaded more than all the other dreadful moments in this thing.

"Billy," she said softly, "it's time to say goodbye to Grandpa."

She turned and saw the two of them as they'd been since leaving the house: the eighty-seven-year-old man and the seven-year-old boy, sitting together, holding hands, saying nothing, just staring ahead. She saw the boy's hand tighten on the man's hand.

"No," whispered the boy.

She felt her own hands shake. She hadn't wanted to bring the boy along, but the sitter had cancelled at the last moment and she didn't dare put this off. If only . . . but, no, it wasn't that really. The clinic had told her they had a woman who'd watch Billy, play with him; he'd probably be better off with her than with that harebrained sitter who did nothing but watch television. It was simply the moment of goodbye she dreaded, whether it happened here or somewhere else.

"Billy . . ."

"No."

God, the two of them were crying now. For an instant she thought about turning the car around and going home. But she knew she couldn't do that, couldn't bear to have the whole thing start over again: putting up with the old man's incoherencies, his fumblings, his constant demands for attention, his messes—it was obscene to have to change diapers on an old man. And she and Harry'd be at each other again—all that yelling—with Harry drinking too much and getting violent and threatening to leave. They didn't have the money to put the old man in a nursing home, and there were hardly any free

107

ones anymore, what with the government cutting back the funds year by year. And it wasn't as if they'd pushed the old man into it. It wasn't until that day when he'd said, "I want to die," that they'd really taken the idea seriously. So why did she have to feel like the villain?

"Dad," she began, trying to force some firmness into her voice, "it's time to . . . oh, no!"

She saw them then, the people starting to descend on the car, maybe twenty people, mostly women, with grim, angry faces. They were carrying signs like battle-axes, the message blurring with the joggling except for that one word she saw over and over: Murderer, Murderer . . .

"Damn it, we're getting out of this car," she yelled. "Right now!"

* * * * * *

Nurse Wyman stifled a yawn and glanced at her watch. It was three in the afternoon and it felt like three in the morning. How would she ever manage to stay awake? She'd had no business staying up for the late, late show, not after working a double shift. But the film had been one of her favorites—*Sweet Desire, Part I*—and she hadn't been able to resist. She was an incurable romantic, there were no two ways about it. That's probably why she'd become a nurse, wanting to become an angel of mercy, just like Florence Nightingale. Only it wasn't like in her childhood books at all: there was so much routine, so much boredom. Well, that's just how real life was. At least she had her books and her movies. And tonight there'd be *Sweet Desire, Part II*.

"Ladies and gentlemen, I'm sorry about the fuss out there . . ."

At the sound of the Director's voice, Nurse Wyman straightened quickly in her chair. Then she realized that his voice came from the next corridor. She remembered that he was conducting another one of his tours for foreign visitors; in that case he wouldn't be coming to her department for another forty minutes or so. She let her body slump.

"They call themselves Pro-Lifers," said the Director, with a theatrical laugh. *"As if we weren't all pro-life. But we must consider the quality of life . . ."*

"Not to mention the sanctity of human choice," muttered Nurse Wyman, absently, the way one talks along with a familiar jingle one has heard often. The Director's voice began to fade as he moved away.

". . . start with the counseling offices. As you must have noted in my report, we insist that each applicant have a minimum of five sessions . . ."

Nurse Wyman stared unhappily at the paperwork stacked in front of her. She had almost gotten up the energy to tackle it when she saw Nurse Anderson approaching with . . . what was the woman's name? . . . Evans?

"You remember Mrs. Evers," said Nurse Anderson, as she placed some papers on the desk.

Nurse Wyman glanced up at the applicant—a young, pretty thing, if one discounted the deep pallor on her face. Evers, yes: she remembered now. Husband killed in a water-skiing accident on the third day of their honeymoon. The woman had been treated for depression for almost a year and a half before she'd applied to the clinic. It was rather romantic, really, someone dying for love this way. Just like in that best-seller, *Love Lasts Forever*.

The forms were all in order, so Nurse Wyman got up from her desk and went to a cabinet, which she unlocked with a key from the chain she wore at the belt of her white uniform. On the top shelf of the cabinet were several small white cups, each containing two green-and-black capsules. She removed one of the cups and handed it to Nurse Anderson.

"The Blue Room?" said Nurse Anderson.

"Yes," said Nurse Wyman, taking from a wall rack a key attached to a blue-painted metal plate.

The three of them walked down the corridor to a door that Nurse Wyman unlocked. Inside was a small rectangular room containing a single bed, a nightstand, and an easy chair. The bed was covered with a blue cotton bedspread and the walls were papered with a blue flowered print. Nurse Wyman noticed that the paper was beginning to peel just a bit in one corner. Still, it was better than in some of the others.

Hearing Mrs. Evers give a small groan, she said: "Is something the matter?"

Mrs. Evers shook her head. "No. It doesn't matter how it looks."

"We do the best we can," said Nurse Wyman, keeping her voice even. It wouldn't be professional to show annoyance. Anyway, one had to make allowances.

"How long do I have the room?"

"We can allow you an hour. After that we'll need the room for someone else."

"Busy day, huh?" said Mrs. Evers with halfhearted sarcasm. She pointed at the door at the opposite end of the room. "That's where they'll take me out."

"Yes," said Nurse Wyman, summoning her professional patience. All the applicants had all these details explained to them well in advance, yet so many insisted on going over everything again here, at the door. "After a doctor has checked on you."

"You can still change your mind," said Nurse Anderson, with obvious emotion. "Once you're inside you won't be able to call out to us—the room is soundproofed—but . . ."

"Why? Why is it soundproofed?"

"To give the applicants some privacy. But if you push that red button there by the bed we'll come immediately. However you'd have to decide before you take the pills. Once you've taken them . . ." Nurse Anderson looked down at the floor.

"I remember now about the button," said Mrs. Evers. "The counselor told me that if I didn't go through with this I would have to wait at least a year before I got another chance."

"That's the rule," said Nurse Wyman. "At least in cases where there is . . . uh . . . no physical illness."

"No physical illness could hurt more than this does."

"Nonetheless . . ."

"I'm not arguing with you," said Mrs. Evers. "There won't be any pain? From the pills, I mean."

"None. It takes only three minutes or so before one loses consciousness. All one feels during that time is some numbness, then drowsiness."

"And there's no chance they won't work?"

"No. As long as you take them both. There's a carafe of water by the bed."

Mrs. Evers took a deep breath. "I'd better get on with it then."

She took two steps to the doorway, hesitated, then walked quickly into the room. As she got to the bed she suddenly bent over, holding her stomach with both hands, and gave a deep, wrenching cry.

"Mrs. Evers," said Nurse Anderson, her voice pleading, "Please recon–"

"Nurse Anderson," hissed Nurse Wyman, as she shut the door quickly, cutting off the sounds of sobbing from within the room. "I don't believe you!"

"I'm . . . I'm sorry."

"That was totally unprofessional. You know we're not allowed to challenge the applicants. Only the counselors can do that. Those poor people have enough on their minds without you trying to confuse them. I'm afraid I'll have to put you on report."

"No, please. I just forgot myself for a moment. The woman's so young."

"That's no excuse and you know it."

"But it's never happened before. It won't happen again. *Please.*"

"I'm sorry, I . . . ." Nurse Wyman stopped, and gave a sigh. "Maybe I am overreacting. You're a good nurse and you're entitled to one mistake. That case we had last month has got me on edge: that nurse who was sneaking the applicants pro-life pamphlets at the door. What a terrible thing to do." She gave Nurse Anderson a sharp look. "You're not one of them, are you?"

"No! You know I'm not."

"Of course you're not. As I say, I'm just overreacting. But you must assure me that something like that won't happen again."

"It won't."

"All right, then."

As the two of them walked back to the desk, Nurse Anderson said: "You know, I think the thing that got me was that I was so sure she wouldn't go through with it. I was so sure the counselors would talk her out of it."

"All they can do is try."

"Which one did she have, do you know?"

"Slattery, I believe."

Nurse Anderson gave a groan. "Not him. The man's incompe—"

"*. . . of course, with the Supreme Court decision of '94, everything became complete chaos. We knew what we couldn't forbid, we just didn't know . . .*"

Nurse Anderson jumped at the sound of the Director's voice; she glanced over her shoulder as if she expected him to be right there, listening to her. Instead he was nowhere in sight.

Nurse Wyman smiled. "His voice does carry, doesn't it. It's all right. He can't hear you."

Nonetheless Nurse Anderson lowered her voice to a whisper. "Slattery is incompetent. You know it. Everybody does."

Nurse Wyman shrugged. "He'll be retiring soon. Anyway, Mrs. Evers was in therapy for well over a year. She must know what she wants by now."

"*. . . the period of experimentation was not all to the bad, I suppose, though we did learn some hard lessons. Nevada's policy of issuing the pills without a prescription was an out-and-out disaster, as anyone with any common sense could have foreseen. California's fourteen-day `reconsideration period' seemed an improvement until the Berofsky murders, and those suicides by that Star Children cult, shocked the nation and forced Congress to formulate a national . . .*"

The Director emerged from a side corridor, nodding briefly to the two nurses while continuing his theatrical gestures, giving the absurd momentary impression that he was lecturing to them. But then his real audience appeared in his train, a group of about fifteen dignitaries who seemed to exhibit every conceivable combination of skin color and style of dress. The group followed the Director away from the nurses.

"*. . . follow me to the Review Board hearing room . . . what? . . . oh, yes, every case. If a counselor feels an extra five sessions are called for, the Board will generally go along with the counselor, but beyond that the Board will generally rule in favor of the applicant, assuming, of course, that the applicant meets the appropriate criteria in terms of physical condition or psychiatric history . . . what? . . . that is a good question. I do remember one such case involving an applicant involved in strategic research. He was asked to wait until . . . no, I'm afraid not. He jumped off a bridge . . . oh, hello there. Ladies and gentlemen, could we move to the side a little bit to let these people through . . .*"

The dignitaries moved to the side, openly gawking, as Nurse Costello led a middle-aged couple through the crowd toward the desk. The woman—Mrs. Lindberg, wasn't it?—had carcinoma of the liver, and her application had been handled quickly: the Board had even agreed to waive three of the five counseling sessions. The woman was terribly gaunt and was having trouble walking, even aided by her husband. It was rather touching the way her husband—a huge, robust man with large workman's hands—held her with such tenderness.

The crowd was gone, along with Nurse Anderson, by the time the three of them reached the desk.

"You know Mr. and Mrs. Lindahl," said Nurse Costello.

"Of course," said Nurse Wyman. "How do you do?"

At that Mrs. Lindahl burst into tears, and Nurse Wyman felt a pang of guilt at the thoughtless phrasing of her greeting. She'd gotten rattled by that episode with Nurse Anderson. But her guilt subsided as she saw that Mrs. Lindahl was smiling through her tears.

"I'm fine," said Mrs. Lindahl. "At least I will be in a few minutes. Finally. You don't know what I've been through these . . . I mean . . . that's silly . . . you're nurses . . . of course you know . . . I just mean I don't think I could have stood it any . . ."

Her words were lost in a fresh burst of tears, and her husband pulled her tighter, to comfort her. Nurse Wyman checked the forms, got the medication, and took them to the doorway of the Pink Room. As the couple glanced inside, the husband said: "Is it all right if I lie there with her, and hold her?"

"Of course," said Nurse Wyman, reassuringly, patting him on the shoulder. She glanced down at the pill cup in her hand and said: "Nurse Costello, would you help Mrs. Lindahl into the room while I have a word with her husband?"

When the wife was out of earshot, Nurse Wyman handed Mr. Lindahl the pills, studying his face as she said: "She must take both pills. If a person took one, it wouldn't be enough. Both pills. Do you understand?"

Mr. Lindahl nodded, but it was obvious he didn't understand her underlying meaning. Good. There had been two cases a couple of months back where a distraught spouse had tried to die along with the applicant, holding back a pill to take after the applicant was unconscious. Both partners had awoken from eight to twelve hours later and the situation had been terrible for everyone. One of these days they'd be able to concentrate enough of the chemical in one capsule. Meanwhile the spouse would just have to be warned.

As the door closed on the couple, Mrs. Lindahl was saying, "Bless you. Bless both of you for the work you're doing . . ."

"Well, that was nice," said Nurse Costello.

"I'll say," said Nurse Wyman. "I can't remember the last time I heard an applicant express any gratitude. I suppose it's understandable, but it would be nice if they thought of us occasionally."

"I can do without the gratitude," said Nurse Costello, "just as long as I don't get the complaints. In that nursing home where I worked, all I got were complaints all day. This place is such a relief after . . . what's wrong?"

Nurse Wyman realized she was frowning. But she wasn't frowning at Nurse Costello, or at the elderly man—Mr. Burke, wasn't it?—approaching with his daughter. She was frowning at the sight of the other nurse, Nurse Morley. Talk about complaints. That nurse was always complaining about something. Today it was some slight she had thought she had gotten from Dr. Mellon. Nurse Wyman hadn't been in the mood to discuss it that morning, and she was even less in the mood to discuss it now. She'd have to find some way to put Nurse Morley off after the applicant had been seen to.

"It's not you, dear," she said to Nurse Costello. "It's just something I have to attend to. You run along now. I do want to tell you, though, that I'm very pleased with your work."

"Oh, thank you."

As Nurse Wyman approached her desk, Nurse Morley said: "You remember Mrs. Burke. And her father, Mr. Carpenter."

Nurse Wyman nodded, avoiding the other nurse's eyes as she got the pills and the key, and led them all down to the Yellow Room. She opened the door, thinking about what excuse she could use to get rid of Nurse Morley, and then noticed that old Mr. Carpenter seemed to be trying to pull his arm loose from his daughter's grip.

"Come on, Dad," said Mrs. Burke.

The old man shook his head.

"*Dad,* come on now," said Mrs. Burke, with exaggerated pleasantness that didn't hide the undertone of exasperation. "We're going to go inside."

Once again the old man shook his head. Mrs. Burke gave a tug on his arm, and he stumbled forward a step before he regained his ground.

"*Dad . . .*"

Nurse Wyman gave a sigh. She could sympathize with the daughter. The cases of old people who were only intermittently lucid were the most difficult of all. Testimony from the family and what testimony there was from the applicant were gone over in great detail, trying to sort out the lucid from the confused, the long-term from the momentary. Mr. Carpenter's case had taken a full ten counseling sessions plus two Board reviews. If he balked now, the family would have to go through the whole exhausting process again, assuming the Board would allow them another review. Nonetheless, the rules had to be observed.

"Just a minute, Mrs. Burke," said Nurse Wyman. "You know the rules. No one is to be forced."

"But . . ." Mrs. Burke started to protest, then seemed to see it was useless. "Dad, *please.*"

The old man shook his head once more.

"Can you give me a minute with him," said Mrs. Burke.

"Of course," said Nurse Wyman. "But just a minute."

Nurse Wyman took a few steps back toward the desk, to give the two of them some privacy, and noticed that Nurse Morley was following.

"Dad, why are you *doing* this to me? We're only here because you said this was what you wanted. You told everybody. Look at all the trouble you've put these people through. Why do you always have to make so much trouble?"

"Nurse Wyman, about Dr. Mellon . . ."

"Not *now,* Nurse Morley."

"You're just doing this to spite me, aren't you, Dad. You like to make me unhappy, don't you. You always have . . ."

"I won't be put off, Nurse Wyman. Something has to be done about that man. Dr. Mellon is downright insulting—not just to me but to the other nurses as well. I'm a professional and I insist on . . ."

". . . do you want to go home, is that it? Well, good, we'll just go then. And then you can explain to Harry why you're doing this to us. You know what Harry will do, don't you? He'll . . ."

". . . and the other day, in front of one of the patients . . ."

Nurse Wyman tuned them all out. She could see Mrs. Burke gesturing to her father off to the side, could see Nurse Morley's insistent mouth working like a spastic clam just in front of her, but she heard none of it. Instead she was reviewing that scene from *Sweet Desire* where the arrogant pirate ripped off Lucinda's bodice and . . .

"Nurse. Nurse!" The insistence of Mrs. Burke's voice finally broke through her reverie. "He's ready now."

Nurse Wyman turned away from Nurse Morley and walked back to the father and daughter. The old man was staring down at the floor and working his hands together nervously. Mrs. Burke was standing next to him, not touching him now.

"Mr. Carpenter," said Nurse Wyman. "Are you ready now?"

The old man gave an almost imperceptible nod.

"Please say so, if you are."

The old man's lips moved. The word was perceptible, though barely so. "Yes."

"All right, then," said Nurse Wyman.

Mrs. Burke let out a sigh of relief. She turned to the nurses.

"I'm sorry for the trouble."

"It's quite all right," said Nurse Wyman. "Old people can be difficult sometimes."

The door to the Yellow Room was barely shut before Nurse Morley started in again: "So I absolutely must insist that you . . ."

". . . *of course, many of your countries will not be able to afford the same kind of individualized attention, but then it's doubtful your people would expect it. As for your governments, the implications for population control can't have . . ."*

Thank goodness, the Director. The sound of his voice had the power to jolt even Nurse Morley, and, as the other stopped in mid-sentence, Nurse Wyman said: "You'll have to excuse me. The Director will be needing me."

Nurse Wyman rushed over to her desk, anticipating her part in the Director's tour. She eyed the rack of keys: yes, the Green Room would be empty now.

". . . *follow me to the Resting Rooms, as we call them, I'm sure you'll be impressed with the privacy and pleasantness of . . ."*

As Nurse Wyman grabbed the key, she glanced at her watch. Still forty-five minutes to go, but after that there'd be a couple of stiff drinks, then a nice dinner, then *Sweet Desire, Part II*, then a nice long weekend to catch up on her sleep.

"Thank God, it's Friday," she muttered as she waved to the Director.

* * * * * *

"Billy seems pretty upset," said the woman who'd been taking care of the boy. She held out a slip of paper. "I've written down the name of a counselor you might . . ."

"Yes, yes," said Mrs. Burke, as she crumpled the paper into her purse and reached for her son's hand. "But right now I just want to get out of this place."

She yanked her son with her as she rushed out of the room and down the stairway. At the street door she paused, looking for protestors, then saw, with relief, that they were gone. She rushed across the street, pushed the boy ahead of her into the car, then got in and started the engine.

It was only after she was a mile from the clinic that she felt herself start to breathe normally again. She turned cautiously to look at her son and saw that he was crying. Suddenly she was crying too. And yelling.

"God damn it, stop it, do you hear me? What about me? I had to be there with him. Do you understand? Your father wants this, and you want that, but *I* was the one who had to be there. How about somebody thinking of me for a change!"

The hysteria in her voice only made the boy cry harder and she knew she had to get control of herself. She took a couple of deep breaths, then gave that up and reached into her purse for some Valium. Fortunately they'd given her more.

When she felt a little calmer, she said: "I'm sorry I yelled at you, Billy. I really am. I know this is hard on you. But you're not being fair. One day you'll understand. Believe me."

Whether because of her words, or because she'd become calmer, or because his tears had run their course, her son gradually quieted. But he kept staring ahead, his forehead wrinkled up, biting at his lip.

"Billy?"

No answer.

"Billy, please speak to me. There was nothing wrong in what we did. I promise you you'll understand that when you're much older."

He turned toward her then, seeming to study her for a moment with an expression she couldn't decipher. When he finally spoke, his voice was flat. He said:

"How old will you be then, Mama?"

Questions

1. In "Death on Demand" three people take their own lives at the Clinic: Mrs. Evers, Mrs. Lindahl, and Mr. Burke. Relative to each of these people, ask yourself whether it was morally right for society to let them/enable them to die as they did. Explain your answers.
2. Imagine yourself in the position of each of those three people. Ask yourself whether you would want society to let you/enable you to die as they did. Is there any difference between your answers here and in #1?
3. The applicants in "Death on Demand" must go through certain procedures before they are allowed to die. What are those procedures? Do you find them adequate? Are there other procedures you think would be better?
4. Do you believe that a person has the right to end his or her own life by positive means? If not, why not? If so, why, and under what circumstances?
5. Do you believe that any system enabling people to die (under certain specified conditions) would be subject to certain abuses? If so, what abuses? Could the abuses be minimized, or would they be so great as to make any such system objectionable?

DISCUSSION

THE RIGHT TO DIE

The story "Death on Demand" imagines a clinic, in the near future, where one can get one's own death "on demand," as now, in many places, one can get abortion "on demand." It is supposed that society gives people who "meet the appropriate criteria in terms of physical condition or psychiatric history" the right to get medical assistance in ending their lives. The conditions/criteria aren't spelled out in the story, but the patients provide examples of what would be allowed. Mrs. Evers has been suffering from severe depression since the death of her husband, a depression, presumably, that did not respond to medical or psychological treatment. Mrs. Lindahl is suffering from terminal cancer. Mr. Carpenter is suffering from intermittant senility and lack of bowel control, as well as other disabilities of old age.

The evolution of the situation portrayed in the story seems to have been this: "Right-to-die" laws were passed on a state-by-state basis, with those laws defining how the means of suicide (only pills are mentioned) were to be dispensed. Nevada allowed people to get the pills without a prescription and without any waiting period. California apparently required both a prescription and a fourteen-day waiting period. Other states, presumably, had different policies. When the pills were involved in a series of murders and a mass cult suicide, Congress stepped in and formulated a national right-to-die law, which established the clinics. Though these clinics seem radical to us, the story supposes they were actually part of a conservative backlash against an even more radical situation. The clinics are, among other things, a way of more carefully controlling who would get the pills and how they would be used.

As far as we can ascertain from the story, the right-to-die procedure goes something like this: The law defines certain medical and psychiatric conditions which make people eligible to be assisted in dying. A person who wants to die has his physician certify his condition, and then the person applies to the clinic. There are a mandatory five counseling sessions in which a counselor talks with the applicant about the decision to die. If the applicant remains determined to die and if the counselor is convinced that the applicant satisfies the legal criteria, the applicant's case goes before a board of review. (If the counselor isn't satisfied, she can request that the applicant have further counseling.) If the board approves the application, the applicant is given a date at the clinic, where he is taken to a small room with a bed and given the pills. He may change his mind up until the moment he swallows the pills (apparently there is no antidote); if he does change his mind, he must wait at least a year before being given another chance to die.

The story invites you to consider the issue of who, if anyone, has the right to die, whether these persons (if any) have the right to ask society to assist them in dying, and how such assistance would/should be implemented. There are other sorts of related cases, not brought up in the story, that we should also consider: the hospital patient with terminal cancer, in excruciating pain, who begs his doctor to give him some injection that will end his life; the same sort of patient who asks his doctor for stronger doses of medication that will kill the pain but will also probably weaken him and shorten his life; and the patient who refuses some treatment that will prolong his misery with no chance of saving his life. All these cases, along with others, come under the heading of euthanasia, or "mercy killing."

SOME DEFINITIONS AND DISTINCTIONS

The term **euthanasia** means deliberately bringing about, either by action or by inaction, the painless death of people with certain incurable conditions, conditions that usually involve great suffering. In order to properly evaluate euthanasia, we need to make two important distinctions.

The first distinction is between active and passive euthanasia, often distinguished by the words "killing" and "letting die." Active euthanasia involves an action intended to cause the person's death. The administering of suicide pills in "Death on Demand" is active euthanasia. A doctor who administers what she knows to be a lethal injection of morphine would be another instance. Passive euthanasia involves intentionally inflicting death by inaction. Not hooking a near-death cancer patient to a respirator or not performing some operation that would give her a few more days of life would be examples of passive euthanasia.

The second distinction is between voluntary and involuntary euthanasia. Voluntary euthanasia involves the consent of the person who is to die; involuntary euthanasia does not. The phrase "involuntary euthanasia" has an awful sound to it, suggesting someone shoving suicide pills down the throat of some protesting, struggling patient. Actually, the phrase generally refers to cases that are much more benign, such as the person who has spent years in a coma, kept alive only by some elaborate machinery; "pulling the plug" would be involuntary euthanasia. Another example would be the case of a terribly deformed infant who will die immediately unless some operation is performed; not operating would be involuntary euthanasia.

In this chapter we shall be concerned primarily with voluntary euthanasia, whether active or passive. We can't exclude involuntary euthanasia entirely, since cases arise in which it's not clear whether the person is acting voluntarily; we need to know how we would feel about that particular kind of involuntary euthanasia. However, cases like those of the deformed infant, where the consent of the person to die is not an issue, will not be discussed here.

In considering the issue of voluntary euthanasia, you'll need to answer at least two categories of questions:

  a. *General moral principle.* Do people have the right to take positive means to end their lives? If so, under what circumstances? Do people have the right to ask society to assist them in this? If so, in what ways?
  b. *Social policy and practices.* (If the answers to the above are, in any sense, positive:) What social system might be implemented to support the right

to die? Would this system be likely to have any unfortunate consequences? If so, what consequences? Would those negative consequences
be so severe as to warrant further limiting the right to die? If so, how
should the right be further limited? Would those consequences be so
severe as to warrant overriding the right altogether?

Questions related to (a) and (b) often get muddled together in right-to-
die discussions. It is important to clarify how you and others feel about (a)
before you think about moving on to (b).

GENERAL MORAL PRINCIPLE

In the previous chapter the following view of morality was suggested:

> . . . To propose moral rules is to imply that such rules should apply even if one
> were in the other person's position . . . moral judgments are "universalizable."
>   A person who, using imagination, discounts his or her particular circum-
> stances, surveys the human condition, and decides what rules all human beings
> should follow is said to be taking the "moral point of view." To express a moral
> preference is to express a preference from the moral point of view.

If you accept this view of morality, try to examine the right-to-die issue
from the moral point of view. Start with your personal preferences. Would
you want to be able/enabled to take your own life under any circumstances?
Under what circumstances? Imagine yourself in various circumstances: You
have a very painful illness that doctors agree is terminal and untreatable. You
have an illness with a slim chance of a cure where the attempted cure would
take months of terrible pain. You are going through a cure that will probably
work but the pain and debility of the cure have made you suicidal. You have
suffered years of debilitating depression for which no psychiatric and medical
treatments have been helpful. You have a terrible depression that makes you
want to die but that others have good reason to believe will be short-term. If
you feel you should have the right to die in any of these circumstances, ask
yourself: Do I have the right to die immediately or should I have to go
through certain processes first? What processes?
    Now imagine that, as you face such situations, you have differing per-
sonal circumstances and personality characteristics. You do or don't have a
sound mind. You are elderly or young, rich or poor. You have a family or no
family. You have a family that desperately wants you to live; you have a family on which you are a burden. You do or don't have a life's work that's important to you, friends to comfort you, the ability to enjoy life under difficult circumstances, a lot of willpower, a great tolerance for pain. Look at all this not
only from the standpoint of the person wanting to take his or her life, but also
from the standpoint of family, friends, and any other members of society who
might be affected.
    As you go through these various cases, you may begin to evolve a com-
plex moral principle with various qualifications and conditions. Keep asking
yourself: Is this now the principle I could be most comfortable with if I didn't
know which of those circumstances I would actually end up in?

In discussing an ethical issue like the right to die, it is helpful to distinguish between two broad types of ethical theory: the consequentialist and the deontological.

Consequentialist ethical theories claim that what makes actions right or wrong is their consequences in terms of increasing or decreasing certain properties that have been identified as intrinsically good or bad. Utilitarianism is one example of a consequentialist theory: It identifies pleasure/happiness as good and pain/unhappiness as bad and judges actions in terms of increasing happiness and diminishing unhappiness.

Deontological ethical theories deny that what makes actions right or wrong is simply consequences. Judeo-Christian ethics, as normally interpreted, has a heavy deontological cast: There are lists of dos and don'ts which can't be entirely accounted for in terms of consequences. (The prohibition against sleeping with your neighbor's wife isn't presented as a rule of thumb, suggesting that in general everyone will be happier if you refrain; it's more like, Don't do it, period.) But it isn't only religious ethics that are deontological. Anyone who believes rights and duties have a weight that can't be accounted for in terms of consequences alone is a deontologist.

To emphasize the differences (and similarities) between the consequentialist and the deontologist, let's consider a familiar "right": the right to free expression. You might assume that the utilitarian (a consequentialist) would be quite casual about this right, denying it to people whenever the expression caused more unhappiness than happiness (when, let us say, there were more people in a particular audience bothered by obscenity than not bothered by it). However, this assumption would be false. Most current versions of utilitarianism talk about judging not individual actions but general rules of action. Traditionally utilitarians have been among the staunchest defenders of free expression, feeling that it is absolutely crucial to the long-term well-being of society. (Among other things, they would argue that free expression is crucial to making people's wants known to government, crucial to the interchange of ideas necessary for scientific advances.) Nonetheless, if it could be demonstrated that a severe limiting of free expression would actually create more long-term happiness for a society, the utilitarian would have nothing further to say against limiting that right.

You might assume that the deontologist would endorse an absolute right to free expression, and this assumption too would be wrong. Few deontologists have proposed any absolute rights. Generally, rights have all sorts of exceptions. Even the staunchest advocates of free speech would deny a person the right to try to provoke one person to kill another, or to yell "Fire!" in a crowd, as a joke.

Though the distinctions between consequentialist and deontological theories are not as sharp as they would first appear, they are real, and they have an important bearing on right-to-die debates.

Most of those who would deny or severely limit a person's right to die are deontologists who are against taking another's life or one's own life. Those who support a broad right to die can be either consequentialists or deontologists. Consequentialists, like utilitarians, would support a broad right to die in terms of avoiding unnecessary pain. Deontologists in this camp might be more limited in their stance against taking a life, and might in addition emphasize some right to self-determination. These philosophies represent different orientations toward the right to die; unless you understand the orientation of those with whom you discuss this issue, you're likely to talk past each other, with neither party feeling that the other "gets the point."

A complicating factor here is that many who take a position against euthanasia are motivated by religious reasons. Yet, people are sometimes reluctant to talk about the religious aspects of this issue. If religion is central, it must be discussed. In Chapter 3 it was argued that the mere fact of God's forbidding something would never be sufficient to make it morally wrong. It would seem that the deontologist should either try to show what's wrong with that argument or come up with another justification for the extremity of his position against taking a life. On the other hand, I don't want to make too much of this point. The only requirement that's been insisted on for having a morality is that one's rules be compatible with taking the moral point of view, and there is nothing contradictory about being a deontologist from the moral point of view. The moral point of view is not equivalent to just adding up wants and satisfying the most possible (to a kind of utilitarianism). It simply entails a commitment that one ought to stand by a rule, whatever one's position. One could certainly decide from that standpoint that no one has the right to actively take his own life. The only question would be whether, if one seriously stripped away from certain prohibitions the commandment-of-God aspect, those prohibitions would have quite the same attraction.

An important difference between consequentialist and deontological ethical theories is the role of motives. Consequentialists aren't uninterested in motives for actions. For instance, encouraging and discouraging certain motives is a way of encouraging and discouraging the actions that tend to result from those motives. For consequentialists, motives are important as means, not ends. For many deontologists, however, particularly those with a religious ethic, the motive is often as important as, if not more important than, the act itself in determining the rightness or the wrongness of the act.

Suppose a man who is on a date with a social worker gives twenty dollars to some homeless person with the sole motive of impressing his date. The consequentialist, stressing the result, would probably say that giving the money was a good thing, even though the motive wasn't so good (that is, wasn't as likely to lead to giving in the long run as would sympathy). To some deontologists, however, the act would not be good at all—it's totally hypocritical—and some might even argue that it would be better not to give money at all than to give it hypocritically.

Motives play a particularly important role in the ethical theories of those deontologists who place severe limits on the right to die.

We've discussed the difference between active and passive euthanasia, between "killing" and "letting die." Many deontologists who disapprove of active euthanasia do approve of passive euthanasia ("letting die"). They feel that while a terminally ill patient does not have the right to take her own life, neither does she have the obligation to endure great discomfort while fighting hopelessly against the natural course of an illness. For instance, she is not required to undergo one painful operation after another when the only result could be a few more days of life. (Similarly with the doctor: She is not allowed to take the patient's life but isn't obligated to implement "heroic" measures.)

In the middle ground between active and passive euthanasia lie some tricky cases: A terminally ill patient is in great pain. Painkillers will weaken the patient, causing him to die sooner. The doctor gives, and the patient accepts, these painkillers. Is this active or passive euthanasia? Is this "killing" or "letting die"?

Here's where the deontologists' emphasis on motives plays a crucial role: Many would say that while the consequence of the act was the shortening of life, the act was not the act of killing because the motive for giving the painkillers was not the shortening of life, but the relief of pain. Thus the giving and taking of such painkillers is morally acceptable (as passive euthanasia) to some deontologists.

SOCIAL POLICY AND PRACTICES

Once you have formulated your moral position on euthanasia, you should ask yourself what social policy and practices should be used to implement such a position. The further you get from the status quo, the more thinking you'll need to do. This will be true particularly if you support active euthanasia.

It's possible, however, that the following thought might occur to someone who supports active euthanasia: "Why bother worrying about some elaborate social mechanism to help people kill themselves? People are capable of killing themselves without that. In fact, why even worry about making suicide legal? Someone who's dead hardly needs to worry about getting punished."

There are a number of reasons someone who believes active euthanasia is morally acceptable might want it made legal. For example, some people don't learn they are terminally ill until they are trapped in hospital beds, too weak to do what is necessary to kill themselves. For people who are capable of taking their own lives, there are other considerations in favor of making suicide legal. Keeping it illegal makes the act furtive, and make those who wish to end their own lives feel like outlaws. Loved ones can't assist or be close to the suicide at the moment of death without putting themselves in legal jeopardy. It bars the person who is to die from doing things that would help others adjust to the death: If the person tries to prepare people, those people would be legally obligated to inform the police, and the police would be obligated to intervene.

There are a number of reasons someone who believes active euthanasia is morally acceptable might want some social mechanism to assist people in dying. It's true that people do successfully kill themselves, but it's also true that people botch suicides. For example: People take the wrong quantity of pills and end up with brain damage; they shoot themselves in the temple and end up blind; they jump off something and end up paralyzed. Even when suicides are successful, they are often violent (obtaining the necessary pills isn't always easy) and for the people who know and love them, discovering successful suicides is traumatic. The answer here wouldn't have to be a clinic, as in the story; it might be a more easily available, relatively gentle means of suicide, along with easily available education on how to utilize those means.

As you try to formulate social policies and practices, you may find that theory may have to be adjusted in practice. For instance, you may find that some policy that was acceptable to you in the abstract is open to too many abuses in practice; you may end up settling for a policy that is more restrictive than you'd like. Is it possible that any social policy/practices would be so open to abuse that you might decide that active euthanasia, though acceptable to you in theory, simply can't be made workable in any form?

Often deontologists who are against active euthanasia argue that any social mechanism aimed at assisting suicides would have horrible consequences. One might wonder why deontologists are speaking in terms of consequences at all, whether they aren't being inconsistent in this. In fact, there's nothing wrong with a deontologist arguing as follows: "I happen to believe that active euthanasia is wrong, apart from any consequences. But I think if you really look at the consequences seriously, you'd see that allowing active euthanasia would be a mistake from that perspective as well."

What emerges in many of these debates is the **slippery slope fallacy:** assuming, without specific evidence, that any move in a certain direction will inevitably lead you to slide past other possibilities to some terrible extreme. The slippery slope fallacy comes up when you are dealing with a continuum of positions, say, A1, A2, A3, A4, A5, where A1 is the status quo and A5 is something obviously bad. The fallacy is to assume, without specific evidence, that there is no way you can move from A1 toward A2 without sliding all the way to A5—so, since A5 is bad, you shouldn't move at all. One example of this fallacy arises in gun control debates: "If you let the government take away the AK-47 assault rifle, pretty soon they'll take away all our rights and we'll be living in a fascist dictatorship." To see how absurd this argument is, turn it around: "We can't let any citizen have any kind of weapon because pretty soon they'll all have tanks and tactical nuclear weapons and be blowing up the whole world."

In real life, we constantly draw boundaries that more or less hold. For example, we eat some sweets without becoming obese; we have a couple of drinks without becoming alcoholics; we have laws against some things without having laws against everything; we pay some taxes without the government taking all our money away. Slippery slope is simply a reflex, lazy way of arguing that is constantly contradicted by life around us.

On the other hand, there are real slippery slopes in life (stepping off a skyscraper would be an obvious example). If you passed a law allowing a certain ten percent of the population to take anything they felt they really needed from the other ninety percent, you might well be creating a situation that would lead to inevitable disaster.

In order to make a nonfallacious slippery slope argument, you must present evidence that demonstrates the existence of a particular danger in a particular case, showing why it is different from the everyday cases in which we do draw boundaries that hold.

With any social institutions there are going to be abuses, and with life-and-death institutions there are going to be life-and-death abuses. For most people, this is an unfortunate but inevitable consequence of having social institutions at all. Ideally, you will anticipate abuses and do your best to formulate policies and procedures that will minimize them. When you evaluate the result, the important question is not, "Will there be abuses?" (there *will* be, of course), but rather, "How many abuses are there likely to be and is that number acceptable?" As you formulate your position here, remember that the minimum required of you, as in any rational endeavor, is consistency. For instance, you can't reject the practice of active euthanasia on the grounds that a few wrongs will be done, and then endorse capital punishment, which obviously would inflict a few wrongs.

READINGS

MARY ROSE BARRINGTON argues in favor of euthanasia.*

Opponents of suicide will sometimes throw dust in the eyes of the uncommitted by asking at some point why one should ever choose to go on living if one once questions the value of life; for as we all know, adversity is usually round the corner, if not at our heels. Here, it seems to me, a special case must be made out for people suffering from the sort of adversity with which the proponents of euthanasia are concerned: namely, an apparently irremediable state of physical debility that makes life unbearable to the sufferer. Some adversities come and go: in the words of the Anglo-Saxon poet reviewing all the disasters known to Norse mythology, "That passed away, so may this." Some things that do not pass away include inoperable cancers in the region of the throat that choke their victims slowly to death. Not only do they not pass away, but like many extremely unpleasant conditions they cannot be alleviated by pain-killing drugs. Pain itself can be controlled, provided the doctor in charge is prepared to put the relief of pain before the prolongation of life; but analgesics will not help a patient to live with total incontinence, reduced to the status of a helpless baby after a life of independent adulthood. And for the person who manages to avoid these grave afflictions there remains the spectre of senile

*From "The Case for Rational Suicide" by Mary Rose Barrington, reprinted by permission from *Voluntary Euthanasia: Experts Debate the Right to Die*, pp. 230–247, edited by A. B. Downing and Barbara Smoker. Copyright © 1986 by Peter Owen, Ltd. Published by Peter Owen Publishers, London and Chester Springs, PA.

decay, a physical and mental crumbling into a travesty of the normal person. Could anything be more reasonable than for a person faced with these living deaths to weigh up the pros and cons of living out his life until his heart finally fails, and going instead to meet death half-way?

It is true, of course, that, all things being equal, people do want to go on living. If we are enjoying life, there seems no obvious reason to stop doing so and be mourned by our families and forgotten by our friends. If we are not enjoying it, then it seems a miserable end to die in a trough of depression, and better to wait for things to become more favourable. Most people, moreover, have a moral obligation to continue living, owed to their parents while they are still alive, their children while they are dependent, and their spouses all the time. Trained professional workers may even feel that they have a duty to society to continue giving their services. Whatever the grounds, it is both natural and reasonable that without some special cause nobody ever wants to die *yet*. But must these truisms be taken to embody the whole truth about the attitude of thinking people to life and death? . . .

It may be worth pausing here to consider whether the words "natural end," in the sense usually ascribed to the term, have much bearing on reality. Very little is "natural" about our present-day existence, and least natural of all is the prolonged period of dying that is suffered by so many incurable patients solicitously kept alive to be killed by their disease. The sufferings of animals (other than man) are heart-rending enough, but a dying process spread over weeks, months or years seems to be one form of suffering that animals are normally spared. When severe illness strikes them they tend to stop eating, sleep and die. The whole weight of Western society forces attention on the natural right to live, but throws a blanket of silence over the natural right to die. If I seem to be suggesting that in a civilized society suicide ought to be considered a quite proper way for a well-brought-up person to end his life (unless he has the good luck to die suddenly and without warning), that is indeed the tenor of my argument . . .

. . . It is frequently said that hard-hearted people would be encouraged to make their elderly relatives feel that they had outlived their welcome and ought to remove themselves, even if they happened to be enjoying life. No one can say categorically that nothing of the sort would happen, but the sensibility of even hard-hearted people to the possible consequences of their own unkindness seems just as likely. . . .

That voluntary euthanasia is in fact assisted suicide is no doubt clear to most people, but curiously enough many who would support the moral right of an incurably sick person to commit suicide will oppose his having the right to seek assistance from doctors if he is to effect his wish. The argument has so far been concentrated upon the person who clearly sees the writing on the wall (perhaps because he has a doctor who is prepared to decipher it) and has the moral courage, whether or not encouraged by a sympathetic society, to anticipate the dying period. Further, this hypothetical person has access to the means of suicide and knows how to make use of those means. How he has acquired the means and the knowledge is obscure, but a determined person will make sure that he is equipped with both as a standby for the future. Yet the average patient desperately in need of help to cut short his suffering could well be a person unaccustomed to holding his own against authority, enfeebled by illness, dependent on pain-killing drugs, having no access to the means of suicide and not knowing how to make use of the means even if they were available; an entirely helpless person, in no way in a position to compass his own death. To acknowledge the right of a person to end his own life to avoid a period of suffering is a mere sham unless the right for him to call on expert assistance is also acknowledged. . . .

JEROME A. MOTTO, a psychiatrist, argues for a limited right to suicide.*

From a psychiatric point of view, the question as to whether a person has the right to cope with the pain in his world by killing himself can be answered without hesitation. He does have that right. . . .

Putting limitations on rights is certainly not a new idea, since essentially every right we exercise has its specified restrictions. . . .

I use two psychological criteria as grounds for limiting a person's exercise of his right to suicide: *(a)* the act must be based on a realistic assessment of his life situation, and *(b)* the degree of ambivalence regarding the act must be minimal. . . .

In the final analysis, then, when a decision has to be made, what a psychiatrist calls "realistic" is whatever looks realistic to *him*. At the moment of truth, that is all any person can offer. This inherent human limitation in itself is a reality that accounts for a great deal of inevitable chaos in the world; it is an article of faith that not to make such an effort would create even greater chaos. On a day-to-day operational level, one contemporary behavioral scientist expressed it this way: "No doubt the daily business of helping troubled individuals, including suicides, gives little time for the massive contemplative and investigative efforts which alone can lead to surer knowledge. And the helpers are not thereby to be disparaged. They cannot wait for the best answers conceivable. They must do only the best they can *now*."

Thus if I am working with a person in psychotherapy, one limitation I would put on his right to suicide would be that his assessment of his life situation be realistic as *I* see it. . . .

The second criterion to be used as the basis for limiting a person's exercise of his right to suicide is minimal ambivalence about ending his life. I make the assumption that if a person has no ambivalence about suicide he will not be in my office, nor write to me about it, nor call me on the telephone. I interpret, rightly or wrongly, a person's calling my attention to his suicidal impulses as a request to intercede that I cannot ignore.

*From "The Right to Suicide: A Psychiatrist's View" by Jerome A. Motto, in *Life-Threatening Behavior*, Vol. 2, No. 3, Fall 1972, pp. 183–188. Printed by Human Sciences Press, Inc., New York, New York 10011. Reprinted with permission.

At times this call will inevitably be misread, and my assumption will lead me astray. However, such an error on my part can be corrected at a later time; meanwhile, I must be prepared to take responsibility for having prolonged what may be a truly unendurable existence. If the error is made in the other direction, no opportunity for correction may be possible.

This same principle regarding ambivalence applies to a suicide prevention center, minister, social agency, or a hospital emergency room. The response of the helping agency may be far from fulfilling the needs of the person involved, but in my view, the ambivalence expressed is a indication for it to limit the exercise of his right to suicide. . . .

It seems inevitable to me that we must eventually establish procedures for the voluntary cessation of life, with the time, place, and manner largely controlled by the person concerned. It will necessarily involve a series of deliberate steps providing assurance that appropriate criteria are met, such as those proposed above, as we now observe specific criteria when a life is terminated by abortion or by capital punishment.

The critical word is "control." I would anticipate a decrease in the actual number of suicides when this procedure is established, due to the psychological power of this issue. If I know something is available to me and will remain available till I am moved to seize it, the chances of my seizing it now are thereby much reduced. It is only by holding off that I maintain the option of changing my mind. During this period of delay the opportunity for therapeutic effort—and the therapy of time itself—may be used to advantage. . . .

ARTHUR J. DYCK argues against euthanasia and for an alternate approach.*

It is important to be very clear about the precise moral reasoning by which advocates of voluntary euthanasia justify suicide and assisting a suicide. They make no moral distinction between those instances when a patient or a physician chooses to have life shortened by failing to accept or use life-prolonging techniques and those instances when a patient or a physician shortens life by employing a death-dealing chemical or instrument. They make no moral distinction between a drug given to kill pain, which also shortens life, and a substance given precisely to shorten life and for no other reason. Presumably these distinctions are not honored, because regardless of the stratagem employed—regardless of whether one is permitting to die or killing directly—the result is the same, the patient's life is shortened. Hence, it is maintained that, if you can justify one kind of act that shortens the life of the dying, you can justify any act that shortens the life of the dying when this act is seen to be willed by the one who is dying. Moral reasoning of this sort is strictly utilitarian; it focuses solely on the consequences of acts, not on their intent.

*From "An Alternative to the Ethic of Euthanasia" by Arthur J. Dyck, in *To Live or To Die*, edited by Robert H. Williams. Copyright © 1973 by Springer-Verlag, Inc. Reprinted by permission of Springer-Verlag, Inc.

Even though the reasoning on the issue of compassion is so strictly utilitarian, one is puzzled about the failure to raise certain kinds of questions. A strict utilitarian might inquire about the effect of the medical practice of promoting or even encouraging direct acts on the part of physicians to shorten the lives of their patients. And, in the same vein, a utilitarian might also be very concerned about whether the loosening of constraints on physicians may not loosen the constraints on killing generally. There are two reasons these questions are either not raised or are dealt with rather summarily. First, it is alleged that there is no evidence that untoward consequences would result. And second, the value of freedom is invoked, so that the question of killing becomes a question of suicide and assistance in a suicide.

A euthanasia ethic . . . contains the following essential presuppositions or beliefs:

1. that an individual's life belongs to that individual to dispose of entirely as he or she wishes;
2. that the dignity that attaches to personhood by reason of the freedom to make moral choices demands also the freedom to take one's own life;
3. that there is such a thing as a life not worth living, whether by reason of distress, illness, physical or mental handicaps, or even sheer despair for whatever reason;
4. that what is sacred or supreme in value is the "human dignity" that resides in man's own rational capacity to choose and control life and death.

From our account of the ethic of euthanasia, those who oppose voluntary euthanasia would seem to lack compassion for the dying and the courage to affirm human freedom. They appear incompassionate because they oppose what has come to be regarded as synonymous with a good death—namely, a painless and deliberately foreshortened process of dying. The term "euthanasia" originally meant a painless and happy death with no reference to whether such a death was induced. . . .

Because of this loss of a merely descriptive term for a happy death, it is necessary to invent a term for a happy or good death—namely, benemortasia. The familiar derivatives for this new term are *bene* (good) and *mors* (death). The meaning of "bene" in "benemortasia" is deliberately unspecified so that it does not necessarily imply that a death must be painless and/or induced in order to be good. What constitutes a good or happy death is a disputable matter of moral policy. How then should one view the arguments for voluntary euthanasia? And, if an ethic of euthanasia is unacceptable, what is an acceptable ethic of benemortasia? . . .

Our ethic of benemortasia acknowledges the freedom of patients who are incurably ill to refuse interventions that prolong dying and the freedom of physicians to honor such wishes. However, these actions are not acts of suicide and assisting in suicide. In our ethic of benemortasia, suicide and assisting in suicide are unjustifiable acts of killing. Unlike the ethic of those who would legalize voluntary euthanasia, our ethic makes a moral distinction between acts that *permit* death and acts that *cause* death. As George P. Fletcher notes, one can make a sharp distinction, one that will stand up in law, between "permitting to die" and "causing death." Jewish and Christian tradition, particularly Roman Catholic thought, have maintained this clear distinction between the failure to use extraordinary measures (permitting to die) and direct intervention to bring about death (causing death). A distinction is also drawn between a drug administered to cause death and a drug administered to ease pain which has the added effect of shortening life. . . .

From the point of view of the dying person, when could his or her decisions be called a deliberate act to end life, the act we usually designate as suicide? Only, it seems to me, when the dying person commits an act that has the immediate intent of ending life and has no other purpose. That act may be to use, or ask the physician to use, a chemical or an instrument that has no other immediate effect than to end the dying person's life. If, for the sake of relieving pain, a dying person chooses drugs administered in potent doses, the intent of this act is not to shorten life, even though it has that effect. It is a choice as to how to live while dying. Similarly, if a patient chooses to forgo medical interventions that would have the effect of prolonging his or her life without in any way promising release from death, this also is a choice as to what is the most meaningful way to spend the remainder of life, however short that may be. The choice to use drugs to relieve pain and the choice not to use medical measures that cannot promise a cure for one's dying are no different in principle from the choices we make throughout our lives as to how much we will rest, how hard we will work, how little and how much medical intervention we will seek or tolerate, and the like. For society or physicians to map out life-styles for individuals with respect to such decisions is surely beyond anything that we find in Stoic, Jewish, or Christian ethics. Such intervention in the liberty of individuals is far beyond what is required in any society whose rules are intended to constrain people against harming others.

But human freedom should not be extended to include the taking of one's own life. Causing one's own death cannot generally be justified, even when one is dying. To see why this is so, we have to consider how causing one's death does violence to one's self and harms others.

The person who causes his or her own death repudiates the meaningfulness and worth of his or her own life. To decide to initiate an act that has as its primary purpose to end one's life is to decide that that life has no worth to anyone, especially to oneself. It is an act that ends all choices regarding what one's life and whatever is left of it is to symbolize.

Suicide is the ultimately effective way of shutting out all other people from one's life. Psychologists have observed how hostility for others can be expressed through taking one's own life. People who might want access to the dying one to make restitution, offer reparation, bestow last kindnesses, or clarify misunderstandings are cut off by such an act. Every kind of potentially and actually meaningful contact and relation among persons is irrevocably severed except by means of memories and whatever life beyond death may offer. Certainly for those who are left behind by death, there can remain many years of suffering occasioned by that death. The sequence of dying an inevitable death can be much better accepted than the decision on the part of a dying one that he or she has no worth to anyone. An act that presupposes that final declaration leaves tragic overtones for anyone who participated in even the smallest way in that person's dying.

But the problem is even greater. If in principle a person can take his or her own life whenever he or she no longer finds it meaningful, there is nothing in principle that prevents anyone from taking his or her life, no matter what the circumstances. For if the decision hinges on whether one regards his or her own life as meaningful, anyone can regard his or her own life as meaningless even under circumstances that would appear to be most fortunate and opportune for an abundant life. . . .

Some readers may remain unconvinced that euthanasia is morally wrong as a general policy. Perhaps what still divides us is what distinguishes a Stoic from a Jewish and Christian way of life. The Stoic heritage declares that my life and my selfhood are my own to dispose of as I see fit and when I see fit. The Jewish and Christian heritage declares that my life and my selfhood are not my own, and are not mine to dispose of as I see fit. . . .

Our ethic of benemortasia has argued for the following beliefs and values:

1. that an individual person's life is not solely at the disposal of that person; every human life is part of the human community that bestows and protects the lives of its members; the possibility of community itself depends upon constraints against taking life;
2. that the dignity that attaches to personhood by reason of the freedom to make moral choices includes the freedom of dying people to refuse noncurative, life-prolonging interventions when one is dying, but does not extend to taking one's life or causing death for someone who is dying;
3. that every life has some worth; there is no such thing as a life not worth living;
4. that the supreme value is goodness itself, to which the dying and those who care for the dying are responsible. Religiously expressed the supreme value is God. Less than perfectly good beings, human beings, require constraints upon their decisions regarding those who are dying. No human being or human community can presume to know who deserves to live or to die.

Questions and Exercises

1. Define euthanasia.
2. Distinguish:
   a. Active and passive euthanasia.
   b. Voluntary and involuntary euthanasia.

3. For each of the following cases decide, Is it euthanasia?, and if so, Is it active/voluntary, active/involuntary, passive/voluntary, or passive/involuntary?
   a. A terminally ill infant is not given an operation that would extend her life by a month (no more).
   b. A physician gives a terminally ill infant a lethal injection.
   c. An elderly woman is killed by a son who wants her money.
   d. A comatose woman who left a will saying she never wanted to "be a vegetable" is taken off the life-support systems.
   e. A terminally ill man knowingly takes an overdose of sleeping pills.
4. Take the moral point of view and develop a moral position (or reconsider your current position) on euthanasia. Explain this position.
5. Explain the difference between a consequentialist and deontological ethic.
6. Is your position in #4 consequentialist or deontological?
7. Whether or not you believe in active euthanasia, outline the social policy/practices that, while allowing active euthanasia, would allow the fewest number of abuses.
8. Do you think that the policy/practices you outlined in #7 would keep abuses down to a relatively small number? Explain.
9. Explain the slippery slope fallacy.
10. Does Barrington think that people have the right to kill themselves whenever they want to? Support your answer with quotes.
11. Does Barrington think it's likely that allowing active euthanasia would result in widespread abuses?
12. Why does Barrington think that society ought to assist people in committing suicide?
13. What are the conditions under which Motto would allow suicide?
14. What do you suppose Motto would think about the clinic in "Death on Demand"? Justify your answer with reference to his article.
15. According to Dyck, what are the major differences between the euthanasia ethic and the benemortasia ethic?
16. Does the benemortasia ethic endorse active euthanasia? Passive euthanasia?
17. Is Dyck a consequentialist or a deontologist? Explain.
18. Does Dyck think that allowing active euthanasia would result in unfortunate consequences? Cite passages from his article in answering the question.
19. Suppose a person who was terminally ill and planning to kill herself spent several weeks visiting people she had known, explaining what she was going to do and saying goodbye. Would this fit Dyck's claim that suicide is a "hostile" act? Explain.

5

The Nature of the Mind

Fiction: Strange Behavior

What first startled us about the civilization on the planet Gamma was not its strangeness but its familiarity. It was as if a piece of southern Europe from the year 2050 had been transported fifty years ahead in time, and millions of miles out into space, to that small planet. Of course, the similarity is not exact. The Italians of fifty years ago did not have quite the same enthusiasm for spherical constructions, nor for the colors pink and orange. Also, the brown-skinned Gammas are nine feet tall and hairless, and they hear through slits located just below their cheekbones. But with all the strange life forms recently discovered in the universe, these minor dissimilarities between the Gammas and the mid-century Italians go almost unnoticed. When we landed on Gamma, we felt as if we had stepped into a living museum.

The technological sophistication of Gamma is virtually the same as that of Earth fifty years ago. But there is one notable difference. The Gammas' skill in robotry is more advanced than is ours even today. In fact, we spent our first six hours on Gamma in the company of robots that we thought to be living beings. In our defense, I should note that the Gammese robots have a tremendous flexibility of response and fluidity of motion and that their metallic parts are covered with a brown, skinlike exterior. It is only when a Gammese robot is standing next to a Gamma that one notices, in the robot, a hint of the mechanical. But I don't think one is thoroughly convinced of the difference between the Gammas and the robots until one has toured the hospitals where the living are treated and the factories where the robots are repaired.

It was from the robots that we got the rudiments of the Gammese language. After letting them know that we were friendly, we coaxed them over to the Q-35 Computer Language Translator. We showed them the green patch on the screen of the Translator's Sensitivity Panel and indicated that they should say aloud the Gammese word for what they saw. The robots said something like "rooga"; the Translator said aloud "green." We said "green" and the Translator said "rooga." We continued this process until we were able to produce, via the Translator, several basic sentences in Gammese. Then the robots realized that the Q-35 was recording all the word translations and would soon enable us to converse by voice alone, without constant reference to the pictures on the Sensitivity Panel. Thereafter, the robots concentrated on teaching the Q-35 their language, responding in quick succession to the series of sights, sounds, textures, tastes, and scents produced by the Sensitivity Panel.

The real Gammas appeared eventually, and we laughed at ourselves for having mistaken the robots for living beings. The Gammas were very friendly and intensely curious about the civilization on Earth. Of course we had more to tell them than they us, for they were like the past to us, and we were like the future to them. The first days on Gamma were a constant series of conferences, largely of a Show-and-Tell variety, as we struggled to make ourselves understood through the less than fluent Q-35 Translator. Fortunately, we had with us an instruction kit filled with models, maps, and photographs designed to aid us in explanations of life on Earth.

With so much on Gamma already familiar to us, we tended to focus our attention on the robots. We became more and more puzzled by what we observed. It was not only that the robots were so lifelike but also that the Gammas seemed to treat the robots as their equals. True, there was a preponderance of robots in jobs that demanded only great strength or great memory; but there were Gammas in such jobs as well. And some Gammese robots held high-level positions in which they supervised the activities of the living Gammas. Furthermore, the Gammas seemed to treat the robots with the same sort of courtesy, affection, or, occasionally, anger that they showed toward other Gammas.

Our most frequent guide was a Gamma whose name is unpronounceable. We simply addressed him as "Mr. A," and the Q-35 made the sound that he recognized as his name. We were eager to question him about the Gammas' attitude toward the robots, but we approached the subject cautiously, not wishing to seem critical. His initial responses to our inquiries were bewildering. It seemed as though he were teasing us.

"Would you say that flesh is so much better than metal?" he asked. "I should think it would be just the opposite."

Or again: "Would you treat someone differently just because he is produced in a factory? Personally, I think our mode of reproduction—which is similar to yours—is rather inefficient and even comical."

Mr. A was asked why only robots had been sent on the potentially dangerous mission of meeting us when we landed on Gamma.

"Because, of course, they are more easily repaired than we are. It is a quality we envy them. Just as they sometimes envy us our greater flexibility."

Phrases like "they envy us" and "they also want" were constantly employed by our guide. Finally Lewis, a member of our group, blurted out the question that all of us wanted to ask.

"Mr. A, do the Gammas really believe that their robots have minds?"

"Of course," said Mr. A, looking puzzled.

"Then that explains the confusion," said Lewis. "We did not mean to say that one should treat a creature differently simply because it is made of a different substance or is produced differently. Rather, we believe that creatures made of metal cannot possibly have minds. On the other hand, you believe they can and do. Now we understand each other better."

We were all quite pleased with the quick and tactful way in which we had solved the mystery. At the same time, we all felt more than a little superior to a people who believed that machines could think. However, Mr. A did not seem pleased. He seemed absolutely bewildered.

"I don't understand," he said. "Please explain yourselves."

"You believe that these robots have minds," said Lewis. "So you treat them as your peers. We don't believe that robots have minds. Therefore, we treat them as we might treat, say, expensive watches. Of course, there is room for disagreement on this point. I mean, one doesn't actually *see* minds."

"Of course you see minds!" said Mr. A.

He was quite emphatic and seemed quite serious. We were all startled.

"Well, one's own mind, yes," said Lewis. "But one doesn't see other minds."

"You do see other minds!"

"No, no. At least not according to our beliefs. We believe that one sees the behavior of other people, but not their minds."

Mr. A glanced toward the Q-35 Translator and then back at Lewis.

"Your words don't seem to translate. What I hear from the Translator makes no sense."

Lewis looked thoughtful for a moment and then continued.

"Does the word 'behavior' make sense to you? The actions of the body?"

"Yes."

"And the word 'pain'?"

"Yes."

"Do you understand me when I say that a person in pain behaves in a special sort of way?"

"Yes. Of course."

"Well, what we call 'pain' is not the behavior but the thing inside."

"What thing inside?" said Mr. A. "There are many things inside."

"I mean the thing that is inside whenever you show the pain behavior."

"Oh, you mean the state of the brain, or the state of the robot's computer?"

"No, no, no. You could observe the brain state or the computer state under certain conditions. I mean the thing that you could never observe no matter how extensively you examined the body. I mean the feel of the pain, the sensation of pain."

"Those last words don't translate."

Lewis was obviously feeling frustrated, but he pressed on.

"Perhaps the example of imagination would be easier. Suppose you close your eyes and imagine something round and orange. Form an image of it.

What we call the 'mental' is not the closing of the eyes or the verbal description 'orange and round' that you might give us. What we call the 'mental' is the round and orange picture inside of you."

"What picture?" said Mr. A.

The conversation went on in this absurd fashion as Lewis tried to phrase the obvious in a way that would be obvious in Mr. A's language. But gradually the truth of the matter began to dawn on us. The reason the Gammas saw no essential difference between themselves and their robots was the Gammas, like the robots, were creatures without minds, without consciousness.

Our words like "think" and "want," and the generic term "mind," had seemed, at first, to translate into Gammese because we constantly correlated our mental events with behavioral patterns. The Gammas had thought all along that we were talking about behavior. In fact, our mental terms didn't translate into Gammese at all, for the Gammas have no minds. They only behave as if they did.

As we were staring at Mr. A in astonishment, it occurred to us that we might be frightening or offending him. We were very vulnerable on this far-away planet. So we turned the conversation from the topic of minds to the topic of interplanetary travel. Our talk of the overtly strange life forms we had encountered on our travels seemed to reestablish our kinship with the Gammese people.

When the subject of minds arose again, as it inevitably did, we tried to deemphasize the dissimilarity between ourselves and the Gammas. We implied that our word "mind" referred to behavior plus that "something else." This allowed us to say that the Gammas and the robots had minds without pretending, as would have been hopeless now, that there was no difference between them and us. Eventually, the whole matter turned into a kind of joke. Mr. A asked us what the "something else" inside the people from Earth did for them. Of course, we had to admit that it produced no overt effects that could not occur without it. After that he began to joke about us as "the people with the something else that does nothing at all." In fact, this phrase threatens to become the general designation for us on Gamma.

* * * * * *

It is truly amazing to observe just how little external difference the lack of mind has made to the Gammese civilization. With only a body and a brain, they have almost managed to keep pace with the civilization on Earth. Without thoughts, they have been able to develop a sophisticated technology that has brought them to the verge of interplanetary travel. Without feelings, they can discriminate between beauty and ugliness, goodness and evil, and they have produced sophisticated treatises on ethics and aesthetics. They act as if they have the normal variety of human emotions, even to the point of enjoying very sentimental love stories.

The only noticeable differences appear in their metaphysical writings, and even these are minor. One philosopher on Gamma began a philosophical treatise with the argument, "I think, therefore I am." Of course, this is not really the same as Descartes's argument. The correct translation would be something like, "I behave (in a thinking way), therefore I exist (as a physical being)."

On Gamma there is a fairly widespread belief in God, though they have their religious skeptics just as we do. They identify God with the universe and claim that He is (or rather behaves as if He is) omnipotent, omniscient, and perfectly good. They certainly do not imagine God to be nonphysical. The word "nonphysical" translates into their language as "not-being" or "nothing," which is to say that it does not translate at all. Some Gammas believe in life after death, which they imagine to be a physical resurrection of the body that occurs at some far distant time. They include the robots in this resurrection. "The robots worship Him as we do," they say, "and our Heavenly Father would not neglect them." Of course, they do not believe that the mind exists during the period between death and the resurrection. Said one philosopher: "To take the mind from the body is as impossible as taking the shape from a flower while leaving its color and weight behind."

I often wonder about our future relations with the Gammas. I doubt that we would provoke hostilities with these creatures. There are enough hostile beings in the universe already, and we need whatever allies we can find. The Gammas may be able to provide us with valuable information about their solar system. And no doubt our scientists and philosophers will want to study the Gammas at great length. But the issues here will be strictly practical. There can be no question of extending moral rights to mindless, unfeeling creatures, whether they are made of metal or protoplasm.

Mr. A was there to bid us goodbye as we prepared to leave the planet Gamma. He told us how much he had enjoyed our visit and how sad he was to see us depart. He said the Gammas would always look forward to visits from the people of Earth. Then he laughed softly:

"We shall always welcome the people with the something else that does nothing at all."

I laughed with him, but in my heart I felt only pity. He did not, could not, possibly understand that the "something else that does nothing at all" is the very essence of life, the point of it, and that it makes all the difference in the world.

Fiction: Life After Life

My funeral was quite moving, I thought. I chose a spot at the front, next to the minister, so that I could observe the faces in the crowd while I listened to the eulogy. There wasn't a dry eye in the house. Reverend Franks reviewed my long career with the Omega Life Insurance Company, my "meteoric rise," as he called it, from messenger boy to president. He said I had always insisted that Omega sold insurance for *living*, not dying: insurance for the happiness of policyholders should they live full term, insurance for the happiness of the loved ones should they not. He was sure that Charlie—my name's Charles R. Smith, but everyone calls me Charlie, even my secretary—that Charlie would want his funeral conducted in the same optimistic, life-loving spirit with which he had conducted his business. That was a nice touch, I thought, and I hoped that the boys from the office were duly appreciative.

Death, said Reverend Franks, was, above all, the opportunity to reflect on life. Though I had lived but fifty years, everyone, he was sure, would agree that my life had been "full term" in the most meaningful sense. I had been not only a business magnate but also a Boy Scout leader, an Elk, and a church deacon. I had been the beloved husband of Ruth and the beloved father of Tim and Marcie, a good provider in life and beyond. I had been a man to whom any friend could turn in legitimate need; a man who could laugh with the fellows and cry, so to speak, for an unfortunate boy; a man who had a fifteen handicap as a golfer but no handicap as a human being.

I was feeling a bit smug at that point, I must admit, and I began to feel more so as Reverend Franks started to speak, somewhat uncomfortably, of his hope for "life after life." Our church has always been vague on that particular issue, tending to stress the vast potential for human moral development in "this life." But I *knew* now, of course, and he didn't. I knew there was life after this life. Or I guess I should say: life after that one.

In all honesty, though, this development was as much of a surprise to me as the next guy. When I got that fish bone caught in my throat and couldn't breathe, and everything started getting dark, I said to myself: This is it, fella. Nothing else, just: This is it, fella. And you know, in the back of my mind, I was a bit pleased with how it was ending. You spend a lot of your life worrying about death and imagining how awful it is going to be. But when the time comes, it's just something you go ahead and do, or rather something that gets done to you, like getting punched in the nose in your first fight. When it happens, it happens quickly, and you're kind of numb, and there isn't that much pain, or fuss, or fear at all.

Then I opened my eyes and I thought: I guess that wasn't it, fella. Ruth was kneeling next to me, wringing her hands and crying, and Tim, who'd been having dinner with us, was yelling into the phone. I said, "I'm all right, Ruth." But she kept on crying, and I realized she was sobbing too loud to hear me. So I got to my feet to show her I was okay. Even that didn't get her attention, so I put my hand on her shoulder. Only then I noticed there wasn't any hand. That was a shocker, I can tell you. I looked down at myself and there was nothing there—no hands, no arms, no feet, no legs, no nothing. I looked in the mirror over the dining room table, and there was nothing there either, just the image of the living room behind me. I looked at Ruth again and there, at her feet, was a body that looked just like mine, only the face was kind of waxy and blue. And I thought: This is too much. You're having some kind of weird dream. You're on the floor, unconscious, dreaming that you're moving around the room without a body. In a little while you're going to wake up in a hospital bed with your body connected to you the way it's supposed to be, and everything will be all right.

But if this was a dream, it was awfully vivid. Tim hung up the phone and helped Ruth over to the couch. He held her as she cried, and occasionally he glanced over her shoulder at the body on the floor, showing little emotion, just as I'd always taught him a boy should do.

And I thought again: Yes, this has to be a dream. You can't be dead. If you are dead, you'd be standing before Saint Peter at the Pearly Gates, getting fitted for your wings, or something like that. But then I thought: Maybe it doesn't happen that fast. Your soul has just left your body. Maybe it takes the Lord a little while. After all, there are people dying in houses all over the world tonight. You could hardly expect the Lord to make the rounds of all those houses so quickly. You'll just have to wait your turn. And maybe you'd better get yourself ready. So I started in with "Our Father Who Art in Heaven" and when I finished that I started singing "Nearer My God to Thee." Only no one appeared except for the policemen and the ambulance attendants. All that commotion distracted me, I guess: the sirens, the chatter, the neighbors gathered outside, the ride to the hospital.

At the hospital they pronounced me dead and gave Ruth a sedative. I wasn't all that concerned about Ruth. I don't mean to say I was unsympathetic. I knew how frightened and unhappy she was, and I knew it would be hard for her to get along without me. But I also knew now that death wasn't the end of everything. Ruth would have a few years of loneliness and fear, but then she would find out that life goes on and on, and she would be with me again. From where I stood, so to speak, that looked like a pretty good deal. Anyway, I had my own problems.

In the days following my death, when I wasn't diverted by my funeral arrangements, I was absorbed with the perplexities of my new situation. It was hard to get used to. Some friend would enter the house and I'd say "hi," and he'd walk right through me. I mean *right through me*. And then I'd look down at where my body had been, and I'd be brought back to reality—whatever that was.

My perception of things was much as it had always been, at least visually. I saw the same shapes, sizes, and colors, in the same three dimensions. And my perception of sounds was about the same. But I had no sense of touch, taste, or smell. I really regretted my lack of taste when I looked at a steak and a beer, not to mention my lack of wherewithal when I glanced at a naked woman. Still, I didn't have hunger anymore, and I wasn't in pain. I just missed those pleasures.

I wasn't able to move objects in any way, which is kind of puzzling when you think about it. Of course, my soul didn't have a body anymore. But if a soul can't move objects, how does it ever move a body? Some special kind of connection, I suppose. In any case, my connection had snapped.

However, if I couldn't move objects, I could move through them without difficulty. I would walk into a wall, get a quick impression of darkness, and then emerge from the other side. I found I was able to rise to a height of about forty feet from the ground, and to move laterally at a top speed of ninety-five miles an hour. I checked that speed when I went into Los Angeles for a Dodger game, two days after the funeral. I had a great time. I was able to move around the infield, getting close-ups of the action, without fear of getting hit by the ball. I had the best "seat" in the house, and it didn't cost me one thin dime.

It goes without saying that I could go anywhere I wanted, unobserved, and observe anything I wanted. I didn't abuse that privilege. The naked woman I mentioned earlier was my wife. Any others I saw were by accident, and I departed almost at once. It was fun, at first, dropping by the office, or a neighbor's house, or Larry's Bar, listening to plans for an ad campaign, or to local gossip, trying to guess along with the fellows on the baseball pools. But as time went on, I found myself less and less interested in those conversations, I suppose because I was not involved in the things they were talking about. Occasionally I heard cutting remarks about me, and those hurt. But perhaps I felt even worse when they stopped talking about me altogether.

The real hurt was from my family. Tim took his share of the inheritance, bought himself a flashy VW van, packed it with surfboards, and left college for the beach. When a friend asked him how he got his money, he said, "My old man kicked the bucket." That's all. No fond recollections, no good words, just "my old man kicked the bucket." I never heard my daughter Marcie talk about me at all. I visited her college dorm once and only once. I mean, you teach a girl what's right and wrong, and how no one will buy a cow if the milk is free, and how pot leads to stronger stuff, and she says, "Yes, Daddy, of course," and then you see what she does when she's away. Just once. I wouldn't want to see any more of it.

But my wife, Ruth, gave me the greatest pain—Ruth, with whom I spent all those years; Ruth, whom I trusted. My old friend Arnold kept dropping by to "pay his respects," which I thought was nice of him until I saw what his respects amounted to. I remember vividly that evening two months ago when Ruth was wearing her black dress, and Arnold was pouring her brandy to boost her spirits, and she started crying, and he hugged her, then kissed her, and she started muttering "No," and he said Charlie would want it this way, which, of course, I didn't, and later they started moving toward the bedroom. I was screaming at her at the top of my lungs, even though I knew she couldn't hear me. Then I turned and stomped out of the house. I haven't been back there since. I'm never going back there.

Later, when I calmed down a bit, I began to think things over. By this time it was obvious that the Lord wasn't coming. Maybe I'd always felt that there wasn't anyone in charge of things—life, I mean—and I was pretty sure of that now. And if my fundamentalist friends had been wrong about heaven and such, I could count myself lucky that those Eastern religions I'd read about had been wrong too. I mean, at least I wasn't reincarnated and wandering around as a skunk or a radish. What was happening to me was quite natural, apparently, and uncontrolled. What I had to do was take things in hand and make my own way, just as I had in my former life. I've never been one to sit on my thumbs, I can tell you.

Now that all the people in my former life had become uninteresting or disappointing to me, it seemed that I ought to try to make some new friends among my own kind. There had to be a lot of other souls around, and surely I would get along with them just fine. I've always been great at making friends.

But the question was: how do you make friends with people who are invisible, untouchable, and make no sounds? All I could see when I looked around me were bodies, no souls. How to make contact? Obviously, I needed some good advice.

In hopes of finding an answer, I started taking some philosophy courses (unofficially, of course) at UCLA. They were no help. I did get a few proofs for the indestructibility of the soul, but that was the last thing I needed. What I needed was a suggestion about how to chat with silent souls, and wouldn't you know those guys would have nothing to say about really relevant topics. I would have asked for my money back if I'd paid any.

After I'd thought about the problem on my own, it occurred to me that extrasensory perception might be the answer. But that didn't help much, considering I didn't know anything about extrasensory perception. The only thing I could think of was to act as if I were yelling to someone. So in my mind I said as forcefully as I could, "Hey there!" "Hello there, guys!" "Speak to me!" "Come in, souls, come in!" For the longest time nothing happened, and I tried everything. I "spoke" loudly and softly, at different times of day, facing in different directions. I would think of departed friends or relatives and speak their names. Or I would simply address myself to strangers. I tried visiting areas where it seemed logical that souls might congregate, such as churches, graveyards, and busy city streets.

Finally, I had some luck of sorts. I was sitting on the shore at Long Beach, watching the water and feeling kind of depressed, when I heard a buzzing, chattering sound, like you might hear over the phone. In desperation I cried, "Speak to me, speak to me!" and then, to my amazement, I heard a voice.

"Who's that?"

"I'm Charlie," I said, "Charlie Smith. Who are you?"

"I'm Mildred."

"Where are you, Mildred, in Long Beach?"

"Long Beach? Heavens no. I'm in Tallahassee."

"Tallahassee?"

It happens like that. You'd think that if you got through to another soul, it would be a soul in your own neighborhood. But that other soul can be anywhere. I remember a teacher at UCLA saying that a soul, being nonphysical, would have no spatial location. I wanted to interrupt her and tell her how wrong she was. I mean, I was a soul, and I was right there in her classroom. But I must admit now that that kind of location doesn't seem to count for much when souls communicate with one another.

I had a pleasant chat with Mildred that day and the next. She invited me to visit her in Tallahassee, and I accepted. It was a pretty easy trip. I could move, as I've said, at ninety-five miles an hour and didn't need to stop and rest. I didn't have to worry about traffic jams, or stop lights, or winding roads. With a few side trips for sightseeing, and getting lost once, I made it in about a day and a half.

I guess I had the absurd feeling that I would *see* Mildred in Tallahassee. Of course, I couldn't. She was a soul and invisible, no matter how close you got. Our communications in Florida were like more phone conversations, only this time they were local calls. Still, we were able to share experiences and see the sights together.

The first few days were fun. Then Mildred reverted to her "normal" routine. It turned out that the only sights she really wanted to see and share were at the television department at Sears. Mildred loved soap operas. She was a real fanatic. When she wasn't watching the soaps, she would listen to women talking about them or peer over someone's shoulder at the pages of *Soap Opera Digest*. It was all too much for me. I wasn't about to spend eternity watching "The Guiding Light" and "One Life to Live." I thought I'd better find a woman with other interests. I'd made contact once, and I was sure I would again.

And I did—this time with Alice in Cheyenne, Wyoming. That visit went badly from the start. All Alice wanted to do was hang around her husband and spy on the women he had taken up with after she'd died. I would have left right away, but I happened to see Alice's picture on the mantelpiece in her house. She was gorgeous, I mean really gorgeous. I'd never been with a woman who looked like that. So I tried to get her interested in me. I told her about my bad experiences with my wife and how I'd decided I should forget about my former life and associate with my own kind. I told her she should forget about her husband and try to have some fun.

I took Alice out on a couple of dates. Her mood seemed to be picking up, and she seemed to be getting to like me. One night, I took her to a drive-in movie. We sat near the front, about twenty feet in the air, over the cars. It was a very romantic, sensual movie. I got really involved in the film. I began to feel a deep regret at not having a body. I was longing for some kind of human warmth.

"Oh Alice," I said, "I wish so much that I could hold your hand."

"It wouldn't be proper," she said. "I've only been widowed for five months."

That was the last straw. An hour later I was heading back to California.

That's the way it's been going. Every soul I meet seems to be interested only in the past. But the past is past, and you can't live on memories. On the other hand, what else can you live on? There doesn't seem to be anything interesting that you can do for, or to, or with, another soul. Or vice versa. It's not much fun floating around like a bubble, not able to do anything in the world.

What on earth am I going to do with myself? I don't know. I've got to figure out something. I've just got to. I'm bored as hell.

Questions

1. Which of the following statements are true of the Gammas?
   a. They act and speak intelligently.
   b. They treat the people from Earth in a friendly way.
   c. They exhibit a good sense of humor.
   d. They have a fairly sophisticated technology.
   e. They write and read love stories.
   f. They philosophize.
   g. They have a religion.
2. Explain the differences between body, brain, and mind. Which of these are the Gammas supposed to have?
3. The narrator of "Strange Behavior" says that the Gammas have no minds. What does she believe the mind to be?
4. What are the Gammas supposed to be missing in not having minds?
5. What outward differences, if any, would there be in the Gammese culture if the Gammas had minds?
6. What conception of mind is implied by "Life After Life"? In what ways is it similar to or different from the conception of mind held by the narrator in "Strange Behavior"?
7. In "Life After Life," Charlie is a disembodied soul. Is a soul any different from a mind? Explain.
8. Charlie says that he can't understand how minds manage to move human bodies. What is his reasoning here?
9. Do you believe that the perceptions and capacities of a disembodied soul would be any different from those described in the story? If so, in what ways do you think they would be different?

DISCUSSION

DUALISM: "THE OFFICIAL VIEW"

The narrator of "Strange Behavior" holds a view of mind and body that seems to be shared by most people in our culture. It is sometimes dubbed "the official view." According to this view, the mind is radically different from any physical object. For one thing, physical objects (including human bodies) are publicly observable, while minds are necessarily private. That is, one can observe another person's body just as one can observe the chairs and tables in a room; but one cannot observe another person's thoughts. Furthermore, physical objects occupy space, while minds do not. A mind is not located in some part of the physical body, nor anywhere else in the physical world. Because the mind is radically different from any physical object, it is claimed, the mind is nonphysical. Persons holding this "official view" of mind and body are called "dualists." **Dualism** is the view that the world is composed of two radically different kinds of things—physical bodies and nonphysical minds.

MATERIALISM: TWO THEORIES

Some of the critics who reject "the official view" are called "materialists." **Materialism** is the view that everything that exists is physical, including the mind. The impulses behind materialism are multiple and will be elucidated throughout this discussion. Some adherents of materialism believe that it is most compatible with a "scientific view" of the world. They believe that the higher life forms evolved from physical matter. In their view, the emergence of physical mind from physical matter is theoretically plausible; but the emergence of nonphysical mind from physical matter is preposterous. Moreover, some of the adherents of materialism believe that their view is supported by considerations of theoretical simplicity. The dualist narrator of "Strange Behavior" has to admit that the "something else" she calls "mind" produces "no overt effects that could not occur without it." In theory, a sophisticated brain–nervous system would be quite sufficient to produce the full range of human behavior. To suppose a spirit (nonphysical mind) is behind the workings of the human body would be as unscientific, materialists say, as to suppose a spirit is behind the workings of a car engine. (Contemporary British philosopher Gilbert Ryle has called dualism "the myth of the ghost in the machine.")

Two forms of materialism that have received considerable attention in the twentieth century are called "behaviorism" and "the identity theory." (It should be noted that the philosophical theory called "behaviorism" differs from the psychological theory of the same name.) First we shall discuss behaviorism, then the identity theory.

The narrator of "Strange Behavior" says that the Gammas are "mindless": "the Gammas have no minds. They only behave as if they did." A behaviorist would disagree with the narrator. The Gammas behave intelligently and kindly, the behaviorist would point out. To behave intelligently and kindly is to be intelligent and kind. The term "mind" designates such characteristics as intelligence and kindness. Therefore, the Gammas do have minds.

According to "the official view," one never sees another mind; at most, one sees the physical behavior of another person. But, says the behaviorist, if we were really talking about unobservable entities when we talk about other minds, then each of us would naturally be skeptical about other minds: We would be reluctant to make judgments about the mental states of others; we would even be dubious about the very existence of other minds. Yet the opposite is the case: We feel certain that other minds exist; we are all quite confident about pronouncing others to be more or less intelligent, kind, or happy. Like all of us, the dualist narrator of "Strange Behavior" makes confident judgments about the supposedly hidden mental states of her associates: "Lewis was obviously feeling frustrated, but he pressed on." Such confidence indicates that the mental states of others are not hidden at all, that other minds are things we can observe. What we observe when we judge other minds is physical behavior.

It is important to recognize that behaviorism is a thesis about the meanings of our mental terms. Since the meaning of a term is determined by how we use it, behaviorism is a thesis about what we mean when we talk about minds. Behaviorism claims to be an accurate report of how we use the generic term "mind" and the more specific mental terms "pain," "kindly," "knowledgeable," and so forth.

According to the proponents of **behaviorism,** when we say that someone has a mind, we are simply saying that the person exhibits or is capable of exhibiting certain complex, overt, physical behavior under certain circumstances. When you have seen someone's behavior, you have seen that person's mind. The mind is nothing more than (certain types of complex, overt) physical behavior.

The behaviorist is not, however, committed to the view that anything that exhibits behavior has a mind, as, for example, plants and amoebae. Note the term "complex" in the definition. The behaviorist is saying that one who exhibits behavior of sufficient complexity has a mind. The kind and degree of complexity necessary for mental behavior would be specified in a full behaviorist account.

The word "overt" in the definition indicates external rather than internal bodily behavior. According to the behaviorist, when we talk about minds we are talking about speech, facial expressions, and the movements of the arms and legs, as opposed to the workings of the liver, heart, or brain. The behaviorist would not deny that a functioning brain is essential to our exhibiting complex, overt, physical behavior. But in the behaviorist view, the mind is not the brain; the mind is behavior.

According to the behaviorist, every particular statement we make about mental states or characteristics is a statement about behavior and dispositions to behave. When we say that someone knows how to ride a bicycle, we are saying that the person is riding a bicycle, has ridden one, or would or could ride one if placed on it. When we say that someone is kind, we are saying that the person is helping others, has helped others, or would help others in a rather wide range of circumstances. And so on, for every statement about mental characteristics.

The behaviorist says that mental characteristics are observable, but not always as readily observable as red hair or blue eyes. One cannot glance at a crowd of pedestrians and immediately determine which ones know how to ride bicycles and which ones are kind. Rather, mental characteristics are observable and physical in the same way in which the fragility of a vase is observable and physical. If a vase breaks at the light touch of a hammer, one has seen that it is fragile. (Of course, there are less drastic tests of fragility.) If someone gets on a bicycle and rides, one has seen that the person knows how. If someone helps others, one has seen that the person is kind. To see the behavior is to see the mind, because the mind is nothing more than behavior.

Whatever plausibility behaviorism may initially have, it is ultimately difficult to defend. We do not use mental terms as the behaviorist claims we use them. Most, if not all, of our mental terms indicate something over and above behavior and dispositions to behave. They indicate events that we are inclined to call "internal" and "private." As Lewis says in "Strange Behavior": "Suppose you close your eyes and imagine something round and orange. Form an image of it. What we call the 'mental' is not the closing of the eyes or the verbal description 'round and orange' that you might give us. What we call the 'mental' is the round and orange picture inside of you."

Similarly, when we say that a person is "in pain," we are talking about something more than the disposition to grimace and groan. We are talking about the sensation, the *feel* of the pain. In the same vein, a person would not be kind unless that person had kindly feelings.

The difficulties with behaviorism are most apparent when that theory is applied to oneself. Sit still, fold your hands, close your eyes, and think, "Two plus two equals four." Now report what you have just thought: "I just thought 'two plus two equals four.' " Is it at all plausible to believe that this statement is merely the report of some behavior or some disposition to behave? Surely your statement doesn't mean "I was sitting still with my eyes closed and my hands folded." Such "behavior" is compatible with a wide range of thoughts—or no thoughts at all. Nor does your statement mean "I was disposed to say the words 'two plus two equals four.' " One is not always disposed to do or say something after each thought. Even if one were, such a disposition is not the crucial fact that you are reporting, but something incidental. The crucial thing that you are reporting is an internal, private event—the thought, "Two plus two equals four."

Put formally, this particular argument against behaviorism is as follows:

1. Behaviorism implies that all talk about minds is talk about behavior.
2. When I report the thought "$2+2=4$," I am not talking about behavior.

3. (Therefore) it's not the case that all talk about minds is talk about behavior (from 2).
4. (Therefore) behaviorism is not true (from 1 and 3).

Such arguments against behaviorism are generally accepted as decisive. However, if behaviorism is not correct, at least one can extract from it a claim that seems to be correct: that many of our mental predicates do imply behavioral components. Consider generosity, for instance. In the absence of all behavior, a person could conceivably be sympathetic, but he or she could not be generous. The term "generosity" implies some physical act of giving. The narrator of "Strange Behavior" makes a similar concession, though overstating it: "We implied that our word 'mind' referred to behavior plus that 'something else.'" A better way to say this would be that some, but not all, of our mental terms refer to behavior in addition to that always essential "something else."

Any adequate theory of mind must make this concession to behaviorism. But for simplicity of exposition, and because not all mental terms imply some sort of behavior, this concession shall not be reiterated as we consider other theories of mind.

Apparently, the mind is not overt physical behavior. But perhaps it is physical nonetheless. There is an internal bodily organ, the brain, that is intimately associated with mental processes. Perhaps the mind and the brain are not two different entities, closely related; perhaps the physical brain *is* the mind. Philosophers who claim that the brain and mind are identical are identity theorists. As has been noted, the identity theory is a form of materialism.

According to the **identity theory,** the mind (that which produces thoughts, images, sensations) is identical with the brain (the mass of nerve tissue inside the skull). Mental events are nothing but electrochemical brain processes. Mental events are "internal" only in the sense that they occur inside the skull. They are "private" only in the sense that brain processes are very infrequently observed.

Unlike behaviorism, the identity theory is not a theory about the meanings of our mental terms. The identity theorist is not claiming that the word "mind" means "brain" or that the word "pain," for example, means "brain state such and such" (where a specific description of a brain state is given). Such a claim would be absurd, because as long as human beings have talked about minds, they have judged other minds according to behavior and have believed that particular sorts of behavior (grimacing and groaning, for example) were typically associated with particular mental states (pain, for example). This is what gave the behaviorist claim some initial plausibility. But human beings were talking about minds before they learned that the brain is the physical organ most intimately associated with thought. (Once it was believed that the heart is the crucial organ of thought.) Even today, when most people do suppose that the brain is crucial for thought, most people haven't the vaguest idea what particular kind of electrochemical process is associated with pain. Surely we do not mean "brain state such and such" when we say "pain."

The identity claimed by the identity theory is factual identity rather than identity of meaning. The words "mind" and "brain" do not have the same meaning, but, says the identity theorist, the mind and brain are, in fact, identical. Questions of factual identity require one to focus not on the meanings of the words, primarily, but on the characteristics of those things to which the words refer. "Is my brother, in fact, the axe murderer that the police are seeking?" would be a question of factual identity. Obviously, such a question could not be decided by considering how we use the phrases "my brother" and "axe murderer." That these two phrases do not mean the same thing does not indicate that they do not refer to the same person. Evidence would have to be gathered as to what is known about my brother and what is known about the axe murderer—evidence that just might reveal that my brother is indeed the axe murderer.

By saying that the mind and the brain are identical, the identity theorist is saying that they are literally one and the same thing. It is easy to misinterpret this claim, because in everyday speech the word "identical" often has the meaning of "very similar." For example, we call some twins "identical," even though they are not one person. They are two different people who are similar in most, but not all, respects; for instance, they occupy different positions in space. However, the identity theorist is not saying that the mind and brain are two different things that are quite similar, but that the mind and the brain are one and the same thing.

The identity theory is widely discussed today, and there are many philosophers who consider it plausible. But there are objections to this theory that seem to have weight.

Critics of the identity theory appeal to what might be called a **principle of nonidentity:** Two things cannot be identical if they have different characteristics.* This principle is one that we seem to accept readily in everyday life. That can't be my pen you have if my pen is blue and the one you are holding is green. My brother can't be the axe murderer if my brother is short and the murderer is tall.

Having claimed that two things having different characteristics cannot be identical, critics of the identity theory go on to claim that mental events and brain events do have different characteristics. Consider, for example, mental images. When one imagines something round and orange, presumably the image is round and orange. But is there a round, orange brain process occur-

---

*This informal wording of the nonidentity principle has the virtue of simplicity, but the phrase "two things" may be confusing. How could two things be one thing (identical), whatever their characteristics? Actually, what is at issue in identity questions is whether *two descriptions* refer to the same thing or to different things. Do the phrases "My brother" and "the axe murderer" refer to the same man? Do the phrases "the mind" and "the brain" refer to the same thing? A more exact statement of the principle of nonidentity would be that if the thing referred to by one phrase has characteristics differing from those of the thing referred to by another phrase, then the two phrases do not refer to the same thing. Once this is understood, the simpler wording of the nonidentity principle allows for less cumbersome exposition.

ring at the same moment? Perhaps there is a round pattern of electrochemical activity: such has been demonstrated in certain experiments on perception. But our best evidence indicates that there is no orange brain event: The brain does not have the range of colors that our images display. If the image is orange and no brain events are orange, then the image cannot *be* a brain event. Mental events and brain events, however closely they might be related, are different things.

Put formally, this argument against the identity theory is as follows:

1. The identity theory implies that the mind and brain have all the same characteristics.
2. Mental images have colors the brain doesn't have.
3. (Therefore) it's not the case that the mind and brain have all the same characteristics (from 2).
4. (Therefore) the identity theory is not true (from 1 and 3).

Few philosophers would consider this objection to be as decisive as the objections leveled against behaviorism. The argument against the identity theory does depend on the reliability of our best *available* evidence concerning the characteristics of the brain. If, in the future, we should discover tiny pictures in the brain that correspond to our mental images, then the identity theory might look very good indeed.

Some identity theorists counter this objection by claiming that our images do not really have colors. The image of orange is not an orange event, they say. Thus the absence of orange in the brain does not show that such an image is not a brain event.

No doubt we do tend to exaggerate the role played by mental "pictures" in our thinking. Clearly, one can think, even imagine, without resorting to such pictures. But sometimes we do have mental images that are analogous to pictures and seem to have shape and color. Stare at a strong light, then close your eyes and consider this afterimage. Doesn't it seem to have color?

In evaluating the identity theory, we have considered only the case of images. What about something like pain? Does pain have the same characteristics as a particular brain process? It is difficult to decide how to approach the question. Obviously, we shouldn't expect a pain to "look like" the visual impression of a brain state. Should we then touch a portion of another's brain to find out if it feels painful to us? Some philosophers say that such conceptual difficulties demonstrate the radical difference between the mind and the brain. Perhaps it only shows that we need to give much more thought to this issue. But the ostensibly clear difference between the mind and brain in the case of images does count against the identity theory.

TWO FORMS OF DUALISM

If the arguments against behaviorism and the identity theory seem convincing to you, you may feel that dualism—"the official view"—is, after all, the most reasonable theory of mind and body. Dualism, you will recall, is the theory that there are physical objects and nonphysical minds. However, a dualist must give some account of the relation between mind and body, and materialists have often claimed that the mind–body relation is a crucial stumbling block for dualism.

There are at least two forms of dualism, which hold different views of the relation between mind and body.

Interactionists believe that nonphysical minds and physical bodies are causally related (have effects on one another). Stubbing the toe causes pain. The desire to wave causes the arm to move.

Parallelists believe that nonphysical minds and physical bodies are never causally related (never have effects on one another). Stubbing the toe may occur just prior to pain, but it does not cause the pain. The desire to wave occurs just prior to the moving of the arm, but it does not cause the arm to move.

Interactionism seems, at first glance, to be a sensible view of mind and body. (In fact, it is probably this specific version of dualism that warrants the label "the official view.") Parallelism, on the other hand, seems ludicrous. Why believe it?

Parallelists invoke the principle that a thing cannot produce characteristics that it does not have. Employing this principle, they say that the nonphysical, containing nothing physical itself, could not produce physical effects. And the physical could not produce nonphysical effects.

The principle that a thing cannot produce characteristics that it does not have seems to be acknowledged in everyday life. A brush that is dipped in clear water could not paint a wall red, because there is no red in the paintbrush. A feather could not topple a sturdy wall, because the feather is not sufficiently powerful.

Suppose that, while watching a knife-throwing act, you learn that the knives in the performer's hand are made of flimsy rubber. You would conclude that the act is a fake. True, each time the man appears to fling a knife, a knife appears in the wooden backdrop, perilously close to the body of his assistant. It seems as though he is throwing the knives, but he is not. The rubber knives do not contain sufficient strength to penetrate the wood. The movements of the man's hand are not causing the knives to appear in the wood; the hand movements are merely correlated with the appearance of the knives. Actually, the knives are hidden in the wooden backdrop and are popping out, handle first, at the appropriate moments. The illusion of the supposed "knife-throwing" act is analogous to what the parallelist sees as the illusion of the relation between mind and body.

The specific impulse to deny causal relations between the physical and nonphysical appears, to some extent, in ghost stories. If a ghost passes through a room, it is not tripped by chairs, nor does it knock them over. It is not stopped by a wall, nor does it dent the wall as it enters.

In "Life After Life," it is quite natural to imagine that Charlie, as a soul, would not interact with physical objects. To Charlie, as to many philosophers, this suggests a philosophical problem about the mind and body: "I wasn't able to move objects in any way, which is kind of puzzling when you think of it. Of course, my soul didn't have a body anymore. But if a soul can't move objects, how does it ever move a body?"

In fact, ghost stories clearly illustrate our confusion about this issue. Though ghosts do not normally interact with the physical world, they do so when the plot demands that they rattle chains or start fires. Ghost stories would be pretty dull if ghosts didn't do such things. But, philosophically, it seems as though we ought to make up our minds on this matter. Could the physical and nonphysical be causally related? Parallelists say no.

Parallelists, of course, are confronted with the following challenge: "If mind and body are not causally related, what accounts for the constant correlations between them? Surely this is not just coincidence!" In the case of the knife-throwing act, we would conclude that the act is a fake: The movements of the man's hand are not causing the knives to appear in the wood. But, having drawn that conclusion, we would suppose some other explanation for the constant correlation between the hand movements and the appearance of the knives. Perhaps there is some mechanism in the backdrop that springs out the knife handles at intervals known to the man; he is timing his arm movements accordingly. Or perhaps there is a third person backstage who presses a button, releasing a knife handle each time the performer's hand moves. We certainly would insist that there is some explanation. We would reject the supposition that the correlations are coincidental.

Parallelists have been unable to provide any satisfactory explanation as to how mind and body happen to be correlated if they are not causally related. Some have said that God causes the correlations, either moment by moment or through some predestined synchronization of mental and physical events. But this supposition won't do. If God is a spirit, then, according to the logic of parallelism, He cannot affect the physical; if He is physical, then He cannot affect the mental. If He is both mental and physical, how do these aspects of God happen to be correlated?

Parallelists are uncomfortable with the idea of extensive, happenstantial correlations between minds and bodies. But they say: "However astounding this may seem, it is more plausible than the theory that nonphysical minds and physical objects are causally related."

THE DILEMMA OF THE MIND–BODY DEBATE

We will gain a clearer perspective on these bizarre and complex controversies if we understand that philosophers are tempted to believe all three of these propositions, but must reject one of them.

    A. The mind and body are causally related.
    B. The physical and nonphysical cannot be causally related.
    C. There are physical bodies and nonphysical minds.

It is tempting to believe *A* because we observe the constant correlations between mind and body, and such correlations generally indicate causal relations. The attraction of *B* has been sketched previously: It doesn't seem as though things as fundamentally different as physical objects and nonphysical minds could have effects on one another. As for *C*, the inclination to believe in minds and physical objects is obvious enough, and the apparently radical dissimilarities between minds and physical objects tempt one to suppose that the mind is not physical.

These three statements, taken together, are inconsistent. They entail the claim that there are nonphysical minds and physical bodies that are, yet can't be, causally related. But any two of these propositions are consistent, and each possible pair yields a different philosophical position:

Statements *A* and *B* are compatible with materialism. According to this view, mind and body could not interact if they were radically different, but they are not radically different. The materialist says that mind and body are both physical. (Of course, the materialist denies *C*.)

Statements *A* and *C* (together with the denial of *B*) are equivalent to interactionism: There are physical bodies and nonphysical minds that are causally related.

Statements *B* and *C* (together with the denial of *A*) are equivalent to parallelism: There are physical bodies and nonphysical minds that are not causally related.

What can we do when we reach such an impasse? We reconsider the positions, the arguments, and the counterarguments (perhaps adding some arguments of our own), and try to determine which position is the most reasonable. We might begin by rejecting the positions that seem to be the less reasonable. Suppose we reject parallelism and behaviorism, narrowing the range of likely positions to interactionism and the identity theory. Then, among other things, we must decide whether it is less reasonable to believe that physical objects and nonphysical minds are causally related or to believe that the mind and the brain have all the same characteristics.

Personal beliefs are also relevant to such an evaluation process. For instance, one's religious beliefs may contradict materialism, though such beliefs constitute a good argument against materialism only if one has good reasons to hold those religious beliefs. Throughout history, many religious polemicists have equated the terms "materialist" and "atheist," though strictly speaking these terms are not equivalent. As is illustrated by the Gammas in "Strange Behavior," a materialist could believe in a physical God. Materialism could even be reconciled with a belief in life after death, in the sense that the physical body, with its mental characteristics, could be resurrected at some future date. But the materialist could not believe in a spiritual God or in a mind that continues to function when the body does not. So it is easy to see why materialism is considered anathema by many theists.

To show that the mind is nonphysical would not be sufficient to show that it survives the death of the body. Further arguments would be needed to support that claim. But to show that the mind is nonphysical would be sufficient to show that it *might* survive the death of the body, a claim that the materialist must deny.

LIFE AFTER DEATH

There are a great number of questions concerning the possibility of, and the possible nature of, an afterlife, many of them raised in the story "Life After Life." Of course, the primary question is: Does the mind survive the death of the body? And there are others: What would survival as a disembodied soul be like? What kind of perceptions would such a soul have, what kind of relations with physical objects? How could such a soul communicate with other souls or, for that matter, with God? Could survival as a disembodied soul be any fun? Charlie, in "Life After Life," finds his disembodied existence to be "hell." Is this because he does not have his mind on higher things? Or is that the way such an existence would inevitably be?

We could not even begin a general discussion of such questions without also introducing the various religious beliefs to which one's answers are so often linked. This we shall not do. Instead, we shall simply consider the kind of rational scrutiny to which we ought to subject our speculations about an afterlife.

Of course, if any topic tempts people toward mystical pronouncements, the concept of an afterlife is it. Ask someone how disembodied souls might communicate and the reply is likely to be "in some mysterious way that we can't even begin to fathom." Although such a response cannot be dismissed as nonsense, one could be forgiven for thinking of it as a glib device to avoid serious thinking. Even if we don't pretend to be able to comprehend all the possibilities of an afterlife, it would not seem overly presumptuous to suppose that we can determine some impossibilities.

If one has a fairly definite conception of how an afterlife is going to be, one ought to try to develop that conception in detail with an eye toward possible difficulties. If one is merely speculating about how an afterlife might be, one ought to try to determine the broad boundaries of the possible and the plausible. In so doing, one should watch out for incoherencies or inconsistencies.

Let us examine, as examples, three general statements implied by "Life After Life":

1. The Person Survives the Death of the Body.

This statement implies that "person" is synonymous with "mind" and, further, that neither of these two terms is definitionally related to "body." The behaviorist would deny the latter claim, but the behaviorist seems to be in error. Statement 1 does not seem to be a contradictory statement.

Statement 1 also implies that the mind (the essence of the person) is, in fact, nonphysical. An identity theorist could not consistently believe this; a dualist, of course, could.

Statement 1 implies the existence of a soul. This is purely a semantic point, though it is a point worth making for the sake of clarification. The word "soul" usually means "a nonphysical mind that survives the death of the body." To claim that a person has a soul is simply to make such claims about the mind; it is not to claim that the person has a mind plus some other thing.

The belief that the mind does survive the death of the body is often, but not always, linked to religious beliefs. Some who believe in an afterlife claim that people have had experiences that are most reasonably interpreted as contacts with disembodied spirits. Some claim that people occasionally have what are most reasonably interpreted as memories of a past life; thus, the mind existed before the birth of the present body and will probably live after the death of the present body. Some claim the "white light" experiences reported by people who have been near death are most reasonably interpreted as contacts with an afterlife. Of course, there are many who doubt that there is an afterlife and are critical of the arguments in favor of it. They claim that there is no persuasive evidence of the existence of a God who will preserve the mind after death. They claim that supposed contacts with spirits and supposed memories of a previous life and supposed glimpses of an afterlife are most reasonably explained naturalistically. They claim that there is evidence that the mind, if not identical with the brain, is dependent on the brain and will cease to function when the brain ceases to function. These are ongoing debates of considerable complexity, and we shall not attempt to deal with them here.

2. A Disembodied Soul Would Have Impressions of Sight and Sound But Would Not Have Impressions of Touch and Taste.

Many people would be inclined to believe this statement. In part, this inclination may result from a more explicit awareness of the role played by the sense organs in our perceptions of taste and touch than in our perceptions of sight and sound. However, it seems to be the case that our perceptions of sight and sound are the effects of light rays and sound waves impinging on the eyes and ears. If, indeed, all our perceptions are the effects of the world on our sense organs, is it reasonable to assume that a disembodied soul would have only limited sensory impressions, as opposed to either the full range of them or none at all?

Still, one might claim that the (image of the) body has an important orientation function with respect to taste and touch that it does not have with respect to sight and sound. I need the impression of a hand to show me what I am feeling; I do not need the impression of eyes to show me what I am seeing. At the very least, sensations of touch and taste would be confusing to a disembodied soul in a way that sensations of sight and sound would not be. If one assumes a benign deity or some principle having to do with the survival of the fittest souls, one might go on to argue that disembodied souls would not have the confusing impressions of touch and taste.

But is it impossible to conceive of some way in which a disembodied soul might receive impressions of taste and touch without confusion? Consider the following supposition: Whenever the disembodied soul had the kind of visual impressions it once had when it put its nose up against some object (object in the center of the visual field, close up), it would experience tactile sensations of that object. Could not the soul thus receive impressions of touch without confusion? Is there something nonsensical about this supposition? Perhaps taste might work in the same way, though the combination of touch and taste might be awkward—if, for example, the soul had to taste whatever it felt.

3. A Disembodied Soul Could, at Best, Communicate With Other Souls by a Kind of Quasi-Verbal "Mental Telepathy."

"Life After Life" makes the following suppositions: that dualism is true; that no mind could directly perceive another mind; that life after death is a natural rather than a supernatural phenomenon; that a disembodied soul would have normal visual and auditory perception of our world; that a disembodied soul would not interact with any physical objects. Of course, it is not claimed that such suppositions are true, nor that this combination of suppositions is even coherent. But, given these suppositions, communication between disembodied souls by a kind of quasi-verbal mental telepathy is the only kind of communication that I can imagine without contradicting one of the suppositions. Even such "mental telepathy" may be inconsistent with the other suppositions. But assuming all these circumstances, an afterlife would seem to be a rather dismal state, even if one were not as shallow an individual as Charlie. Perhaps you can do better than this. Perhaps my judgments are only indicative of some triviality and lack of imagination on my part.

Many theists, of course, believe that after the death of the body, the soul joins God and other souls in a community of spirits that either goes on forever or lasts until a time when all bodies will be resurrected. Can one make sense out of this supposition of a community of souls? One suggestion (borrowed, in part, from a philosophy called "idealism") would be that after death, God links these bodiless human souls and Himself together through something analogous to coordinated dreams. God would present these souls with the kind of images they would have if they lived together in some magnificent physical world. Each soul would receive sensory images that would represent other souls: It would seem as if every other soul had some sort of body and could gesture, talk, and so forth. This suggestion may seem a bit too "earthly" for some theological tastes, and it might be offensive in its implication of an image body for God. Still, one might be able to work out something like this along more "spiritual" lines. In any case, this conception of the afterlife would be "other-worldly" in the sense that it is hard to imagine experiencing simultaneously this community of souls and our world.

Philosophers have not done much speculation about the possible nature of an afterlife, and theologians do not often subject their conceptions of an afterlife to careful scrutiny. Here, at least, is one rather engaging area of philosophical speculation in which the beginner can advance ideas without the annoying feeling that all such ideas, along with objections to them, can be found in some volume in the library.

READINGS

RENÉ DESCARTES (1596–1650): a dualist view.*

. . . since on the one hand I have a clear and distinct idea of myself in so far as I am only a thinking and not an extended being, and since on the other hand I have a distinct idea of body in so far as it is only an extended being which does not think, it is certain that this "I"—that is to say, my soul, by virtue of which I am what I am—is entirely and truly distinct from my body and that it can be or exist without it. . . .

. . . there is a great difference between the mind and the body, in that the body, from its nature, is always divisible and the mind is completely indivisible. For in reality, when I consider the mind—that is, when I consider myself in so far as I am only a thinking being—I cannot distinguish any parts, but I recognize and conceive very clearly that I am a thing which is absolutely unitary and entire. And although the whole mind seems to be united with the whole body, nevertheless when a foot or an arm or some other part of the body is amputated, I recognize quite well that nothing has been lost to my mind on that account. Nor can the faculties of willing, perceiving, understanding, and so forth be any more properly called parts of the mind, for it is one and the same mind which as a complete unit wills, perceives, and understands, and so forth. But just the contrary is the case with corporeal or extended objects, for I cannot imagine any, however small they might be, which my mind does not very easily divide into several parts, and I consequently recognize these objects to be divisible.

PIERRE GASSENDI (1592–1655) objecting to Descartes's interactionism.†

One thing I note, and that is that you say *that nature teaches you by the sensation of pain, hunger, thirst, etc., that you are not lodged in the body as a sailor in a ship, but that you are very closely united with it and, so to speak, intermingled with it so as to compose one whole along with it. For if that were not the case,* you say, "*when my body is hurt, I who am merely a thinking thing would not feel pain, but should perceive the wound with the mere understanding, just as the sailor perceives by sight when something is damaged in his vessel, and when my body has need of food or drink, I should clearly understand this fact, and not have the confused feelings of hunger and thirst. For all these sensations of hunger, thirst, pain, etc., are in truth none other than certain confused modes of thought which are produced by the union and apparent intermingling of mind and body.*"

This is indeed quite right; but it still remains to be explained, how that *union and apparent intermingling,* or *confusion,* can be found in you, if you are incorporeal, unextended and indivisible. For if you are not greater than a point, how can you be united with the entire body, which is of such great magnitude? How, at least, can you be united with the brain, or some minute part in it, which (as has been said) must yet have some magnitude or extension, however small it be? If you are wholly without parts, how can you mix or appear to mix with its minute subdivisions? For there is no mixture unless each of the things to be mixed has parts that can mix with one another. Further, if you are discrete, how could you be involved with and form one thing along with matter itself? Again since conjunction or union exists between certain parts, ought there not to be a relation of similarity between parts of this sort? But what must the union of the corporeal with the incorporeal be thought to be? Do we conceive how stone and air are fused together, as in pumice stone, so as to become a fusion of uniform character? Yet the similarity between stone and air which itself is also a body, is greater than that between body and soul, or a wholly incorporeal mind. Further, ought not that union to take place by means of the closest contact? But how, as I said before, can that take place, apart from body? How will that which is corporeal seize upon that which is incorporeal, so to hold it conjoined with itself, or how will the incorporeal grasp the corporeal, so as reciprocally to keep it bound to itself, if in it, the incorporeal, there is nothing which it can use to grasp the other, or by which it can be grasped.

G. W. F. LEIBNIZ (1646–1716): a parallelist view.*

Having established these things, I thought I had reached port. But when I began to think about the union of the soul with the body, it was like casting me back into the open sea, for I found no way to explain how the body causes anything to take place in the soul, or vice versa, or how one substance can communicate with another created substance. So far as we can know from his writings, Descartes gave up the struggle over this problem. But seeing that the common opinion is inconceivable, his disciples concluded that we sense the qualities of bodies because God causes thoughts to arise in our soul on the occasion of material movements and that, when our soul in its turn wishes to move the body, God moves the body for it. And since the communication of motion also seemed inconceivable to them, they believed that God imparts motion to a body on the occasion of the motion of another body. This they call "the System of Occasional Causes." . . .

Imagine two clocks or watches which are in perfect agreement. Now this can happen in three ways. The *first* is that of a natural influence. This is the way with which Mr. Huygens experimented, with results that greatly surprised him. He suspended two pendulums from the same piece of wood. The

*Extracts from *G. W. Leibniz Philosophical Letters and Papers,* by LeRoy E. Loemker, 1957, pp. 746, 750–752. Reprinted by permission of Mrs. LeRoy Loemker.

continued strokes of the pendulums transmitted similar vibrations to the particles of wood, but these vibrations could not continue in their own frequency without interfering with each other, at least when the two pendulums did not beat together. The result, by a kind of miracle, was that even when their strokes had been intentionally disturbed, they came to beat together again, somewhat like two strings tuned to each other. The *second* way of making two clocks, even poor ones, agree always is to assign a skilled craftsman to them who adjusts them and constantly sets them in agreement. The *third* way is to construct these two timepieces at the beginning with such skill and accuracy that one can be assured of their subsequent agreement.

Now put the soul and the body in the place of these two timepieces. Then their agreement or sympathy will also come about in one of these three ways. The *way of influence* is that of the common philosophy. But since it is impossible to conceive of material particles or of species or immaterial qualities which can pass from one of these substances into the other, this view must be rejected. The *way of assistance* is that of the system of occasional causes. But I hold that this makes a *deus ex machina* intervene in a natural and ordinary matter where reason requires that God should help only in the way in which he concurs in all other natural things. Thus there remains only my hypothesis, that is the *way of pre-established harmony*, according to which God has made each of the two substances from the beginning in such a way that, though each follows only its own laws which it has received with its being, each agrees throughout with the other, entirely as if they were mutually influenced or as if God were always putting forth his hand, beyond his general concurrence. I do not think that there is anything more than this that I need to prove—unless someone should demand that I prove that God is skilful enough to make use of this foresighted artifice, of which we see samples even among men, to the extent that they are able men. And, assuming that God can do it; it is clear that this way is the most beautiful and the most worthy of him.

GILBERT RYLE: a behaviorist view.*

The official doctrine, which hails chiefly from Descartes, is something like this. With the doubtful exceptions of idiots and infants in arms every human being has both a body and a mind. Some would prefer to say that every human being is both a body and a mind. His body and his mind are ordinarily harnessed together, but after the death of the body his mind may continue to exist and function.

Human bodies are in space and are subject to the mechanical laws which govern all other bodies in space. Bodily processes and states can be inspected by external observers. . . .

*Excerpts from *The Concept of Mind* by Gilbert Ryle. Copyright © 1949 by Gilbert Ryle. Reprinted by permission of HarperCollins Publishers. Quotations from Gilbert Ryle, *Concept of Mind*, by arrangement with Century Hutchinson, Limited, London.

But minds are not in space, nor are their operations subject to mechanical laws. The workings of one mind are not witnessable by other observers; its career is private. Only I can take direct cognisance of the states and processes of my own mind. A person therefore lives through two collateral histories, one consisting of what happens in and to his body, the other consisting of what happens in and to his mind. The first is public, the second private. . . .

Such in outline is the official theory. I shall often speak of it, with deliberate abusiveness, as "the dogma of the Ghost in the Machine." I hope to prove that it is entirely false, and false not in detail but in principle. It is not merely an assemblage of particular mistakes. It is one big mistake and a mistake of a special kind. It is, namely, a category-mistake. It represents the facts of mental life as if they belonged to one logical type or category (or range of types or categories), when they actually belong to another. . . .

I must first indicate what is meant by the phrase "Category-mistake." . . .

A foreigner visiting Oxford or Cambridge for the first time is shown a number of colleges, libraries, playing fields, museums, scientific departments and administrative offices. He then asks "But where is the University? I have seen where the members of the Colleges live, where the Registrar works, where the scientists experiment and the rest. But I have not yet seen the University in which reside and work the members of your University." It has then to be explained to him that the University is not another collateral institution, some ulterior counterpart to the colleges, laboratories and offices which he has seen. The University is just the way in which all that he has already seen is organized. When they are seen and when their co-ordination is understood, the University has been seen. His mistake lay in his innocent assumption that it was correct to speak of Christ Church, the Bodleian Library, the Ashmolean Museum *and* the University, to speak, that is, as if "the University" stood for an extra member of the class of which these other units are members. He was mistakenly allocating the University to the same category as that to which the other institutions belong. . . .

It is perfectly proper to say, in one logical tone of voice, that there exist minds and to say, in another logical tone of voice, that there exist bodies. But these expressions . . . indicate two different senses of "exist." . . .

. . . When we describe people as exercising qualities of mind, we are not referring to occult episodes of which their overt acts and utterances are effects; we are referring to those overt acts and utterances themselves. There are, of course, differences, crucial for our inquiry, between describing an action as performed absentmindedly and describing a physiologically similar action as done on purpose, with care or with cunning. But such differences of description do not consist in the absence or presence of an implicit reference to some shadow-action covertly prefacing the overt action. They consist, on the contrary, in the absence or presence of certain sorts of testable explanatory-cum-predictive assertions. . . .

A drunkard at the chessboard makes the one move which upsets his opponent's plan of campaign. The spectators are satisfied that this was due not to cleverness but to luck, if they are satisfied that most of his moves made in this state break the rules of chess, or have no tactical connection with the position of the game, that he would not be likely to repeat this move if the tactical situation were to recur, that he would not applaud such a move if made by another player in a similar situation, that he could not explain why he had done it or even describe the threat under which his King had been.

Their problem is not one of the occurrence or non-occurrence of ghostly processes, but one of the truth or falsehood of certain "could" and "would" propositions and certain other particular applications of them. For, roughly, the mind is not the topic of sets of untestable categorical propositions, but the topic of sets of testable hypothetical and semi-hypothetical propositions. The difference between a normal person and an idiot is not that the normal person is really two persons while the idiot is only one, but that the normal person can do a lot of things which the idiot cannot do. . . .

U. T. PLACE defends the identity theory against the argument that since our mental images have properties, such as colors, which our brain processes do not, mental images cannot be brain processes.*

. . . In the case of cognitive concepts like "knowing," "believing," "understanding," "remembering" and volitional concepts like "wanting" and "intending," there can be little doubt, I think, that an analysis in terms of dispositions to behave is fundamentally sound (see Ryles's *Concept of Mind* and Wittgenstein's *Philosophical Investigations*). On the other hand, there would seem to be an intractable residue of concepts clustering around the notions of consciousness, experience, sensation and mental imagery, where some sort of inner process story is unavoidable. It is possible, of course, that a satisfactory behaviouristic account of this conceptual residuum will ultimately be found. For our present purposes, however, I shall assume that this cannot be done and that statements about pains and twinges, about how things look, sound and feel, about things dreamed of or pictured in the mind's eye, are statements referring to events and processes which are in some sense private or internal to the individual of whom they are predicated. The question I wish to raise is whether in making this assumption we are inevitably committed to a dualist position in which sensations and mental images form a separate category of processes over and above the physical and physiological processes with which they are known to be correlated. I shall argue that an acceptance of inner processes does not entail dualism. . . .

. . . the "phenomenological fallacy" is the mistake of supposing that when the subject describes his experience, when he describes how things look, sound, smell, taste or feel to him, he is describing the literal properties of objects and events on a peculiar sort of internal cinema or television screen,

*From "Is Consciousness a Brain Process?" by U. T. Place, in *British Journal of Psychology*, February 1956, Vol. XLVII, pp. 49–50. Reprinted by permission of The British Psychological Society and the author.

usually referred to in the modern psychological literature as the "phenomenal field." If we assume, for example, that when a subject reports a green after-image he is asserting the occurrence inside himself of an object which is literally green, it is clear that we have on our hands an entity for which there is no place in the world of physics. In the case of the green after-image there is no green object in the subject's environment corresponding to the description that he gives. Nor is there anything green in his brain; certainly there is nothing which could have emerged when he reported the appearance of the green after-image. Brain processes are not the sort of things to which colour concepts can be properly applied.

The phenomenological fallacy on which this argument is based depends on the mistaken assumption that because our ability to describe things in our environment depends on our consciousness of them, our descriptions of things are primarily descriptions of our conscious experience and only secondarily, indirectly and inferentially descriptions of the objects and events in our environments. It is assumed that because we recognize things in our environment by their look, sound, smell, taste and feel, we begin by describing their phenomenal properties, i.e., the properties of the looks, sounds, smells, tastes and feels which they produce in us, and infer their real properties from their phenomenal properties. In fact, the reverse is the case. We begin by learning to recognize the real properties of things in our environment. We learn to recognize them, of course, by their look, sound, smell, taste and feel; but this does not mean that we have to learn to describe the look, sound, smell, taste and feel of things before we can describe the things themselves. Indeed, it is only after we have learnt to describe the things in our environment that we can learn to describe our consciousness of them. We describe our conscious experience not in terms of the mythological "phenomenal properties" which are supposed to inhere in the mythological "objects" in the mythological "phenomenal field," but reference to the actual physical properties of the concrete physical objects, events and processes which normally, though not perhaps in the present instance, give rise to the sort of conscious experience which we are trying to describe. In other words when we describe the after-image as green, we are not saying that there is something, the after-image, which is green, we are saying that we are having the sort of experience which we normally have when, and which we have learnt to describe as, looking at a green patch of light.

Once we rid ourselves of the phenomenological fallacy we realize that the problem of explaining introspective observations in terms of brain processes is far from insuperable. We realize that there is nothing that the introspecting subject says about his conscious experiences which is inconsistent with anything the physiologist might want to say about the brain processes which cause him to describe the environment and his consciousness of that environment in the way he does. When the subject describes his experience by saying that a light which is in fact stationary appears to move, all the physiologist or physiological psychologist has to do in order to explain the subject's introspective observations is to show that the brain process which is causing the subject to describe his experience in this way is the sort of process which normally occurs when he is observing an actual moving object and which therefore normally causes him to report the movement of an object in his environment. . . .

C. B. MARTIN doubts that disembodied existence is a meaningful concept.*

. . . We shall soon question whether the notion of a disembodied spirit is meaningful, but first let us consider a simple case that reveals the oddity of identifying such spirits. John and Henry are brothers who know a great deal about one another's past. Something unfortunate happens: John gets the idea he is Henry, and Henry gets the idea he is John. John seems to remember doing what Henry did, and Henry seems to remember doing what John did. They are put away for treatment. Later a friend asks, "Is John all right now?" and if John has come out of his delusion under the treatment we can answer, "Yes." But now suppose John and Henry die before the treatment has had any effect and a friend asks, "I wonder if John is all right now?" If John and Henry are disembodied spirits what possible criteria for their identity could be appealed to in order to answer the nightmare question? Yet divine judgment demands an answer. . . .

The question "Can men live on after death without their bodies?" is like a request to people empty places. These colorless shades that cast no shadow and stir no curtain intrude without notice the privacy of my most private place. They may live by multitudes under my clothing or under my skin. How many angels on the head of a pin? How many souls inhabit my limbs? And just what kind of nonsense is this if nonsense it be?

At first sight the question "Can I, myself, survive death without a body?" seems easily settled in the affirmative by the simple means of a slight feat of the imagination. Surely I can imagine the following scene. I am lying on my deathbed with the members of my family gathered around me. My breathing becomes more difficult until I can breathe no more. The doctor closes my eyes, and still I see his face and hear the weeping. Without effort or resistance I find myself moving above the bed and now, owning no body, I view the body that was my own.

What I can imagine to be true of myself must be conceivable of others. How then can there be any serious confusion in the notion of disembodied existence when I seem to be able to imagine this disembodied state so easily? The imagination *can* play conceptual tricks. People sometimes dream or think that they can imagine with ease themselves to have *really* been someone else and not just *like* someone else. This is to imagine nonsense. Therefore, I see no prima-facie objection to arguing, as I shall attempt to do, that what might at first be thought to be clearly imaginable is really a confusion. . . .

*From *Religious Belief* by C. B. Martin, 1959, Cornell University Press. Copyright by C. B. Martin. Reprinted by permission of the author.

When I describe for myself my disembodied state, is this describing my mental life without a body? Not necessarily. There are many things that I can describe, without having to mention anything else, that cannot exist by themselves. I can describe a thing's shape without having to mention its size. From this it does not follow that I have described or can describe a thing that has shape but no size. Similarly, I can describe my mental life without mentioning anything about my body. It does not follow that I have described or can describe my mental life existing without a body. . . .

The question "Can experiences and intellectual processes exist without a body?" can be reformulated "Can one formulate a statement that is *only* about an experience or intellectual process?"

At first, the answer seems obviously "Yes." The statement "I am in pain" or the statement "I shall think about survival" seem to be clear examples. But each statement makes reference to an individual who is in pain and who has decided to think about a problem. The pain experience and the decision have been ascribed to something that might not have been in pain and might not have made that decision, and that might not have been at that time in any way conscious, though not for that reason nonexistent. I do not know how to ascribe an experience to an individual that cannot be thought to have been able to exist without any experience at that time. . . .

Questions and Exercises

1.   Materialism   Dualism
   Behaviorism   Identity theory   Interactionism   Parallelism
   a. What is the difference between materialism and dualism?
   b. What is the difference between behaviorism and the identity theory? Why are they both considered forms of materialism?
   c. What is the difference between interactionism and parallelism? Why are they both considered forms of dualism?
2. Give the reasoning behind being an interactionist.
3. What reasoning would a parallelist give for believing interactionism is false?
4.   Identity of meaning   Identity theory
       Factual identity   Behaviorism
   a. Explain the two phrases listed on the left.
   b. Connect those phrases with the appropriate terms on the right, and then explain why you made those connections.
   c. How does one argue for or against identity of meaning? Show how this relates to the debate concerning the appropriate theory.
   d. How does one argue for or against factual identity? Show how this relates to the debate concerning the appropriate theory.

5. "Suppose you close your eyes and imagine something round and orange. . . . What we call the 'mental' is not the closing of the eyes or the verbal description 'orange and round' that you might give us. What we call the 'mental' is the round and orange picture inside of you." Which theory of mind would this be an appropriate argument against? Explain.

6. "The mind and body are causally related" and "The physical and non-physical cannot be causally related." Are these two statements consistent with one another? Explain.

7. What does Descartes believe to be the difference(s) between mind and body?

8. What problem(s) does Gassendi find with Descartes's view of mind and body?

9. Leibnitz considers three ways in which one could account for the mind and body being synchronized with one another. What are they? Which one does he think is most reasonable and why?

10. What does Ryle mean by a "category mistake"? How does he think such a mistake has affected our concept of mind?

11. What does Place mean by the "phenomenological fallacy"? How does he think the fallacy affects the case for or against the identity theory?

12. a. If two brothers (with bodies) got amnesia, could we tell who was who? If so, how?

   b. If two identical twins (with bodies) got amnesia, could we tell who was who? If so, how?

   c. If two identical twins who were disembodied spirits got amnesia, could God tell who was who? If so, how?

13. "To take the mind from the body is as impossible as taking the shape from a flower while leaving its color and weight behind," says a Gammese philosopher. How do you think C. B. Martin would feel about this statement?

6

Appearance and Reality

Fiction: Why Don't You Just Wake Up?

I'm in the living room at home, and Dad's there, all serious, saying, "John, where's your mind these days—you've got to wake up," and I think I wake up, and I'm at my desk at home. I straighten up and yawn and pick up my history book, and just then Mom comes in, saying, "Johnny, you're just not concentrating—you've got to wake up," and I think I wake up, and I'm sitting in class. I look around, and Teresa's sitting next to me looking all upset, saying, "John, what's with you these days—why don't you just wake up," and I think I wake up, and I'm lying in bed in my dorm room.

It was all dreams within dreams within dreams, and what I thought was waking was just more dreaming. I lie in my dorm bed and wonder who is going to come in next and wake me from this, only no one comes in, and the digital clock blinks slowly toward seven-thirty, and I guess this must be real.

It doesn't seem real, though. Nothing does these days. Everything that happens seems sort of vague somehow and out of focus and not all that important. I have trouble concentrating—taking things seriously—and everybody's on my case. That's the reason, I think, for all those dreams about dreaming and waking.

One reason, anyway. The other is that philosophy class and all that talk about Descartes and whether all reality could be a dream. That's not helping much either.

I'm late picking up Teresa again, and she's had to wait, and there won't be time for us to get coffee together. She gives me that exasperated look I see a lot these days, and we walk across campus without talking. Finally, she says:

"I don't know why I took that stupid philosophy class. I can't wait 'til it's over."

I know it's not really the class she's annoyed at. It's me and the way I've been lately. I know I should say something nice. But I'm feeling pushed and kind of cranky.

"I like the class," I say, to be contrary.

"You do not."

"I do. It's kind of interesting."

"Interesting. Right. Like I really want to sit around all day wondering whether I'm dreaming everything in the world."

"Maybe you are."

"Sure." She shakes her head. "That's so stupid."

"Just because you say 'stupid' doesn't make it wrong. How do you know you aren't just dreaming this all up?"

She glares at me, but her eyes begin to dart the way they always do when she's thinking hard. She's not in the mood for this, but I've gotten her mad.

"Because . . . I know what dreams look like. They're all hazy. Not like the world looks now."

"You mean what you can see of it through the smog."

"Funny."

I know what she means, though. A few weeks back I would have said that being awake looked a lot different from dreaming. But the guy in class is right. That's just a matter of how things look. It doesn't prove how things are.

"Look," I say, "nobody's denying that what we call 'dreaming' looks different from what we call 'being awake.' But is it really different? Maybe 'being awake' is just a different kind of dream."

"Yeah, well, if I'm making all this up, how come we're talking about something I don't want to talk about?"

"Because you're not in control of this dream any more than you are your dreams at night. It's your unconscious doing it."

"This is so much bullsh. . . ."

"Why?"

"It's crazy. You're standing here trying to convince me that everything is my dream while you know you're real. That doesn't make any sense."

"Yeah, it does. I'm saying you can't know that I really exist, I can't know that you . . ."

I stop suddenly, because something scary is happening. It's like a ripple moving through the whole world, coming from the horizon to my left, but moving fast as if the world is really much smaller than it appears. And where the ripple is, everything becomes elongated and out of focus. The ripple passes over Teresa, distorting her for a moment, like a fun house mirror. Then it's gone, and everything's back to normal.

"John, are you okay?" says Teresa, giving me a worried look. "You look white as a sheet."

"I don't know. I just got the weirdest feeling. I guess I'm okay."

"John, are you on something?"

"No. I told you. Really."

She looks at me for a moment and decides I'm telling the truth.

"Come on," she says, taking my hand. "The last thing you need right now is philosophy class. Let's go get something to eat and then sit in the sun for awhile. I bet you'll feel better."

"Hey, Ter, I'm sorry I'm being such a jerk. I . . ."

"Don't worry about it, John. It's okay. Come on."

Later I do feel better. I feel like things are almost back to normal. But my night is full of dreams within dreams, and the next day the world seems full of unreality once again. And then, at midday, the world ripples again.

I go to the university health service, and of course the doctor thinks it's drugs, and we go round and round on that until I insist that he test me and then he begins to believe I'm not lying. He becomes nicer then, and more concerned, and schedules some tests and an appointment with a specialist he'd like me to see, though he's "sure it's nothing, just exhaustion."

Walking across campus, I see the world ripple again and suddenly I realize what it all looks like. It's like when you are watching a movie in class, and the movie screen ripples, distorting the image, and suddenly you're aware that it wasn't a world in front of you at all, but just an illusion on a not-very-large piece of material. I put my arm out to feel the ripple, only my arm ripples too because it's part of the movie.

I don't know what's happening; and I'm afraid. At night I keep myself from sleeping because the idea of dreaming is something I suddenly find disturbing. In the morning I'm exhausted, but I stumble off to class because I want something to divert my attention, but once there I have trouble paying attention. I guess the professor must have asked me something I didn't hear because I feel Teresa nudging me in the ribs, and hear her say, "Come on, John, wake up."

I look up then at the professor standing behind his lectern, and just above and in back of him a dark line seems to appear in the wall. It looks like the slow fissure of an earthquake, except that the edges fold back against the surface of the wall like the edges of torn paper, and I see that behind the tearing there is nothing at all, just darkness. Then I see that the tear isn't in the wall at all but in my field of vision because as it reaches the professor he begins to split apart and then the lectern and then the head of the student in the front row. On both sides of the tear the world distorts and folds and collapses. The fissure moves downward through the students and then, as I glance down, through my own body. No one is moving or screaming—they take no more notice than movie characters on a torn movie screen would. In a panic I reach out and touch Teresa, then watch as she and my hand distort, as everything, absolutely everything, falls away.

* * * * *

It is night. It's always night. A night without stars, without anything—just an infinite emptiness falling away on every side. And so I float, an invisible being in a nonexistent world.

How long have I been like this? I don't know. It feels like years, but that's just a feeling because there is nothing here by which to mark the time.

I try to remember how it was, but my memories are such pale things, and they grow more pale as time drags on.

I would pray, but there is nothing to pray to. And so I hope, for hope is all I have: that one day, as inexplicably as once I did, I will begin to dream the world again.

Questions

1. According to the story "Why Don't You Just Wake Up?" which of the following are real and which illusion:
   a. John's father talking to John.
   b. The college campus.
   c. John's feelings of fear.
   d. The exasperated expression on Teresa's face.
   e. Teresa's feelings of annoyance.
   f. Endless darkness.
   g. Teresa's mind.
   h. John's body.
   i. John's mind.
2. Critique the following arguments: This world can't be just my dream because:
   a. what I'm seeing right now looks much more vivid than it does when I am asleep and dreaming.
   b. I can't control what the world is like.
   c. I just asked my friend if I were dreaming this all up and she said, "No."
3. What reasons would you give for believing that the world is not just your dream?

DISCUSSION

COMMONSENSE BELIEFS

The idea that "reality" is just a dream appears in literature and religion back to ancient times. The story "Why Don't You Just Wake Up?" imagines one variant of this possibility: that the world is just a dream of mine, and that nothing exists outside that dream. Let's each ask ourselves the following questions: Is it possible that the world is just my dream? Is there any way I can prove that this is not so?

Before taking up those questions, let's clarify them a bit. Presumably you believe in the existence of the following:

1. Other minds
2. Physical objects
3. Your own mind

To believe in the existence of a mind is, at a minimum, to believe that there exists a collection of thoughts, images, emotions, and sensations. To believe in the existence of a physical object is to believe in the existence of some such thing as a tree, a hand, a river, a flash of lightning, or a molecule *and* to believe that such a thing would or could continue to exist if all minds ceased to exist. (In other words, dreams or desires could not exist in the absence of the mind: such things, then, are mental.)

The possibility that the world is a dream challenges some of these "commonsense" beliefs, but which ones? Imagine that you dream you are a handsome or beautiful movie star getting out of your limousine at the Academy Awards, with people cheering you and snapping pictures. Then imagine you wake up in your same old bedroom, wearing pajamas or nightgown or underwear, nobody cheering, nobody (we hope) snapping pictures. What has remained constant from dreaming to waking? Very little. The location has changed, the objects have changed, even your body has changed. The one constant has been that the same mind (in some sense) was dreaming and waking. Similarly in the story. The only thing left after the narrator's dream has ended is the mind that was dreaming it. Everything else—all other minds, all human bodies, including his own, and all other physical objects—turns out to be illusion. The possibility one might be dreaming challenges the existence of the world outside one's mind—what philosophers have dubbed the **external world.**

DOUBTING THE EXTERNAL WORLD

The possibility that the world is a dream is likely to evoke from us the same response it evoked from Teresa in the story: "That's so stupid. . . . I know what dreams look like. They're all hazy. Not like the world looks now."

All of us constantly distinguish dreams from reality, and we don't find any particular difficulty with this. True, while we are dreaming we can be confused about whether we are dreaming or awake, but when we are really awake, it's obvious that we are.

How do we distinguish dreams from reality? In both dreams and waking life, we seem to see, hear, touch, taste, and smell things. But in dreams, perhaps, those sensory impressions are not as vivid and persistent as in waking life. More strikingly, the experiences of waking life are more consistent from episode to episode. In a series of dream episodes, one may be able to fly, then be able to walk, then be able to walk but not be able to fly, and so forth. In a series of waking experiences, one's abilities to act are more fixed. In waking life, impressions of a burning building are followed by a familiar set of long-term impressions that continue through subsequent episodes: fire engines, smoking ashes, cold ashes, clearing away debris, rebuilding. Such need not be the case when one merely dreams that a building is burning.

In most cases, then it seems that we can easily distinguish dreams from reality. Dreams can be distinguished from waking life by their relative haziness and relative inconsistency from episode to episode. However, consider two meanings of the word "dream":

1. Dreams are experiences that are hazy and relatively inconsistent.
2. Dreams are experiences that are purely mental and do not represent things existing outside the mind.

Perhaps the preceding commonsense view of waking and dreaming indicates that there is no serious problem about determining when we are dreaming in the first sense. But is this sufficient to show that we are not always dreaming in the second sense? "Why Don't You Just Wake Up?" implies not. The story grants our normal distinction between experiences that are hazy and inconsistent and those that are not, but it undercuts this distinction as evidence for what is only in our minds and what is not. It issues the following challenge: How do you know that what we experience when we are "awake" isn't as much a product of our minds as what we experience when we are dreaming (in sense 1)? How do we know that reality isn't a dream (in sense 2)?

Consider some other objections to the possibility that the world is just a dream:

QUESTION: How could I perceive images if there were no objects?

REPLY: Your mind could invent them, as in dreams.

QUESTION: How can this chair hold me if it is only an imaginary chair?

REPLY: What is sitting on the chair might be an imaginary body, and, as we know from dreams, imaginary chairs are quite adequate to support imaginary bodies.

QUESTION: If everything I perceive is imaginary, why can't I create a more pleasant world through acts of will?

REPLY: To say that the world consists of mental images is not to say that these images are within your conscious control. You can't control your dreams, but you don't therefore deny that dreams are mental.

QUESTION: How can I be dreaming? Just now, I asked my friend if I was dreaming and she said no.

REPLY: Maybe you're just dreaming that your friend is here telling you no.

You begin to see what is so insidious about the possibility that one is dreaming everything up. It seems to undercut the evidence against itself by raising the possibility that the evidence is merely illusion.

PROVING MY OWN MIND

We have seen how the possibility that I might be dreaming challenges my belief in the external world. Is there a comparable problem with the internal world? That is, is there a problem justifying my belief in the existence of my own mind? It seems not, and here we can borrow an argument from Descartes, whose name is mentioned in the story.

Descartes was a seventeenth-century French philosopher who subjected his basic beliefs to the kind of critical scrutiny in which we have been engaged here. Initially, he decided that there were serious grounds for doubting his belief in physical objects and other minds. But Descartes thought there were no serious grounds for doubting his own existence; he could be absolutely certain that he existed. He said: "I think, therefore I am" or, in Latin, "Cogito ergo sum"; the claim is often referred to as the **cogito.** (A similar claim can be found in the fifth-century writings of Saint Augustine.)

This traditional, shorthand formulation of the "cogito" seems to indicate that Descartes was presenting an argument with "I think" as premise and "I exist" as conclusion. In fact, what Descartes argued was that one cannot be in error about one's existence as a thinking being, one's existence as a mind. Descartes noticed that one's belief in one's own mind seemed to be immune to the sorts of challenges or doubts that infect one's other beliefs. "Perhaps I am mistaken in thinking that others think." "Perhaps I am mistaken in thinking that physical objects really exist." "Perhaps I am mistaken in thinking that I think." In the third statement, and the third statement only, the conclusion is reaffirmed in the doubting. The very act of doubting my existence proves it.

The "cogito" can be applied to more specific first-person statements, and a consideration of such statements helps clarify the nature of the "cogito." "I seem to see a chair" appears to be an indubitable statement. One cannot be wrong about seeming-to-see, as opposed to seeing, and seeming-to-see is an experience, a mental state. "I am distressed" appears to be an indubitable statement. My seeming-to-be distressed is necessarily a kind of distress, and distress is a mental state. All statements about my present mental states would seem to be indubitable.

Descartes's "cogito" seems to me to be correct if it is properly restricted in scope, but one should be clear about these restrictions.

Descartes's "cogito" is not a proof to each of us that Descartes existed. To each of us, Descartes is another mind. Your "cogito" could not be a proof to me that you exist, and vice versa. I have no direct experience of your thoughts, and you have no direct experience of mine.

My "cogito" does not prove that I have a particular body or, indeed, any body at all. The body is a physical object, and the existence of physical objects is in question at this point. The "cogito" does not prove that I have a particular past or, in fact, any past at all; that I think does not guarantee the reliability of my memory impressions. Insofar as my proper name, Tom Davis, is linked with a particular physical or mental past, my "cogito" does not prove that Tom Davis exists. Perhaps I am Descartes, Napoleon, or Norman Mailer, and I am merely hallucinating that I am Tom Davis. What the "cogito" does guarantee is that there now exist certain thoughts, images and sensations that I may define as "my mind."

CAN WE PROVE AN EXTERNAL WORLD?

Having proved the existence of my own mind, can I prove the existence of the external world? There are philosophers who say no. They hold a position called **solipsism,** which says that the only thing one can prove exists is one's own self. The solipsist accepts Descartes's "cogito" but claims that one cannot prove the existence of the external world.

The solipsist argues as follows: It is theoretically possible that everything one has ever experienced has been a total invention of one's mind (as in dreams). Since one can judge things only according to one's experience, and since one cannot get "outside" one's experience to determine its source, one cannot know whether the experience reflects an external world or whether it is merely an invention of one's mind. One cannot show that an external world is more likely to exist than not to exist.

The problem of the external world is a difficult one, and the argument of the solipsist is forceful. Can we satisfactorily answer the solipsist? Can we formulate an argument that shows that the existence of an external world of physical objects and other minds is more likely than its absence?*

Before we attempt any kind of proof, let's talk a little about what a proof might involve.

Note that we can't prove everything. If no statements are accepted without proof, it will be impossible to prove anything. For example, consider any statement and call it A. If that statement is not acceptable without proof, then we shall have to form an argument in which A is the conclusion and another statement (or statements) B is the premise. This will show that A is true if B is true, but what is the proof for B? Now we will need another argument in which C is the premise and B is the conclusion. This will show that A is true if B is true, and B is true if C is true. But what is the proof for C? Now we shall have to give an argument for C and so on, ad infinitum. Since this process of proof can never be completed, and A remains doubtful until the process is completed, we shall never prove A. If we are required to prove everything, then we can prove nothing.

Any theory must begin with **axioms**—statements accepted without "proof." In fact, this whole discussion has presupposed an unmentioned axiom: that our fundamental principles of reasoning are reliable—that any contradictory statement is false, that no statement can be both true and false, that certain forms of argument are such that the conclusion follows from the premises, and so forth. This general axiom has been presupposed by the "cogito," by the skeptical argument of the solipsist, and by the very attempt to engage in rational discussion.

---

*Descartes is of no further help to us. He did offer a proof of an external world, but it is not satisfactory. First Descartes presented the "ontological argument" for the existence of a perfect God. Then he went on to argue that a perfect God would not deceive him by presenting him with appearances that were all illusory. Thus, Descartes's experiences must represent an external world. As is explained in Chapter 2, the ontological argument is fallacious. With it the rest of Descartes's argument collapses.

Some skeptics, more extreme than the solipsist, have challenged the reliability of our principles of reasoning. They have demanded a proof of the reliability of these principles. Of course, this demand could not be met. Any supposed proof would simply assume its conclusion since, as proof, it would assume the principles of reasoning that have been questioned. What we have here is a choice: Either we assume the reliability of our principles of reasoning and go on reasoning about various matters, or we do not assume this and we treat all statements as mere babble. Of course, we are assuming the reliability of these principles.

But is this axiom concerning the reliability of our principles of reasoning "mere assumption"? I am inclined to say emphatically no. These principles of reasoning seem to be "self-evident": One simply "sees" that they are correct.

A second general axiom has been presupposed in this discussion: that appearances do exist now (of a chair, of distress, and so on). One could not argue for this claim without simply assuming the conclusion: Any purported proof would have to assume the existence of appearances. But are there rational grounds for doubting this statement? I would say no. The axiom that appearances do exist now seems to me "self-evident."

Employing these two axioms, we have considered and then accepted the "cogito." It seemed that one could not be in error in believing that one's own mind exists. Would it be correct to say that we advanced one step and then were halted by the problem of the external world? To say we "advanced one step" might be misleading. The "cogito" is not a proof of some additional entity not stated in the axioms. The "cogito" simply enabled us to use principles of reasoning to clarify the statement that there are now appearances. For example, we noted that the word "distress" indicates nothing more than a certain kind of appearance. The statement "I exist as a thinking being" is really equivalent to the statement "There are thoughts," which is equivalent to the statement "There are appearances."

In a sense, then, at the point at which we confront the problem of the external world, what we have claimed are two general axioms. The solipsist also accepts these axioms. He asks us for a proof of the existence of physical objects and other minds. But, instead of attempting a proof, why not make the statement "There are physical objects and other minds" an axiom and claim that it is self-evident?

This possibility, though tempting, is troublesome. At what point should one stop claiming that statements are self-evident axioms and start offering proofs for them? Surely, there is some such point. Many of us would be inclined to scoff if someone claimed that the existence of a benign, omnipotent, omniscient God was self-evident. And we would howl in disbelief if someone claimed as self-evident the statement that there is life on exactly sixteen other planets. What guidelines should we use in determining which statements are self-evident and which are not?

What we might do is determine what essentially distinguishes our two general axioms from other beliefs that almost no one would be inclined to call self-evident. These characteristics could be used as tests to determine which other statements, if any, qualify as self-evident. It seems that our two general axioms share at least the following essential characteristics:

1. They are believed with the deepest conviction.*
2. No conceivable experimental evidence would count against them.
3. It seems unimaginable that they are false.

Clearly, the statement that there is an omnipotent, omniscient, benign God would be disqualified by the third and second characteristics, if not by the first. Even if one has a deep religious faith, one can *imagine* there not being such a God, even if one is sure there is such a God, just as one can imagine the floor collapsing, even if one is sure that it will not. One can imagine future experiential evidence that would count against the existence of such a God—for example, an afterlife encounter with a being who is powerful but unable to accomplish a difficult task or with an omnipotent being who acts immorally. Obviously, the statement that there is life on exactly sixteen other planets fails to pass any of these tests.

How does the concept of "external world" withstand these three conditions of self-evidence? At the very least, the third condition presents a serious problem. The implication of "Why Don't You Just Wake Up?" and the subsequent discussion is that we can at least imagine there being no external world. If we can imagine there being no external world, then a claim for the self-evidence of the statement "There are physical objects and other minds" would seem weak.

What else could we try?

One approach that won't work is to employ the kind of evidence we use in everyday life to prove that something "really" exists—looking, touching, asking other people, etc. As we have seen, the possibility that we are dreaming undercuts such reality checks by raising the question of whether they too are only a dream.

Similarly there is no way we can somehow peek outside our experience to see if there is something causing it. Whatever we perceive is, or at least could be, only our experience.

What about treating the external world as the most reasonable hypothesis explaining why we have the experiences we do? Let's ask along with that: Why am I so inclined to believe in an external world?

Perhaps one general consideration that sways us toward a belief in the external world is the stark contrast between the relative poverty of those thoughts obviously created by one's mind and the richness of those experiences that seem to be imposed upon one. When I intentionally produce a mental image, it tends to be hazy and simple, and its content tends to be exhausted at a glance. But much of the experience that seems to come from outside is

---

*There is the temptation to word this in terms of "universal conviction." But such wording would assume the existence of other minds at a point where their existence is in question. Note that the conversational "we" employed in this discussion of skepticism does not assume what is at issue since it can be taken as merely hypothetical. It would assume what is at issue only if it led to statements that could not be rephrased as first-person statements.

complex, endlessly explorable, and full of surprises. A similar contrast exists between the ideas that are obviously mine and those that seem to come from others. Through apparent conversations with others, I gain knowledge that I was not conscious of possessing before. Many of those ideas that seem to come from elsewhere are barely comprehensible to me (for example, Einstein's theory of relativity, Russell's *Principia Mathematica*, Joyce's *Ulysses*). It seems absurd to suppose that all these ideas are really just products of my own mind.

Of course, the solipsist isn't suggesting that this complexity is coming from my conscious mind. He suggests that it could be produced by the unconscious mind. But is that an equally reasonable hypothesis?

Note, first, that the concept of the unconscious mind is a murky one. We need something like that concept to account for phenomena like the following: My mind seems to be processing information even when I'm not aware it's doing so (the solution to the problem I was thinking about yesterday suddenly pops into my head); or, some people act as if they intend to do things they are not aware of intending (a friend engages in self-destructive behavior without seeming to realize it). There is a temptation to view the unconscious as a full-blown second mind deep down below (sort of like the troll under the bridge in fairy tales). But there are alternatives to thinking of the unconscious as a second mind. The brain, for instance, might perform the information processing functions (as a computer would) and deliver the results to consciousness. (Note that the brain is not something the solipsist is allowed, since it is a physical object, part of the external world). A lot of unconscious intentional activity could be analyzed as habit: If I act self-destructively without realizing it, that doesn't have to mean that deep down inside of me is the intention to self-destruct. It could mean that I once felt self-destructive and set up behavioral habits. Or, more likely, that I was simply trained to act in self-destructive ways by antagonistic parents.

If we do try to think of the unconscious as analogous to the conscious mind, the resulting concept seems to verge on the self-contradictory: awareness without awareness, thought without consciousness.

The solipsist is suggesting that it is equally reasonable to suppose that the world of experience comes from the unconscious as from the external world. But the concept of the unconscious seems to be either close to contradictory or a placeholder for causes that either the solipsist can't employ (the brain) or which won't do the work he wants the unconscious to do (habits). It's questionable whether the all-experience-comes-from-the-unconscious hypothesis even makes sense. It's more questionable whether it is as reasonable as the hypothesis that much experience comes from the external world.

Approaching this from a slightly different direction, let's ask ourselves what a one-mind universe would look like. I don't know about you, but I see an image of a bubble floating around in the darkness with video pictures projected inside it. Obviously this won't do because we need some source for the pictures. So mentally we might add a kind of ghostly video camera, and perhaps a computer, to the bubble. Among other things, either this computer contains every bit of information in every library in every language, or somehow (as in "Please Don't Tell Me How the Story Ends") it contains only the information I will happen to look up. Why? How? Saying "it just does" isn't satisfactory. Again, we're not simply asking whether this is possible. We're asking whether it is the most reasonable view.

When I try to complete a picture of a one-mind universe, just at the point where it seems to make some sense, I find it's no longer a one-mind universe at all: It isn't one mind with a huge unconscious, but a mind plus another huge mind (a kind of God) which has actively thought everything up and is feeding me some of the information. But if we reach that point we already have an external world of sorts: God, in addition to my mind. Now we can ask if that is the most reasonable view. What is the evidence for there being such a God? Does it make sense to suppose that there would be a God plus one human mind? If there are other minds, does it make sense to think that there are also physical objects?

People have taken all sorts of different positions concerning the nature of the external world. Philosophers called "idealists" have argued that what exists in the world are God and minds and no physical objects. Other people believe the world consists of God, minds, and physical objects, while still others believe in minds, physical objects, but no God. At this point, though, we are debating what the external world is really like, not whether there is one.

READINGS

RENÉ DESCARTES (1596–1650) gives reasons for doubting the existence of the external world and then presents the "cogito."*

Everything which I have thus far accepted as entirely true and assured has been acquired from the senses or by means of the senses. But I have learned by experience that these senses sometimes mislead me, and it is prudent never to trust wholly those things which have once deceived us.

But it is possible that, even though the senses occasionally deceive us about things which are barely perceptible and very far away, there are many other things which we cannot reasonably doubt, even though we know them through the senses—as, for example, that I am here, seated by the fire, wearing a winter dressing gown, holding this paper in my hands, and other things of this nature. And how could I deny that these hands and this body are mine, unless I am to compare myself with certain lunatics whose brain is so troubled and befogged by the black vapors of the bile that they continually affirm that

*From *Meditations on First Philosophy* by René Descartes, translated by Lawrence J. LaFleur. Copyright © 1951 by Macmillan Publishing Company; copyright renewed © 1979. Reprinted by permission of Macmillan Publishing Company.

they are kings while they are paupers, that they are clothed in gold and purple while they are naked; or imagine that their head is made of clay, or that they are gourds, or that their body is glass? But this is ridiculous; such men are fools, and I would be no less insane than they if I followed their example.

Nevertheless, I must remember that I am a man, and that consequently I am accustomed to sleep and in my dreams to imagine the same things that lunatics imagine when awake, or sometimes things which are even less plausible. How many times has it occurred that the quiet of the night made me dream of my usual habits: that I was here, clothed in a dressing gown, and sitting by the fire, although I was in fact lying undressed in bed! It seems apparent to me now, that I am not looking at this paper with my eyes closed, that this head that I shake is not drugged with sleep, that it is with design and deliberate intent that I stretch out this hand and perceive it. What happens in sleep seems not at all as clear and as distinct as all this. But I am speaking as though I never recall having been misled, while asleep, by similar illusions! When I consider these matters carefully, I realize so clearly that there are no conclusive indications by which waking life can be distinguished from sleep that I am quite astonished, and my bewilderment is such that it is almost able to convince me that I am sleeping.

So let us suppose now that we are asleep and that all these details, such as opening the eyes, shaking the head, extending the hands, and similar things, are merely illusions; and let us think that perhaps our hands and our whole body are not such as we see them. Nevertheless, we must at least admit that these things which appear to us in sleep are like painted scenes and portraits which can only be formed in imitation of something real and true, and so, at the very least, these types of things—namely, eyes, head, hands, and the whole body—are not imaginary entities, but real and existent. For in truth painters, even when they use the greatest ingenuity in attempting to portray sirens and satyrs in bizarre and extraordinary ways, nevertheless cannot give them wholly new shapes and natures, but only invent some particular mixture composed of parts of various animals; or even if perhaps their imagination is sufficiently extravagant that they invent something so new that nothing like it has ever been seen, and so their work represents something purely imaginary and absolutely false, certainly at the very least the colors of which they are composed must be real.

And for the same reason, even if these types of things—namely, a body, eyes, head, hands, and other similar things—could be imaginary, nevertheless, we are bound to confess that there are some other still more simple and universal concepts which are true and existent, from the mixture of which, neither more nor less than in the case of the mixture of real colors, all these images of things are formed in our minds, whether they are true and real or imaginary and fantastic.

Of this class of entities is corporeal nature in general and its extension, including the shape of extended things, their quantity, or size and number, and also the place where they are, the time that measures their duration, and so forth. That is why we will perhaps not be reasoning badly if we conclude that physics, astronomy, medicine, and all the other sciences which follow from the consideration of composite entities are very dubious and uncertain; whereas arithmetic, geometry, and the other sciences of this nature, which treat only of very simple and general things without concerning themselves as to whether they occur in nature or not, contain some element of certainty and sureness. For whether I am awake or whether I am asleep, two and three together will always make the number five, and the square will never have more than four sides; and it does not seem possible that truths so clear and so apparent can ever be suspected of any falsity or uncertainty.

Nevertheless, I have long held the belief that there is a God who can do anything, by whom I have been created and made what I am. But how can I be sure but that he has brought it to pass that there is no earth, no sky, no extended bodies, no shape, no size, no place, and that nevertheless I have the impressions of all these things and cannot imagine that things might be other than as I now see them? And furthermore, just as I sometimes judge that others are mistaken about those things which they think they know best, how can I be sure but that God has brought it about that I am always mistaken when I add two and three or count the sides of a square, or when I judge of something else even easier, if I can imagine anything easier than that? But perhaps God did not wish me to be deceived in that fashion, since he is said to be supremely good. But if it was repugnant to his goodness to have made me so that I was always mistaken, it would seem also to be inconsistent for him to permit me to be sometimes mistaken, and nevertheless I cannot doubt that he does permit it.

At this point there will perhaps be some persons who would prefer to deny the existence of so powerful a God, rather than to believe that everything else is uncertain. Let us not oppose them for the moment, and let us concede according to their point of view that everything which I have stated here about God is fictitious. Then in whatever way they suppose that I have reached the state of being that I now have, whether they attribute it to some destiny or fate or refer it to chance, or whether they wish to explain it as the result of a continual interplay of events or in any other manner; nevertheless, since to err and be mistaken is a kind of imperfection, to whatever degree less powerful they consider the author to whom they attribute my origin, in that degree it will be more probable that I am so imperfect that I am always mistaken. To this reasoning, certainly, I have nothing to reply; and I am at last constrained to admit that there is nothing in what I formerly believed to be true which I cannot somehow doubt, and this not for lack of thought and attention, but for weighty and well-considered reasons. Thus I find that, in the future, I should withhold and suspend my judgment about these matters, and guard myself no less carefully from believing them than I should from believing what is manifestly false if I wish to find any certain and assured knowledge in the sciences.

It is not enough to have made these observations; it is also necessary that I should take care to bear them in mind. For these customary and long-standing beliefs will frequently recur in my thoughts, my long and familiar acquaintance with them giving them the right to occupy my mind against my will and almost to make themselves masters of my beliefs. I will never free myself of the habit of deferring to them and having faith in them as long as I consider that they are what they really are—that is, somewhat doubtful, as I have just shown, even if highly probable—so that there is much more reason to believe than to deny them. That is why I think that I would not do badly if I deliberately took the opposite position and deceived myself in pretending for some time that all these opinions are entirely false and imaginary, until at last I will have so balanced my former and my new prejudices that they cannot incline my mind more to one side than the other, and my judgment will not be mastered and turned by bad habits from the correct perception of things and the straight road leading to the knowledge of the truth. For I feel sure that I cannot overdo this distrust, since it is not now a question of acting, but only of meditating and learning.

I will therefore suppose that, not a true God, who is very good and who is the supreme source of truth, but a certain evil spirit, not less clever and deceitful than powerful, has bent all his efforts to deceiving me. I will suppose that the sky, the air, the earth, colors, shapes, sounds, and all other objective things that we see are nothing but illusions and dreams that he has used to trick my credulity. I will consider myself as having no hands, no eyes, no flesh, no blood, nor any senses, yet falsely believing that I have all these things. I will remain resolutely attached to this hypothesis; and if I cannot attain the knowledge of any truth by this method, at any rate it is in my power to suspend my judgment. That is why I shall take great care not to accept any falsity among my beliefs and shall prepare my mind so well for all the ruses of this great deceiver that, however powerful and artful he may be, he will never be able to mislead me in anything. . . .

I suppose, accordingly, that everything that I see is false; I convince myself that nothing has ever existed of all that my deceitful memory recalls to me. I think that I have no senses; and I believe that body, shape, extension, motion, and location are merely inventions of my mind. What then could still be thought true? Perhaps nothing else, unless it is that there is nothing certain in the world.

But how do I know that there is not some entity, of a different nature from what I have just judged uncertain, of which there cannot be the least doubt? Is there not some God or some other power who gives me these thoughts? But I need not think this to be true, for possibly I am able to produce them myself. Then, at the very least, am I not an entity myself? But I have already denied that I had any senses or any body. However, at this point I hesitate, for what follows from that? Am I so dependent upon the body and the senses that I could not exist without them? I have just convinced myself that nothing whatsoever existed in the world, that there was no sky, no earth, no minds, and no bodies; have I not thereby convinced myself that I did not exist? Not at all; without doubt I existed if I was convinced or even if I thought anything. Even though there may be a deceiver of some sort, very powerful and very tricky, who bends all his efforts to keep me perpetually deceived, there can be no slightest doubt that I exist, since he deceives me; and let him deceive me as much as he will, he can never make me be nothing as long as I think that I am something. Thus, after having thought well on this matter, and after examining all things with care, I must finally conclude and maintain that this proposition: I *am*, I *exist*, is necessarily true every time that I pronounce it or conceive it in my mind. . . .

But I, what am I, on the basis of the present hypothesis that there is a certain spirit who is extremely powerful and, if I may dare to say so, malicious and tricky, and who uses all his abilities and efforts in order to deceive me? Can I be sure that I possess the smallest fraction of all those characteristics which I have just now said belonged to the nature of body? I pause to consider this attentively. I pass and repass in review in my mind each one of all these things—it is not necessary to pause to take the time to list them—and I do not find any one of them which I can pronounce to be part of me. Is it characteristic of me to consume nourishment and to walk? But if it is true that I do not have a body, these also are nothing but figments of the imagination. To perceive? But once more, I cannot perceive without the body, except in the sense that I have thought I perceived various things during sleep, which I recognized upon waking not to have been really perceived. To think? Here I find the answer. Thought is an attribute that belongs to me; it alone is inseparable from my nature.

I am, I exist—that is certain; but for how long do I exist? For as long as I think; for it might perhaps happen, if I totally ceased thinking, that I would at the same time completely cease to be. I am now admitting nothing except what is necessarily true. I am therefore, to speak precisely, only a thinking being, that is to say, a mind. . . .

BERTRAND RUSSELL (1872–1970) argues for the existence of other minds and physical objects.*

What grounds have we for inferring that our percepts and what we recollect do not constitute the entire universe?

. . . When we speak to people, they behave more or less as we should if we heard such words, not as we do when we speak them. When I say that they behave in a similar manner, I mean that our perceptions of their bodies change in the same sort of way as our perceptions of our own bodies would in correlative circumstances. When an officer who has risen from the ranks gives the word of command, he sees his men doing what he used to do when he heard the same sounds as a private; it is therefore natural to suppose that they have heard the word of command. One may see a crowd of jackdaws in a newly-ploughed field all fly away at the moment when one hears a shot; again it is natural to suppose that the jackdaws heard the shot. Again, reading a book is a very different experience from composing one; yet, if I were a solip-

*From *The Analysis of Matter* by Bertrand Russell (1927). Reprinted by permission of Routledge.

sist, I should have to suppose that I had composed the works of Shakespeare and Newton and Einstein, since they have entered into my experience. Seeing how much better they are than my own books, and how much less labour they have cost me, I have been foolish to spend so much time composing with the pen rather than with the eye. All this, however, would perhaps be the better for being set forth formally.

First, there is a preliminary labour of regularizing our own percepts. I spoke of seeing others do what we should do in similar circumstances; but the similarity is obvious only as a result of interpretation. We cannot see our face (except the nose, by squinting) or our head or our back; but tactually they are continuous with what we can see, so that we easily imagine what a movement of an invisible part of our body ought to look like. When we see another person frowning, we can imitate him; and I do not think the habit of seeing ourselves in the glass is indispensable for this. But probably this is explained by imitative impulses—i.e. when we see a bodily action, we tend to perform the same action, in virtue of a physiological mechanism. This of course is most noticeable in children. Thus we first do what someone else has done, and then realize that what we have done is what he did. However, this complication need not be pursued. What I am concerned with is the passage, by experience, from "apparent" shapes and motions to "real" shapes and motions. This process lies within the perceptual world: it is a process of becoming acquainted with congruent groups—i.e. to speak crudely, with groups of visual sensations which correspond to similar tactual sensations. All this has to be done before the analogy between the acts of others and our own acts becomes obvious. But as it lies within the perceptual world, we may take it for granted. The whole of it belongs to early infancy. As soon as it is completed, there is no difficulty in interpreting the analogy between what we perceive of others and what we perceive of ourselves.

The analogy is of two kinds. The simpler kind is when others do practically the same thing as we are doing—for instance, applaud when the curtain goes down, or say "Oh" when a rocket bursts. In such cases, we have a sharp stimulus, followed by a very definite act, and our perception of our own act is closely similar to a number of other perceptions which we have at the same time. These, moreover, are all associated with perceptions very like those which we call perceptions of our own bodies. We infer that all the other people have had perceptions analogous to that of the stimulus to our own act. The analogy is very good; the only question is: Why should not the very same event which was the cause of our own act have been the cause of the acts of the others? Why should we suppose that there had to be a separate seeing of the fall of the curtain for each spectator, and not only one seeing which caused all the appearances of bodies to appear to applaud? It may be said that this view is far-fetched. But I doubt if it would be unreasonable but for the second kind of analogy, which is incapable of a similar explanation.

In the second kind of analogy, we see others acting as we should act in response to a certain kind of stimulus which, however, we are not experiencing at the moment. Suppose, for example, that you are a rather short person in a crowd watching election returns being exhibited on a screen. You hear a burst of cheering, but can see nothing. By great efforts, you manage to perceive a very notable result which you could not perceive a few moments earlier. It is natural to suppose that the others cheered because they saw this result. In this case, their perceptions, if they occurred, were certainly not *identical* with yours, since they occurred earlier; hence, if the stimulus to their cheering was a perception analogous to your subsequent perception, they had perceptions which you could not perceive. I have chosen a rather extreme example, but the same kind of thing occurs constantly; someone says "There's Jones," and you look round and see Jones. It would seem odd to suppose that the words you heard were not caused by a perception analogous to what you had when you looked round. Or your friend says "Listen," and after he has said it you hear distant thunder. Such experiences lead irresistibly to the conclusion that the percepts you call other people are associated with percepts which you do not have, but which are like those you would have if you were in their place. The same principle is involved in the assumption that the words you hear express "thoughts."

The argument in favour of the view that there are percepts, connected with other people, which are not among our own percepts, is presupposed in the acceptance of testimony, and comes first in logical order when we are trying to establish the existence of things other than our own percepts. . . .

The argument is not demonstrative, either in the one case or in the other. A conjuror might make a waxwork man with a gramophone inside, and arrange a series of little mishaps of which the gramophone would give the audience warning. In dreams, people give evidence of being alive which is similar in kind to that which they give when we are awake; yet the people we see in dreams are supposed to have no external existence. Descartes' malicious demon is a logical possibility. For these reasons, we may be mistaken in any given instance. But it seems highly improbable that we are always mistaken. . . .

We have been considering hitherto, not the external world in general, but the percepts of other people. We might say that we have been trying to prove that other people are alive, and not mere phantoms like the people in dreams. The exact thing we have been trying to prove is this: Given an observed correlation among our own percepts, in which the second term is what one would naturally call a percept of our own bodily behaviour, and given a percept of similar behaviour in a physical object not our own body but similar to it, we infer that this behaviour was preceded by an event analogous to the earlier term in the observed correlation among our percepts. This inference assumes nothing as to the distinction of mind and body or as to the nature of either.

In virtue of the above argument, I shall now assume that we may enlarge our own experience by testimony—i.e. that the noises we hear when it seems to us that other people are talking do in fact express something analogous to what we should be expressing if we made similar noises. This is a particular case of the principle contained in the preceding paragraph. I think the evidence for other people's percepts is the strongest we have for anything that we do not perceive ourselves; therefore it seems right to establish this, so far as we can, before proceeding to consider our evidence for "matter"—i.e. for existents satisfying the equations of physics. This must be our next task; but it will be well to begin with common-sense material "things" conceived as the causes of perceptions.

Having now admitted the percepts of other people, we can greatly enlarge the group constituting one "physical object." Within the solipsistic world, we found means of collecting groups of percepts and calling the group one physical object; but we can now enrich our group enormously. A number of people sitting near each other can all draw what they see, and can compare the resulting pictures; there will be similarities and differences. A number of stenographers listening to a lecture can all take notes of it, and compare results. A number of people can be brought successively into a room full of hidden roses, and asked "What do you smell?" In this way it appears that the world of each person is partly private and partly common. In the part which is common, there is found to be not identity, but only a greater or less degree of similarity, between the percepts of different people. It is the absence of identity which makes us reject the naïve realism of common sense; it is the similarity which makes us accept the theory of a common origin for similar simultaneous perceptions.

. . . Suppose a room arranged with a man concealed behind a curtain, and also a camera and dictaphone. Suppose two men came into the room, converse, dine, and smoke. If the record of the dictaphone and the camera agrees with that of the man behind the curtain, it is impossible to resist the conclusion that something happened where they were which bore an intimate relation to what the hidden man perceived. For that matter, one might have two cameras and two dictaphones, and compare their records. Such correspondences, which are only more extreme forms of those with which primitive common sense is familiar, make it inconceivably complicated and unplausible to suppose that nothing happens where there is no percipient. If the dictaphone and the hidden man give the same report of the conversation, one must suppose some causal connection, since otherwise the coincidence is in the highest degree improbable. But the causal connection is found to depend upon the position of the dictaphone at the time of the conversation, not upon the person who hears its record. This seems very strange, if its record does not exist until it is heard, as we shall have to suppose if we confine the world to percepts. . . .

I shall assume henceforth not only that there are percepts which I do not perceive, connected with other people's bodies, but also that there are events causally connected with percepts, as to which we do not know whether they are perceived or not. I shall assume, e.g., that if I am alone in a room and I shut my eyes, the objects in it which I no longer see (i.e. the causes of my visual percepts) continue to exist, and do not suddenly become resurrected when I re-open my eyes.

Questions and Exercises

1. Explain the concept of the "external world." What would, and wouldn't, be part of that world?
2. On what basis do we normally distinguish dreams from reality? What does it mean to say that reality might also be a dream?
3. Explain Descartes's "cogito" argument.
4. Say to yourself, "I think, therefore . . . exists," filling in your name. Is this a good argument?
5. "If we had to prove everything, we couldn't prove anything." Explain this statement.
6. What's the problem with saying that the existence of the external world is "self-evident" and requires no argument?
7. Critique the following claim: "To believe there is no external world is as reasonable as to believe there is."
8. Descartes says: ". . . how can I be sure but that God has brought it about that I am always mistaken when I add two and three or count the sides of a square, or when I judge something even easier. . . ?" What problems would Descartes get into if he held to this line of reasoning?
9. What purpose does the supposition of an evil spirit play in Descartes's philosophical inquiry?
10. What is Russell's argument for the existence of other minds?
11. How does Russell's concept of a physical object change before and after he has argued for the existence of other minds?

7

Logic

Fiction: Philosophy Is Murder: A Nebuchadnezzar Hulk Mystery

I've pulled plenty of stunts on Nebuchadnezzar Hulk over the years. You might say that's one of my jobs. Hulk is a genius, but he's as lazy and contrary as he is smart. Someone has to make sure that he keeps working. After all, Hulk is the sole support of a four-story house filled with hundreds of expensive orchids, a plant nurse who feeds the orchids, a French chef who feeds Hulk, and an assistant detective—me—who is no genius but is ingenious, particularly at pulling stunts that get Hulk working.

I must say I hesitated this time. To admit to Hulk's office, unannounced, a gaudily dressed six-foot blonde carrying a poodle, a night-club dancer wanting help for her underpaid philosophy-professor husband—that seemed to be going a bit far. But I decided Hulk needed a real shocker. A week before, with our bank balance well below six figures, Hulk had returned a $10,000 retainer because the twelve directors of the Granite Corporation had had the audacity to insist that he come to their offices rather than the other way around. I don't begrudge Hulk his idiosyncrasies, like never leaving the house on business and never missing his four hours a day in the plant rooms. But he's made exceptions to his rules in the past, and he should have made an exception for the Granite Corporation. Now I would let him know quite vividly what he could expect in the way of cases if he continued to be so stubborn.

Hulk was sitting at his desk, reading *Principia Mathematica*, when I ushered the dancer into the office.

"Sir, allow me to introduce Miss Gloria Lovely. That's 'L-O-V-E-L-Y.' Actually, that's her stage name. She is a night-club dancer currently working at the Starlight Lounge. She is married to Heinrich Bergmann, an existentialist who is suspected of murder, and she is here to engage your services on his behalf. I told her we didn't have a case at the moment, and you'd probably be happy to have the work."

Mrs. Bergmann couldn't have done better if I'd coached her. She shifted the poodle to her left arm, extended her right hand to the man who avoids shaking hands with anyone, and murmured:

"It's a pleasure to meet you, Mr. Hulk. Or may I call you Nebuchadnezzar?"

I thought for a moment Hulk's jaw was going to drop, but he managed to stop. He stared at Mrs. Bergmann for a moment, keeping his hands on his book, and then slowly lifted his seventh of a ton out of his chair.

"Madame. My assistant, Mr. Crocker, has been known to dabble in the inane before, but never in the occult. Allow me to say that you are a truly extraordinary creature. Now, if you will excuse me. Arnie, be sure this woman is not paid from office funds for her acting here today. As you are so cleverly reminding me, they are not up to the challenge."

He was halfway to the door when her fist struck the desk.

"Mr. Hulk!"

Hulk turned around, his eyebrows raised in surprise.

"Obviously, you and Mr. Crocker regard me as a joke," she went on angrily, "but this certified check for $5,000 is no joke. Nor is my husband's situation. He is in serious trouble and needs your help!"

"Indeed," said Hulk. "If this is a performance, Mrs. Bergmann, it is most certainly a commanding one. But don't you think the existentialist touch strains credulity?"

Her voice softened a bit now that she had his attention.

"My husband, Mr. Hulk, is a professor at Fountain College. His specialty is existentialism, and he has published several articles on Sartre's early work. He has maintained to his colleagues that his marrying me was Gide's *acte gratuit,* a gratuitous act demonstrating his complete freedom of choice. It is a conceit of his to which I don't object, since we have a good marriage in any case. My husband's interests in life are not purely intellectual. And it helps that I am not as devoid of intelligence as you seem to think I am. I have a degree in philosophy from Fountain, but no one hires female philosophy majors unless they minor in stenography. I happen to find what I do much more enjoyable, not to say lucrative, than secretarial work. It goes without saying that my tastes are not terribly conventional."

"You say that your husband is suspected of murder. Whose murder?"

"Professor William Lanchaster, chairman of the philosophy department at Fountain, was shot to death in his study at his home last Thursday evening."

Hulk looked at Mrs. Bergmann, then at me, then back at her. He nodded slightly and started back to his desk.

"Arnie, please find a place for that dog other than this office and the kitchen. Mrs. Bergmann, please take a seat. What may I offer you to drink?"

Obviously my joke had backfired, but it had us moving in the right direction. After all, the point had been to get Hulk working, and now he was working. We had a murder case, and we had a $5,000 retainer. So I was feeling rather pleased with myself as I returned to his office, without the poodle, and sat behind my desk. I reached for my notebook, signaling Hulk I was ready.

"Now then, Mrs. Bergmann," said Hulk, "suppose you tell me about the events related to the murder in what seems to you the most logical order."

Mrs. Bergmann took a sip of her drink and began:

"Fountain College, Mr. Hulk, has, or had, a five-person philosophy department: Heinrich Bergmann, my husband; William Lanchaster, the deceased, who taught logic; Herbert Lord, history of ancient philosophy; Beatrice Trilling, history of modern philosophy; and Reggie Stout, contemporary American and British philosophy.

"Fountain, like many small private colleges, is having financial difficulties, and the trustees have undertaken a considerable reduction of faculty positions. Every faculty member is theoretically vulnerable: Fountain is an experimental college and has never had a tenure or seniority system.

"A couple of months ago, the trustees affirmed Lanchaster's position and directed him to eliminate one member of the philosophy department. Since that time, there has been a great deal of nasty politicking among the philosophers. Eventually, Lord, Trilling, and Stout banded together to try to eliminate my husband. They have even gone so far as sending willing students to Lanchaster to complain about my husband. He's particularly vulnerable because he's an unorthodox personality, even for Fountain, and because existentialism is viewed with some contempt by most professional American philosophers.

"Professor Lanchaster was to announce his decision to the members of the department, individually, at his home, on Thursday evening. He asked Lord to come at 7:00, Stout at 7:30, my husband at 8:00, and Trilling at 8:30. This schedule has been confirmed by the department secretary.

"Lord says he arrived at 7:00 and left at 7:30. He claims that Lanchaster told him that he, Lord, would be retained and that my husband was to be fired. Of course, Lord maintains that Lanchaster was alive when he left. There was no one else in the house to confirm this or to tell of any arrivals or departures. Professor Lanchaster's children are grown, and his wife had been out of town for several weeks visiting a sick sister. The only other visitor that we know of was Lanchaster's niece, Lisa Williams, who stopped by the house at 7:25, with a friend, to pick up some books. Her friend, apparently, can confirm her presence at the library for the rest of the evening. When Lisa arrived, Lord answered the door at Professor Lanchaster's request, he says, and gave her a bundle of books that was on the table in the hallway.

"Stout says that he did not come to the house at 7:30. He arrived instead at 8:30 and found Beatrice Trilling outside the door. Stout has produced a typewritten note that he claims was put in his mailbox at the college that day asking him to come at 8:30 rather than 7:30. The note had apparently been typed on a departmental typewriter and was unsigned. Stout says he assumed that one of the secretaries had typed it at Lanchaster's direction.

"Stout and Trilling say that they rang the bell for several minutes and then entered the house. They say the door was slightly ajar. They found Lanchaster's body and called the police. After the police arrived, Trilling told them she had passed my husband in Lanchaster's neighborhood as she was going to her appointment.

"My husband, I regret to say, has acted stupidly. He now claims that he got back late from an out-of-town lecture, arrived at the Lanchaster house at 8:15, discovered the body, but left without reporting the murder. He has an elaborate rationale for leaving the scene, but the plain fact is that he panicked. When the police questioned him, he first denied being in the Lanchaster neighborhood, then denied being in the house, before telling the police what he now says is the truth.

"The police asked my husband how he thought he could get away with denying his presence at the house, since his appointment was part of a schedule known to the whole department. My husband said that he knew of no schedule. Apparently, Lanchaster did not make a point of telling each person that he was seeing the others. Stout, Trilling, and Lord knew about the schedule because they had talked with one another. My husband was not in on their conversations.

"Unfortunately, my husband's admission makes plausible the assumption that he went to Lanchaster's house with a gun, killed him, and then left, all with a reasonable expectation that no one would ever know he had done it.

"The police have not arrested my husband. They are obviously aware of the other possibilities. The medical examiner places the time of death between 7:45 and 8:15. Trilling or Lord could have faked the note to Stout and killed Lanchaster during Stout's appointment time. Or Stout could have kept his appointment and typed the note himself.

"But my husband is the prime suspect. The police are suggesting that Lanchaster might have typed the note to Stout and asked my husband to come at 7:30 so that they would have an hour to discuss my husband's dismissal. Lord says Lanchaster told him that my husband was to be fired, and Stout and Trilling say that they had hints of this.

"I don't like the situation at all. The police are obviously antagonistic toward my husband, as are the other professors in the department. And one of those others is the murderer. If some piece of planted evidence should show up—well, it would certainly be all over for my husband. I want you to clear him by finding the murderer for us."

Mrs. Bergmann had moved forward in her chair during this recital. Now she let out a breath and leaned back. After a pause, Hulk began to speak. He was scowling.

"I must admit, Madame, that I can't help sharing the negative attitude of the police. Whether or not we assume your husband is the killer, his ineptitude is amazing. Is he an utter idiot? This is a man who has been employed to teach reason to the young. I find myself astounded."

Mrs. Bergmann stared at Hulk for a moment, and then, much to my surprise, she laughed.

"Mr. Hulk, you may have heard the story of how Thales, the Greek philosopher, fell into a ditch while gazing at the stars. My husband is like that. He can develop very impressive arguments concerning the existence of God, free will, and the nature of the unobservable world. But ask him which foot fits his left shoe, and he is lost. It is part of his charm for me, but I must admit that I'm less than charmed with him at the moment. However, I'm not asking you to like him. I'm asking you to prove him innocent."

"Are you so sure of his innocence?" said Hulk. "Obviously you don't have any evidence in his favor that the police will accept."

"True. But I know my husband. He is not a violent man. And, quite frankly, he wouldn't have the courage."

"Mrs. Bergmann, you should know that I do not shield murderers. I do not, in the end, hide evidence from the police. If I go after a murderer, I find him, and if it turns out to be your husband, the police shall know about it. Nor will I return your retainer. Are you sure you want to engage me on those terms?"

"I'm quite certain."

"Satisfactory. Tell me, what do the police know about the murder weapon?"

"Lanchaster did not own a gun, and none of the suspects is known to have owned one. It seems that Lanchaster was shot with one of those handguns you can order by mail. As far as I know, the police have not found it."

"You said that the three other suspects disliked your husband. How did the deceased feel about him?"

"They weren't close, but I think Professor Lanchaster was quite fond of him. A case of opposites attracting, perhaps. Lanchaster was a very precise, proper person, but not dogmatic. I think he enjoyed my husband's flamboyance. Of course, there was no question of competition. My husband posed no threat to Lanchaster's position at the college."

"And Mrs. Lanchaster? How does she feel about you and your husband?"

"Mrs. Lanchaster has always been very kind to both my husband and me."

"Do you think you could persuade her to admit Mr. Crocker to the house?"

"To the house, yes. But I'm afraid questioning Mrs. Lanchaster would be unadvisable. The doctor has ordered her to rest. Lisa Williams, the niece, who is a friend of ours, is staying with her. She could show Mr. Crocker around. Professor Lanchaster was quite a fan of yours, as a matter of fact. He used some of your cases as exercises in his introductory classes. He referred to you as a fellow logician doing battle outside the ivory tower. That's how I happened to think of your name. Yes, I'm quite sure that Mrs. Lanchaster would admit a representative of yours."

Hulk glanced at the clock and noticed that it was time to do battle in the plant rooms. He rose from his chair.

"Very well. Please arrange it, and call Mr. Crocker. If you will excuse me now, I have an appointment. But please stay a few more minutes. Mr. Crocker will need some more information from you."

* * * * *

Mrs. Bergmann arranged to have me visit the Lanchaster house the next afternoon. Before visiting the house, I made inquiries at police headquarters and at the philosophy department of Fountain College.

Inspector Shultz wasn't very philosophical about my visit. He loses any composure he has at the sound of Hulk's name or at the sight of me. I suppose I can't blame him. It never makes him look good when Hulk solves a case that Shultz can't. Shultz let me cool my heels for an hour outside his office before letting me know the only thing he was planning to show me was the door.

Professor Stout, who was now acting chairman of the department, showed me into his office immediately—once he realized I was questioning a secretary about a certain typewriter. He was soon joined by Professors Lord and Trilling. Stout looked like a radical from the sixties who had lost his causes but had managed to hang on to his faded jeans. Lord looked like the professors you see in cartoons: balding head, glasses, sport coat with patches on the sleeves, a slightly confused look on his face. Professor Trilling was a Bella Abzug look-alike: heavy-set, with a booming voice.

Even though you know it does no good, you never get out of the habit of looking into eyes, trying to find the guilt there. Stout looked cynical, Lord nervous, and Trilling ferocious, but no one looked guiltier than the others. I told them what I'd found, but, when it became apparent that they intended to ask all the questions, I left. One thing was clear to me: They were all happy to have Bergmann on the hot spot and weren't about to help him.

My next stop was the Lanchaster house. Lisa Williams opened the door seconds after my first ring. She was a nice-looking girl, about eighteen. She greeted me with a finger to her lips and signaled me to follow her to the study, which was at the back of the house. Once we were inside the room, she shut the door carefully.

"Betty—Mrs. Lanchaster—is sleeping. You are Mr. Crocker, aren't you?"

"That's right. I appreciate this."

"Gloria and Heinrich are my friends."

I looked around the study. It was mostly old mahogany and old books. There was a large desk on the far side of the room, facing the door, with a chair behind it, and two other chairs to the side and front of it.

"Your uncle was sitting in the desk chair when he was shot?"

"Yes. The police say he was shot by someone sitting in that other chair, there, in front of the desk."

I walked over to the desk and found the bullet hole in the padded back of the desk chair. I looked quickly at the papers and books scattered on the desk.

"Is the room the same as it was that evening? Did the police take any-thing?"

"As far as I know, everything is here."

I inspected the area around the desk and noticed that the cord of the desk phone had been torn from the wall. I held up the frayed cord.

"Was this done on the evening of the murder?"

"Yes. At least, this phone was working that afternoon when I called my uncle. I know he was on this line, because he was looking for the books I wanted while holding the phone."

"Those were the books you came by to get that evening? Why don't you tell me about that."

"There's nothing much to tell," she said. "I needed some books for a paper I'm writing. My uncle said he'd be busy and wouldn't be able to see me, but he would put the books on the hall table and leave the front door unlocked. When I rang the doorbell, Lord answered the door and handed me the books. Then I left. I was with a friend all evening at the library, as I told the police."

"Did Lord say anything when he gave you the books?"

"No. He just met me at the door with them and handed them to me before I could say a thing. He obviously knew I was coming for them."

"Did you think it strange that Lord should answer the door?"

"No. My uncle was lame and often asked people to do little things for him so that he wouldn't have to move around too much. And Lord was always anxious to please him."

"How did Lord seem to you?"

"The same as always."

I looked more closely at the items on the desk. There were some books on logic, including one written by Lanchaster, some journal reprints, a draft of a paper on some logical controversy, and notes on a logic exam he'd been preparing. I also went through the desk drawers. There was nothing among the papers that seemed to bear on the murder.

"I assume the police found nothing that indicated which professor was to be fired?"

"No."

"Professor Lanchaster didn't tell his wife?"

"No. The police asked her that."

"All right. Is there a working phone around here I can use? I'm supposed to call Hulk for instructions."

She took me to the kitchen, which was at the front of the house, and I dialed Hulk from there. Hulk didn't want a report on my entire day, just on what I had found in the house. That took only a few minutes.

"I'm heading back now, unless you want me to do something else here," I told him.

There was a long pause. "Photographs," he said finally. "I want photos of every paper, of all writing on or in that desk. When you are finished, take the film to Lew's shop. Tell Lew I want the photographs developed tonight. Offer him the usual bonus."

"Will do," I said, wondering what Hulk could be after.

* * * * *

They were all in place in the office by 4:00, when Hulk came down from the plant rooms: Stout, Lord, and Trilling seated together on Hulk's right, Lisa Williams in the center, Heinrich and Gloria Bergmann on Hulk's left, and Inspector Shultz and Sergeant Joe Kurz in the back row. I'd never seen an existentialist before, but had I imagined one, he would have looked just like Heinrich Bergmann. His long hair and beard, jeans, and shirt were all black. The only contrasts were the brown eyes and the nicotine-colored skin at the center of all that hair.

"All right, Hulk, they're all here," said Inspector Shultz. "They have been told that you have no official standing and that they are not legally obligated to answer any of your questions. However, we have asked for their cooperation. What do you have?"

"I don't have any questions," said Hulk. "What I have is something to show all of you. Arnie, if you please."

$$D \supset B$$
$$D \supset (B \supset W)$$
$$B \supset (W \supset S) / \therefore D \supset S$$

$$M \equiv N / \therefore \sim N \vee M$$

$$A \supset B$$
$$C \supset D$$
$$(B \vee D) \supset E$$
$$\sim E / \therefore \sim (A \vee C)$$

$$\sim R \vee \sim S$$
$$A \supset (R \cdot S) / \therefore \sim A$$

$$\sim (M \cdot N)$$
$$(O \cdot T) \vee (M \cdot N)$$
$$(M \cdot N) \vee (R \cdot L)$$
$$O \supset (I \cdot D)$$
$$D \equiv S / \therefore$$

Ont. Arg.

I gave each person in the room a copy of the photograph of a sheet of paper shown here.

"The reason I have no need to ask questions," said Hulk, "is that Professor Lanchaster has given us the answer we are looking for."

Puzzled exclamations burst out all over the room.

"What kind of nonsense is this?" said Shultz. "What is this picture?"

"This is a picture of a page from Professor Lanchaster's desk pad," said Hulk. "And it is not nonsense. Quite the opposite. Before he died, Lanchaster wrote on his desk pad all that we need to solve his murder."

Switching parodies, in mid-mystery, from Rex Stout to Ellery Queen, I interrupt the story to issue:

A CHALLENGE TO THE READER

You now have all the clues necessary to solve the mystery. A little deduction will indicate "whodunit." Some additional reflection should enable you to give a full explanation of the crime. (For instance, when and why was the phone torn out of the wall?) For those readers who have had no philosophy or logic, the following information should suffice:

The relevant logic problem is the one at the lower right-hand side of the paper, the one without a solution filled in:

$$\sim (M \cdot N)$$
$$(O \cdot T) \vee (M \cdot N)$$
$$(M \cdot N) \vee (R \cdot L)$$
$$O \supset (I \cdot D)$$
$$D \equiv S / \therefore$$

The conclusion you want is a conjunction of all the letters that can be deduced from the premises, without any letter being repeated. The conclusion should not contain "not," "or," or "if–then." The conclusion should have the following form: A and B and C, and so on. *The letters you can deduce from these premises can be rearranged to form a message.* If this appears to be a formidable task, it won't be if you take a moment to read the following instructions: A, B, C, and so on, stand for distinct statements. But you could not know which, if any, specific statements these letters symbolize. Therefore, you have to concern yourself with the letters themselves.

Here are the meanings of the symbols:

"$\sim$ A" means "not A"
"A $\cdot$ B" means "A and B"
"A $\vee$ B" means "A or B"
"A $\supset$ B" means "If A, then B"
"A $\equiv$ B" means "If A, then B, *and* if B, then A"
"/ $\therefore$" means "therefore" (having the same meaning as a line drawn
          under the premises)

The parentheses group symbols together, acting as a kind of punctuation. For instance:

"(A $\cdot$ B) $\vee$ (C $\cdot$ D)" means "either both A and B, or both C and D"

Start by deducing what letters you can; put those in the conclusion. Then use those letters to deduce others; add those to the conclusion.

Symbolic logic simply formalizes the logic we use every day, and you can do the logic informally. For instance:

$$A \cdot B$$
$$(A \cdot B) \supset (C \cdot D)$$
$$\overline{A \cdot B \cdot C \cdot D}$$

REASONING: The first premise gives us both A and B; these can be put in the conclusion. The second premise says that, if we have both A and B, we can get both C and D. Since we have A and B, we also get C and D. These are added to the conclusion.

$$\sim A$$
$$A \vee B$$
$$\overline{B}$$

REASONING: The first premise gives us not A; since this is a negative statement, it won't be part of the message. But the first premise is helpful in conjunction with the second premise, which says either A or B. Since we know it's not A, it must be B.

Also: "Ont. Arg." = "Ontological Argument" = Descartes's proof for the existence of God (originally from Anselm).

The people in the room began to study the photograph intently. No one came up with the answer. Shultz was the first to speak.

"We're not here to play games, Hulk. If you've got an answer, let's have it."

"What's written at the bottom of the page?" asked Lisa. " 'Ont. Arg.' "

"Ontological argument," said Stout.

"Is that some kind of clue?" asked Mrs. Bergmann.

"Indeed it is," said Hulk. "Ladies and gentlemen, consider the taxing, not to mention frightening, predicament of a man who knows he is going to die and wants to leave a clue as to the name of his murderer. If it is too obvious, the murderer will remove it. If it is too obscure, no one will notice it. Professor Lanchaster got his clue past the murderer but almost erred on the side of subtlety. I have been told that Professor Lanchaster admired my work, and I flatter myself with the supposition that he took a chance that someone, perhaps his wife, would bring me into the case. In any event, it is fortunate that I did get involved. Had the situation been left to the police department, the clue would have gone undetected."

"All I've gotten so far is talk," said Shultz.

"You will also get a murderer, Inspector. A man wants to leave a clue as to the identity of his murderer. He would hardly write out the name. So what would he do instead? He'd devise some word association, perhaps. Here the abbreviation 'Ont. Arg.' stands out on a sheet otherwise devoted to logic exercises. As Professor Stout has noted, this abbreviation stands for 'ontological argument.' None of the books and papers on Lanchaster's desk had any connection with the ontological argument. Perhaps a clue lay there.

"What is the ontological argument? The four professors here can tell you better than I, but, briefly, it is an argument that claims that the actual existence of God is necessarily implied by the mere definition of God. It is a proof concerning God. God . . . why not *Lord*? A good association. I thought: Lord is the killer."

"Hulk, you're an idiot," said Professor Trilling.

"How so, Professor?"

"The proof you refer to is Anselm's ontological proof, also used by Descartes. But it is not the only ontological proof. Sartre has another, a proof for the existence of Being, independent of consciousness. In fact, Bergmann has written an article on it. Perhaps Lanchaster was indicating Bergmann."

"More likely it is only a random scribble," said Stout. "If it isn't, it might as well be. No, Hulk, that gets you nowhere."

"I doubt very much that it was random," said Hulk. "I believe it was written intentionally as a clue. But it was invented in haste, and Lanchaster saw the ambiguity. So he came up with something else, a clue hidden among the logic exercises on his desk pad. Fortunately, that clue is not ambiguous.

"The philosophers here know how introductory logic courses proceed. Students learn to translate normal sentences into symbols that express their logical form. Look." Hulk lifted up a large sheet of paper on which he had printed the symbols and pointed to them as he explained. "Letters like A and M replace basic sentences. Other symbols stand for the logical connectives: $\sim$ means 'not'; $\cdot$ means 'and'; v means 'either . . . or'; $\supset$ means 'if–then'; and $\equiv$ means 'if either, then the other.' For example, 'If Joe gets paid, then Joe buys groceries' can be symbolized as A $\supset$ B. Or, 'Either Joe goes to work, or he does not go to work' can be symbolized as Mv $\sim$ M.

"Having learned such symbolization, the students are then taught a series of valid argument forms. A valid argument is an argument such that, if the premises are true, then the conclusion must be true. For example, 'A $\supset$ B; A; therefore ($\therefore$) B' is a valid argument form, and any argument having that form is valid. 'If the sun shines, then the grass will grow; the sun shines; therefore, the grass will grow' is a valid argument having that form.

"Students then analyze more complex arguments. If the conclusion of an argument can be derived from the premises by employing a series of valid argument forms, then that more complex argument is valid. If not, then there are definite procedures for showing the argument to be invalid.

"Consider the example at the center of Lanchaster's desk pad. This is a typical example of a logic exercise at a point in the course where the ability of the student to translate from English to logical symbolism is assumed. Only the symbolized argument is given. The conclusion of the argument is given. The student is asked to determine whether the argument is valid.

"Now consider the example at the lower right-hand side of the desk pad. No conclusion is given, as if one were being invited to draw a conclusion. Of course, it could be that Lanchaster was simply interrupted there, but a little work shows that such was not the case. The solution to the murder is there.

"Of course, in a sense, there is no single answer to any logic problem. '$\sim$ (M $\cdot$ N),' for example, can be deduced from the premises and would be a 'solution.' Also, since any letter can be deduced from itself, any letters in the conclusion could be repeated indefinitely. But, presumably, a message would be a conjunction of all the individual letters that could be deduced from the premises, with no repetition of any letters. Such, indeed, is the case.

"Let us work out this solution. Since the argument is fairly simple, we can do it informally.

"The second premise says, 'Either both O and T or both M and N.' The third premise says, 'Either both M and N, or both R and L.' Since the first premise says 'not M and N,' we can deduce the other pairs of letters. That gives us O and T and R and L. The fourth premise says, 'If O, then both I and D.' Since we already have O, we can deduce I and D. The last premise says that whenever we have D, we have S, and vice versa. Since we have D, we can deduce S. The conclusion, then, is O and T and R and L and I and D and S.

"Appropriately, Lanchaster, professor of logic, used his own tools to name his murderer. He gave us a problem whose solution is an anagram, giving us his statement: ITS LORD."

Lord was staring at Hulk without speaking, his fingers playing at his lips. Everyone else was staring at Lord. Shultz motioned Sergeant Kurz to move in Lord's direction and then turned to Hulk.

"I don't get it, Hulk. Lanchaster died instantly and obviously didn't write his message after the killer left. Do you mean to tell me that Lord was stupid enough to sit there while Lanchaster jotted down notes that would convict him?"

"Inspector, it would not be the first time that one of this group of supposedly educated people has exhibited blatant stupidity. But, no, Lord wasn't that stupid.

"Presumably Lord had some early hint from Lanchaster that he would be dropped from the department, and Lord planned to kill Lanchaster should that be the decision. He was taking an awful chance, killing him when he did. But he did not want to act before the final decision had been confirmed. Had he waited longer, others would have learned of his dismissal.

"Of course, the time of his appointment was known to the others, so he had to commit the crime in such a way that another would be blamed or, at the very least, that others would be suspected. He sent a note to Stout and perhaps even verified that Stout would be coming late. Would you care to comment, Professor Stout?"

Stout glanced quickly at Lord. "Yes," he said. "He knew I had gotten the note. We discussed it."

"Thank you," said Hulk. "Lord had also decided to kill fairly close to 8:00. That way, both Stout and Bergmann would be suspects. He did not know, of course, that Professor Bergmann would be so helpful with his panic and his bumbling stories.

"Lord arrived at 7:00, learned that he was to be fired, pulled a gun on Lanchaster, and waited. But then a problem arose. The doorbell rang. It was Lisa Williams, who had come to pick up her books. No doubt Lord had locked the door upon entering the house. But he did not dare let the doorbell go unanswered. Miss Williams knew Lanchaster would be there, the lights in the house were on, and the car was in the driveway. For his part, Lanchaster had to cooperate or jeopardize the life of his niece. He told Lord that she had come for the books and told him where they were.

"Lord did not dare let Lanchaster go to the door: He might pass a message to his niece. He saw only one danger in leaving a lame man alone in the room—the phone. So he pulled the phone cord from the wall. It was the broken cord that first made me suspect that there might be a message among the things on the desk.

"Perhaps Lord quickly searched for a message when he returned to the room. Perhaps he didn't think of that possibility. In any case, Lanchaster had hidden his message well. It would not have been spotted by someone afraid and in haste, even a colleague who knew his symbolic logic.

"Lord then waited in the study with Lanchaster for another fifteen or twenty minutes before killing him. All of you know the rest. I am certain that a jury will find the accusation, 'ITS LORD,' in the deceased's own handwriting, sufficient evidence to convict, especially given the cogency of the hypothesis I have outlined. Would you care to comment, Professor Lord?"

"No," said Lord, still rubbing his lips.

"Rest assured, sir, that you will be convicted and sent to prison for the rest of your life. Perhaps the prison authorities will let you teach Plato and Aristotle in prison. If so, I hope that the inmates enjoy your courses. I suspect, from Professor Lanchaster's decision, that your students at Fountain did not. But in prison, at least, you will have tenure."

"Damn you, Hulk, damn you!"

Many men have tried to get at Hulk in that office and none has succeeded yet. Lord certainly didn't, though he made quite a try for a man of his size. I intercepted him, wrestled him to the floor, and held him while Sergeant Kurz put on the cuffs.

* * * * *

Hulk refuses to talk business at dinner, so I waited until we were drinking coffee in the office to tell him.

"While you were in the plant rooms, a messenger arrived with a package from Mrs. Bergmann. It was the second check for $5,000 we'd expected. It has been put in the safe and will be deposited tomorrow. Mrs. Bergmann also sent you a present. It's a copy of an article by her husband on Sartre's ontological proof. The major question seems to be: Is the phenomenon of Being itself the Being of the phenomena, or is it merely a phenomenal representation, non-identical with, but indicating the nature of, the Being of the phenomena? I haven't quite made up my mind. Perhaps we could discuss the matter after you've read the article."

"Rubbish. They should fire the whole department at Fountain and hire four logicians. At least that is a sensible subject."

"You're just prejudiced because you are a fellow logician, even if you are doing battle outside the ivory tower. But that reminds me, sir. There is one point about the case that hasn't been cleared up to my satisfaction—something you said when you were disclosing the murderer."

"Yes? What was that?"

"You said, 'If Joe gets paid, then Joe buys groceries.' What I want to know is: Did Joe get paid?"

"Phooey. Go amuse yourself elsewhere."

It is a shame to be living with a genius and yet have to do without intellectual conversation. Fortunately, my interests are not purely intellectual. I grabbed my hat and headed for the Starlight Lounge.

Questions

1. Trace the steps in Hulk's reasoning from his first search for evidence to his proposed solution to the crime.
2. Is it implausible to suppose that the exercise yielding the message "ITS LORD" was written prior to Lord's appearance in the study? Explain.

   If one assumes that it was, what account might one give of the crime?
3. Compare your preliminary solution with those of Hulk and of the other students. (Don't simply assume that Hulk's explanation must be correct.) Are these various explanations equally reasonable? Discuss.
4. Do the following logic exercise as you did the exercise in the mystery story. Here you will need to derive some negative statements in the course of your reasoning (for example, ~ 0), and you may find it convenient to put these in the conclusion as you proceed. But when you have completed your reasoning, cross out any negative statements in the conclusion. The remaining conjunction of letters can be arranged to form a one-word admonition. As before, there should be no double letters in the conclusion.

   In reasoning out logic problems, one does not usually follow the written order of the premises. In this case, it would be a mistake to begin with the first one. Look over the premises and choose a reasonable starting point.

$$(K \cdot N) \supset \sim O$$
$$\sim O \supset T$$
$$I \cdot \sim A$$
$$(K \cdot N) \vee A$$
$$H \vee (B \cdot L)$$
$$\underline{\sim (B \cdot L)}$$
$$?$$

DISCUSSION

ARGUMENTS, DEDUCTIVE AND INDUCTIVE

Philosophers, indeed all "rational" individuals, should be able to give arguments for their beliefs. An **argument** consists of a statement that is the conclusion and one or more additional statements that are the premises. The premises are offered as evidence in support of the conclusion.

There are deductive and inductive arguments. It is convenient to define these types of arguments in terms of their valid forms.

A **valid deductive argument** is an argument such that if the premises are true, then the conclusion *must* be true. Two examples of valid deductive arguments are:

> (1)   All students are human.
>   <u>All humans are mortal.</u>
>   All students are mortal.

> (2)   All students are human.
>   <u>All humans have three heads.</u>
>   All students have three heads.

A **valid inductive argument** is an argument such that if the premises are true, then the conclusion is *probably* true, but not necessarily so. Two examples of valid inductive arguments are:

> (3)   <u>All human beings observed have lived less than 500 years.</u>
>   All human beings live less than 500 years.

> (4)   <u>All human beings observed have lived less than 20 years.</u>
>   All human beings live less than 20 years.

Questions of validity and invalidity concern only the relation between the premises and the conclusion. To show that an argument is valid is not to show that the premises are true. It is to show that one should rely on the conclusion *if* the premises are true. Thus, with any argument you need to know two things:

Is it valid?

Are the premises true?

A valid argument with true premises is called a **sound argument.** Arguments "1" through "4" are all valid. But only "1" and "3" are sound.

Note that if a deductive argument is valid and the premises are true, then the conclusion must be true. However, if an inductive argument is valid and the premises are true, then the conclusion is probably true, but not necessarily so. What accounts for this difference?

The conclusion of a valid deductive argument contains no information that is not contained, at least implicitly, in the premises. In a sense, the conclusion of a valid deductive argument is merely a repetition of the premises. Thus the conclusion could not possibly be false if the premises are true.

On the other hand, the conclusion of a valid inductive argument does contain information not contained in the premises. Thus, it is conceivable that the premises of such an argument could be true and the conclusion false. In the examples of induction given above, the premises contain information about the human beings who have been observed, whereas the conclusions are statements about *all* human beings. What is true of the human beings we have observed is likely to be true of all human beings, but it need not be. In a valid inductive argument, the premises provide good evidence for the conclusion, but they do not guarantee its truth absolutely.

ASSESSING DEDUCTIVE ARGUMENTS

In assessing deductive arguments, one examines argument forms. "Philosophy Is Murder" has already introduced you to how arguments are formalized. The letters "A," "B," "C," and so on, stand for distinct statements. These letters are merely place markers, and it does not matter which one is used to represent a particular statement. However, within a single argument, a particular letter should be used for only one particular statement whenever that statement occurs.

Other symbols are used to represent what are called "logical connectives": "and," "or," "if–then," and so on. "~ A" means "not A." "A · B" means "A and B." "A v B" means "A or B." "A ⊃ B" means "if A, then B." "A ≡ B" means "if A, then B, *and* if B, then A." Parentheses group symbols together, acting as punctuation marks. For instance, "(A · B) v (C · D)" means "either both A and B or both C and D."

The premises are separated from the conclusion by a line drawn under the premises or by a slash mark and three dots in triangular form. The line or the dots mean "therefore." "These premises, *therefore* this conclusion."

The following arguments have the same form:

It is raining	It is snowing
It is cool	It is warm
It is raining and it is cool	It is snowing and it is warm

The form of these arguments is:

$$\frac{\begin{array}{c} A \\ B \end{array}}{A \cdot B}$$

(Or, "R; S; therefore R · S." Remember that the letters are merely place markers.)

Every argument of this form is valid. How do we know that this is a valid argument form? Our knowledge of validity is based on our knowledge of the meanings of the logical connectives. The word "and" implies that the statement "A and B" will be true if, and only if, "A" is true and "B" is true. Given this definition, it is impossible for "A and B" to be false if "A" is true and "B" is true.

There are technical methods for determining which basic argument forms are valid. With any complex argument, if the conclusion can be derived from the premises by employing a series of valid argument forms, then the complex argument has been shown to be valid. Consider, for example, the argument used in solving the mystery in "Philosophy Is Murder":

$$(\sim M \cdot N)$$
$$(O \cdot T) \lor (M \cdot N)$$
$$(M \cdot N) \lor (R \cdot L)$$
$$O \supset (I \cdot D)$$
$$\underline{D \equiv S}$$
$$O \cdot T \cdot R \cdot L \cdot I \cdot D \cdot S*$$

"R and L and O and T" can be deduced from the first three premises by employing the valid argument form: "A v B; ; A; therefore, B."

"I and D" can be derived from "O" and the fourth premise by employing another valid argument form: "A $\supset$ B; A; therefore, B."

The fifth premise has the same meaning as: "(D $\supset$ S) $\cdot$ (S $\supset$ D)." "D $\supset$ S" can be derived from that statement by employing the valid argument form: "A $\cdot$ B; therefore, A." Then "S" can be derived from "D" and "D $\supset$ S," by employing a valid argument form already mentioned: "A $\supset$ B; A; therefore, B."

In this case, formalization may seem to complicate the obvious. But in the case of more complex arguments, these symbolic techniques make precise and mechanical a process of evaluation that would be difficult, if not impossible, to do informally.

There are formal techniques for proving deductive arguments to be either valid or invalid. There are no simple, informal techniques for demonstrating validity, but there is one such technique for demonstrating invalidity, and you may find it useful on occasion.

Consider the following argument:

> If I am Superman, then I can leap tall buildings.
> I am not Superman.
> _____
> Therefore, I cannot leap tall buildings.

Here the premises are true, and the conclusion is true. Perhaps the argument seems to be valid; perhaps the conclusion seems to follow from the premises. But this argument is, in fact, invalid.

Remember that if an argument is valid, then every argument having that form is valid. Also, if an argument is valid, that means that it is impossible for

---

*For the benefit of those who have had, or may later have, a course in formal logic, it should be noted that this, and not the exercise with the conclusion omitted, would typify a logic exercise. As Hulk says: "This is a typical example of a logic exercise . . . the symbolized argument is given . . . the conclusion of the argument is given . . . the student is asked to determine whether the argument is valid." As Hulk also states: ". . . there is no single answer to any logic problem. '~ (M · N),' for example, can be deduced from the premises and would be a 'solution.' Also, since any letter can be deduced from itself, any letter in the conclusion could be repeated indefinitiely." This mystery story employs a special, and rather limited, "logical game" that would not be found in any logic textbook.

an argument of that form to have true premises and a false conclusion. Thus, if we can construct an argument that has the same form as the above and that has obviously true premises and an obviously false conclusion, we will have shown that argument to be invalid.

First, we determine the form of the argument. In the above case, it is:

$$A \supset B$$
$$\underline{\sim A}$$
$$\sim B$$

Now we construct an argument of this form, having obviously true premises and an obviously false conclusion. For example:

> If I am Superman, then I am a man.
> I am not Superman.
> _____
> I am not a man.

The premises are obviously true: Superman is male, and I am not Superman. The conclusion is obviously false: I *am* male. Thus, we have shown the initial argument to be invalid—it does not have a form such that the truth of the premises guarantees the truth of the conclusion. Every argument of the form "$A \supset B$; $\sim A$; therefore, $\sim B$" is invalid.

Note that the manufactured argument used to demonstrate invalidity need not have the same subject matter as the original argument. It is only necessary that it have the same form and that it have obviously true premises and an obviously false conclusion. The following argument would do just as well:

> If this is 1942, then this is the 20th century.
> This is not 1942.
> _____
> This is not the 20th century.

Another argument is given below as an exercise. Try to prove it invalid using the techniques we have discussed. That is, first determine the form of the argument, and then construct a "counter-example," an argument having the same form with obviously true premises and an obviously false conclusion. Compare your proof with that given in the footnote on p. 202.

> If I am nice to people, then people are nice to me.
> People are nice to me.
> _____
> I am nice to people.

EVALUATING INDUCTIVE ARGUMENTS

Evaluating inductive arguments is a much trickier business than evaluating deductive arguments. It is difficult to say precisely how the premises and conclusion are related in valid inductive arguments. It is often difficult to determine the degree of support that certain premises give a certain conclusion. This is not to say that we ought to disdain induction: Most of us trust induction and use it quite well; indeed, we must use induction if we are to gain any new knowledge. This is only to say that induction is difficult to formalize.

If we know that we have examined ninety-nine out of a hundred beans in a jar, and that all the ones we have examined have been green, we can conclude that the probability that all the beans in the jar will be green is ninety-nine percent. But when we make a judgment about all human beings based on the ones we have observed, we have no idea how many human beings there have been and will be. In such cases, we say our conclusions are "highly probable" or "fairly probable," and even these vague probability assessments can be matters of dispute. When we come to assessing the probability of, say, Einstein's general theory of relativity, the issue becomes enormously complex. Nonetheless, we do seem to come to considerable agreement on our inductive judgments.

Perhaps the simplest way to explain the nature of inductive reasoning is to consider its use in "Philosophy Is Murder." Detectives are often called "masters of deduction." In fact, however, most of their reasoning is inductive. On the basis of certain facts, they form conclusions concerning other matters; and where conclusions contain more information than is contained in the premises, such reasoning is inductive. Furthermore, the guilt of a criminal is never established with absolute certainty. The law requires only that guilt be proved "beyond a reasonable doubt"—which is to say, with a high degree of probability. And where we are dealing with probabilities, we are dealing with induction.

The instances of induction in the story, as in everyday life, are numerous. For instance, to conclude from Lanchaster's wound and from the bullet hole in the back of his chair that Lanchaster had been shot with a gun is to use induction. This conclusion is not the only one theoretically compatible with those premises. The premises would be true if the bullet had been thrown into the air somewhere across town, had landed and bounced erratically through the streets, had bounced into the Lanchaster house, and had struck the deceased. But induction tells us that such a theoretical possibility is so unlikely that we need not consider it seriously. In such an instance, the conclusion seems so obvious that we may not think of ourselves as reasoning at all, but we are. And the reasoning is inductive.

Hulk learns that the phone was torn from the wall on the evening of the murder. He concludes that there is a possibility that Lanchaster had been left alone by the murderer at some point, and a more remote possibility that he had left some kind of message. True, Hulk is dealing with mere possibilities here, but induction tells him that such possibilities are at least worth investigating. He isn't going to tell Crocker to search the bedroom or the lawn for a message.

Hulk finds the logic exercise and deduces the message "ITS LORD." Conceivably, it is pure coincidence that these letters can be deduced from this logic exercise. But inductive reasoning would convince all of us that this coincidence is unlikely beyond a reasonable doubt.

However, in preliminary readings of the story, some students have taken issue with Hulk's "total hypothesis." Some have favored an alternate account:

The logic exercise was constructed before Lord ever arrived at the house. It was not constructed as a message. Rather, it was a sort of doodle by a logician who was preoccupied with the unpleasant task of having to fire an associate. Lord arrived and argued his case until 7:30. At the time Lisa Williams arrived, Lord had not yet drawn the gun, nor had he torn out the phone. A bit later, Lanchaster started to phone Stout to find out what was keeping him. At that point, Lord tore out the phone and drew his gun.

There is no difference of opinion here over "whodunit." But this does provide an interesting example of an inductive controversy. Which hypothesis is the more reasonable, and how much more reasonable is it? This I shall leave to your consideration.

> Re: the exercise on page 200.
> If I am nice to people, then people are nice to me.
> People are nice to me.
> ─────────────────────────────
> I am nice to people.
> The form of the argument is:
> $A \supset B$
> $\underline{B}$
> A
> Here is an argument having that form which has obviously true premises and an obviously false conclusion.
> If I am Superman, then I am a man.
> I am a man.
> ─────────────────────
> I am Superman.
> Or:
> If this is 1942, then this is the 20th century.
> This is the 20th century.
> ─────────────────────────────
> This is 1942.
> Any argument of the form "$A \supset B$; B; therefore, A" is invalid.

READING

IRVING COPI: What is logic?

Logic is concerned with reasoning. Its concern is to distinguish good reasoning from bad, or better from worse. Logic is both an art and a science. As a science logic investigates, develops, and systematizes principles and methods that can be used to distinguish between correct and incorrect reasoning. The science of logic has its own professional jargon and technical notation, like other advanced sciences such as mathematics, physics, and chemistry. But as an art, logic can be equated with "logical ability" and includes a whole family of related skills that have many applications. Among those applications are problem solving, weighing evidence, marshaling evidence and constructing arguments for or against a disputed proposition, analyzing a problem into components that may usefully be dealt with separately, detecting and exposing mistakes in reasoning (including one's own), and clarifying issues, often through defining or redefining the key terms on which disputes frequently turn. In studying informal logic, our aim is to develop and strengthen these skills.

These logical skills are valuable and important. Each of us is a constant target for those who want to influence our beliefs, our actions, and the way we feel about things. In our free society, others cannot simply demand that we think, act, and feel as they tell us to. They must attempt to persuade us. Often they have their own benefit or advantage in mind rather than ours. So we should not let ourselves be too easily persuaded. We should believe only on the basis of evidence, act only in ways for which we have good grounds for acting, and our feelings or attitudes should be in harmony with our most deeply held commitments and sense of self. In general, we ought to let our beliefs be guided by the careful weighing of argument and evidence. Where a proposed action could have serious consequences, we should have good reason for taking such an action. Here is where logical skills can protect us from being unduly influenced by media commercials, slanted "news" stories, and politicians' promises.

Another benefit of developing our logical skills comes when we try to understand complex situations and to think things through. As the greatest American philosopher, Charles Sanders Peirce, remarked long ago, "The object of reasoning is to find out, from the consideration of what we already know, something else which we do not know."* To achieve this object, to extend our knowledge by reasoning, we must reason well rather than poorly. In order to infer correct and useful conclusions from what we already know, we must possess and apply the logical skills that constitute the art of logic. As Peirce went on to remark, "We come to the full possession of our power of drawing inferences, the last of all our faculties; for it is not so much a natural gift as a long and difficult art."† Indeed, sometimes in the process of reasoning we find that we are working with less than maximum effectiveness: depending on slogans rather than using our intelligence, avoiding the work of thinking by appealing only to habit, stereotypes, stale maxims, and vague generalities.

Finally, logical skills are valuable because they contribute to both fruitful cooperation and effective leadership. We live in communities with others, and some of our needs and wants can be satisfied only by the effort of many people working together toward common goals. That presupposes agreement on goals and on ways to achieve them. In reaching such agreement, one must try to avoid being persuaded on insufficient grounds by others. Here the recogni-

---

*Charles Sanders Peirce, "The Fixation of Belief," 1877, reprinted in Irving M. Copi and James A. Gould, *Readings on Logic,* Second Edition (New York: The Macmillan Company, 1972), p. 60.
†Ibid., p. 59.

tion of bad reasoning is important. But it is also important to be able to persuade others to agree on what is the best route to the best goal. Careful, constructive, *logical* thinking is not only a basis for productive collaboration, but the hallmark of effective and dependable leadership.

Questions and Exercises

1. Do the following logic puzzles with the mystery story and the exercise on page 196 in mind. (Explain the meaning of each premise and the reasoning behind each step in your deduction.)
   a. When will school be . . . ?
      i. $(O \cdot V) \supset E$
      ii. $M \vee R$
      iii. $L \supset N$
      iv. $U \equiv T$
      v. $\sim L \supset T$
      vi. $O \cdot \sim L$
   b. I live in San Francisco. . . .
      i. $(C \cdot L) \supset (I \cdot F)$
      ii. $\sim B \supset C$
      iii. $A \vee B$
      iv. $(O \cdot R) \supset (N \cdot I)$
      v. $Q \vee T$
      vi. $\sim B$
2. Explain your answer to each of the following:
   a. Can a valid deductive argument have false premises? *Y*
   b. Can a valid deductive argument have a false conclusion? *Y*
   c. Can a sound deductive argument have a false conclusion? *N*
   d. Can a sound inductive argument have false premises? *N*
   e. Can a sound inductive argument have a false conclusion? *Y*
3. Prove the following arguments invalid:
   a. If Louis is at the party and Grace is at the party, then there will be an argument; Louis will be at the party; therefore, there will be an argument.
   b. If it's vacation, then I'm not in school; if I'm not in school, then I'm not studying; therefore, if I'm not studying, then it's vacation.
4. Think of some problem you tried to solve recently (finding lost keys, fixing some piece of machinery, reuniting angry friends, whatever).
   a. Describe the reasoning process you went through.
   b. Explain how your reasoning was inductive or deductive or some combination of both.
5. According to Copi, what are the benefits of developing logical skills?

8

Methodology

Part 1: Understanding Philosophy Argumentation

One thing you will probably find different about philosophy is the degree to which it involves arguments. It's important that you learn to recognize arguments and to distinguish them from other passages in the text.

Often this text starts off with a problem: Are things this way or that way? Then it presents Position A, which says things are this way, and Position B, which says things are that way. (There will be more than two positions on some issues.) Then the text tries to clarify the problem or positions, giving you a better understanding than you would have gotten from a few simple statements. Then arguments are presented.

Roughly, then, as you read, you should be aware of at least four categories of passages in the text:

1. Problems
2. Positions
3. Clarifications
4. Arguments

Let's discuss these distinctions in terms of what could be an everyday sort of debate. You and your friends are talking, and you touch on the subject of whether human beings are really capable of caring about one another. This is a *problem:* a general sort of question you want answered. One of your friends says, "Everyone is out for number one." This is a *position:* a general statement that attempts to answer the question.

Suppose you are not quite clear about what your friend is claiming. You ask her: "What do you mean by that?"

"I mean, everyone is completely selfish," says your friend. "People just care about themselves."

Your friend has just attempted to clarify her original position—put it in other ways, give more detail, define terms. If this is done at all well, you now understand her position just a little better than you did when she first stated it. (If you don't understand it well enough, keep asking.)

"Why do you think that?" you ask your friend, wanting to know the reasons for her belief. You are asking your friend for an argument: additional statements (premises) which support the truth of the original statement (the conclusion).

When you ask someone for an argument, you might not get it. Let's consider two ways in which your friend might fail to fulfill your request.

If your friend said, "Why shouldn't I?" or "It's obvious," your friend would be **ducking the question**—that is, avoiding answering the question. You requested reasons, and you're not getting any.

Suppose, with the air of producing an argument, your friend says, "Because no one cares about anything but himself." Your friend is **begging the question:** presenting a version of the conclusion as if it were an additional statement in support of the conclusion. "No one cares about anything but himself" is equivalent to your friend's earlier statement, "People just care about themselves." If we believed the one, we'd believe the other. One isn't an additional reason for believing the other.

What's the difference between clarification and begging the question? If I want to understand a statement better and you give me equivalent statements, that's clarification. If I want additional reasons for believing a statement and you give me equivalent statements, that's begging the question.

If you don't elicit any kind of argument from your friend, you're entitled to ignore her claim. The burden of proof is on the person who makes the claim. But suppose you think her claim is wrong, and you want to give an argument against it. You say something like this: "I think you're wrong that everyone is selfish. Think about the Bay Area earthquake. People were helping each other all over the place."

You have given an argument. Let's see what it involves. Your friend has argued that everyone is completely selfish, which seems to imply that absolutely every person on every occasion is selfish. And being selfish seems to imply not helping another person. A clear instance of a person helping another seems to disprove your friend's statement that everyone is completely selfish.

Your argument involves a couple of logical concepts that should be made explicit:

Logical incompatibility: Two statements are logically incompatible if the truth of one implies the falsity of the other and vice versa. "It's raining"/"it's not raining," "Des Moines is the capital of Iowa"/"Des Moines is not the capital of Iowa," "I'm standing on my head"/"I'm not standing on my head" are pairs of logically incompatible statements.

Logical implication: If statement A implies statement B, that means that if A is true, then B must be also be true. "Norman is a novelist" implies that

"Norman has written something of book length." (Note that the second statement does not imply the first: Norman could have written a cookbook.
However, if the second statement read, "Norman has written a single book-
length piece of prose fiction, then the implication would goes both ways.
When the implication both statements, they are logically equivalent.)

The argument you presented was this:

1. "Everyone is completely selfish" implies that absolutely everyone on
   every occasion is selfish.
2. "Absolutely everyone on every occasion is selfish" implies that no one
   ever helps another.
3. It's not the case that no one ever helps another.
4. (Therefore) it's not the case that everyone is selfish (from 1, 2, and 3.)

The word "therefore" indicates the conclusion and the numbers in
parentheses after the conclusion indicate the statements from which the conclusion was deduced. (This convention comes in handy when dealing with a
series of statements containing several conclusions.)

If we substitute letters like A and B for the simple statements in the
above, we can represent the argument as follows:

1. A implies B.
2. B implies C.
3. Not C.
4. (Therefore) not A (from 1, 2, and 3).

There are several things to note about the reasoning here. If statement A
implies statement B, and statement B implies statement C, it follows that statement A implies statement C. This kind of reasoning is important in attempting
to determine what a statement is really saying, to determine whether it is reasonable or not.

Also, if a statement implied by some statement is false, it follows that the
original statement is false. That is, if C is implied by A and C is false, then A
must be false. This sort of reasoning is often used in trying to disprove a statement.

At this point, your friend might concede your argument, perhaps retreat-
ing from "Everyone is out for number one" to "Most people are out for number one." (You can then debate that modified claim if you wish.)

Suppose instead that your friend says the following: "Yes, people help
others sometimes. But only for the happiness of helping."

This is the kind of debate maneuver that drives people crazy. You seem
to have made some good points, but instead of conceding anything to you,
your opponent keeps changing her claim, often with an attitude of "See, I'm
still winning."

In such situations, keep in mind that the burden of proof is on the person
making the claim, not the person who questions it. It's up to her to prove her
point; it's not up to you to disprove it. Your failure to disprove doesn't constitute proof. To believe otherwise is to commit the fallacy of appeal to igno-

rance: assuming that because a statement can't be disproved, it must be true. (Appeal to ignorance is part of the mentality of people who thrive on *National Enquirer*–type stories: "What do you mean that wasn't a real spaceship in the sky last night? Prove it.")

On the other hand, maybe your friend isn't trying to pull some trick on you; maybe she's in the process of trying to clarify to herself what she means. This swinging back and forth between clarification and argument happens often in philosophy; the act of giving arguments brings up further points that need clarification. The thing to do at this point (something you will learn to do as you learn to do philosophy) is to assume the temporary role of referee or moderator:

"Okay," you say, "let's get this straight. I thought when you said that everyone was out for number one, you meant no one helps anyone else. But you seem to agree with me that that statement is false. What you're really saying is that people do help others. But the sole motive for helping others is the happiness one gets out of helping."

If this statement is accepted, you have gained quite a bit. You both agree on the point you were trying to make, and now you are a little closer to figuring out what your friend is claiming. Note some important differences between what the claim seems to be now and what it seemed to be before. The original claim seemed to imply that people never do good things; now it's possible that they do all sorts of good things, just not for good motives. (Obviously the second situation is preferable to the first.) Also the old claim seemed to be about how people behave, and behavior is fairly easy to observe. The new claim, however, seems to be about motivation and that may be difficult, if not impossible, to decide—especially if your friend brings in unconscious motivation. (Remember the burden of proof is on your friend.)

Let's imagine just one more step in this debate:

You say: "I still don't agree with you. I don't think the only motive people have for helping others is the happiness they get out of helping. There have been people who have knowingly given up their lives to help someone else. How could that be if their only motive was their own happiness?"

Your friend says: "But it was what they wanted to do. Dying for that other person was happiness to them."

Though it would take a little more questioning to be sure, it looks now as if your friend's claim is really a **tautology:** a trivial, purely verbal truth. Your friend is now using the word "happiness" to refer not to a particular feeling, but to whatever a person happens to do. Thus "People do things only for the happiness they get" really means something like "People do only what they do," which is true, but trivial, and has absolutely nothing to do with whether or not people are selfish.

This is a tricky point. To understand it better, let's review the evolution of your friend's claim. Your friend has said, (1) "Everyone is selfish," which you took to mean (1a) "No one ever does anything for someone else." When you challenged 1a, your friend's statement seemed to become (1b) "People help others only for the feeling of happiness they get from helping." When that was challenged, your friend defended the claiming by labeling anything a person does as happiness, which makes her claim equivalent to (1c): "People do only what they do."

Why would anyone be so silly as to argue for 1c? Presumably your friend doesn't realize what she's doing. She thinks she's saying something like 1b and doesn't see that she's defending it in a way that turns it into 1c. This happens fairly frequently when people are arguing abstract issues. If you or someone you're talking with seems to be defending some claim in a way that seems absolutely impervious to argument, check to make sure that the claim hasn't become a tautology.

Questions and Exercises

1. What is an argument?
2. What is the difference between argument and clarification?
3. What is begging the question?
4. What is the difference between clarification and begging the question?
5. What is the difference between ducking the question and begging the question?
6. What is the fallacy of appeal to ignorance?
7. Complete the following sentences:
   a. "A logically implies B" means that if A is true, then B. . . .
   b. "A is logically incompatible with B" means that if A is true, then B. . . .
8. The discussion describes two acceptable ways of reasoning involving logical implication. Do the examples below match either of those ways of reasoning? Explain.
   a. 1. A implies B.
      2. B implies C.
      3. (Therefore) C implies A (from 1 and 2).
   b. 1. A implies B.
      2. Not B.
      3. (Therefore) not A (from 1 and 2).
9. Which of the following statements are tautologies? Explain. (Some statements may be tautologies under one interpretation and not tautologies under another.)
   a. Whatever goes up must come down.
   b. Whatever will be will be.
   c. There is too much evil in the world.
   d. Evil is a very bad thing.
   e. Either God exists or He doesn't.
   f. We're not directly aware of what goes on in our unconscious minds.
   g. Each of us is an individual.

Part 2: How to Write a Philosophy Paper

Introduction

When I returned to school after working for several years, I approached my first philosophy papers by sitting down at the typewriter about 10 P.M. on the evening before the paper was due, skimming over the assignment, and then beginning to type, expecting a polished paper to emerge from the machine in a couple of hours. Instead I would find myself at 4 A.M. with a splitting headache, an ashtray full of cigarette butts (I smoked then), and a floor full of crumpled sheets of paper, each with a different version of the introductory paragraph.

Eventually, as a student, and then as a teacher, I learned better, and I'd like to share some of what I learned with you. My advice—much of which could be applied to most types of papers—will be organized according to the following steps: interpreting the assignment and developing a preliminary outline; developing ideas and expanding the outline; and drafting and polishing.

Sample Assignment

Assume you are given the following reading:

> The argument is: Physical evil brings moral good into being, and in fact is an essential precondition for the existence of some moral goods. . . .

> The real fallacy in the argument is in the assumption that all or the highest moral excellence results from physical evil . . . this is completely false. Neither all moral goodness nor the highest moral goodness is triumph in the face of adversity or benevolence toward others in suffering. Christ Himself stressed this when He observed that the two great commandments were commandments to love. Love does not depend for its possibility on the existence and conquest of evil. [Further] the "negative" moral virtues which are brought into play by the various evils—courage, endurance, charity, sympathy and the like—besides not representing the highest forms of moral virtue, are in fact commonly supposed by the theist and atheist alike not to have the value this . . . argument ascribes to them. We—theists and atheists alike—reveal our comparative valuations of these virtues and of physical evil when we insist on state aid for the needy; when we strive for peace, for plenty, and for harmony within the state.*

And the following assignment:

> Write a five-page paper critically evaluating the passage above; relate the ideas in the passage to those we have discussed in class.

*From H. J. McCloskey, "God and Evil," *Philosophical Quarterly*, Vol. X, No. 39, (1960): 106, 108, 109, 113. Reprinted by permission of the author.

Interpreting the Assignment and Developing a Preliminary Outline

The first step is to interpret the assignment in a way that gives us a preliminary structure of the paper—a structure we can use to organize our thinking. What this structure should be depends in part on some fundamentals of paper writing.

Every paper should have an introduction and a summary. I advocate the view that the introduction (give or take a little decoration) should simply announce what the paper will cover, and the summary should remind the reader what's been covered. The more you let content slip over into either of those two sections, the more likely you are to lose control of the structure of the paper.

We need to decide, in the case of our particular assignment, what sections should go between the introduction and summary—comprising the "body" of the paper. Critical evaluation is something we are clearly required to do. It's also clear that we're supposed to relate the reading to the class material. That's two sections. In addition, any time one does a critique of a reading, it's good practice to summarize the reading—that's a third section. In terms of ordering the sections, the summary obviously should go before the critique. Since critiquing seems to be our main assignment and the class material we bring in might be relevant to that, let's put the critique section last and the class material section just before it. Thus the following preliminary outline emerges:

Introduction

Summary of reading

Relation of reading to class discussion

Critical evaluation of reading

Summary

In the above outline I have skimmed over some organization questions that might have given you trouble if you'd had to develop this outline on your own. Should the class material be grouped with the summary or the critical evaluation, or does it stand on its own? If it is a separate section, should it go before or after critical evaluation? In the beginning, as you're developing confidence in your ability to organize the material, just remember that no decision at this stage is irreversible. If you find that the way you've chosen to divide and order the sections isn't working, go back and try another method. Here are a few tips: Read the assignment carefully to see if it gives you a kind of outline for the body of the paper; many will. (The one above is only mildly helpful; a better one would have asked you to summarize the reading, relate it to the class material, and then critically evaluate the reading.) If material A is necessary to discuss material B, you should handle material A first (for example, summary before critique). The main point of the paper generally should be discussed in the last section of the body. If you can't decide if material should constitute a separate section (for example, relation to course material), try it first as a separate section. In general, beginners don't include enough sections.

A preliminary outline is valuable because it provides an overall structure for the paper and guides the development of your ideas. It gives guidance and some assurance on that most crucial of questions: "How am I going to write five @#! pages about that?" Allowing, say, half a page for the introduction and summary, you can now think of a one-and-a-half-page essay on each subtopic—a lot less intimidating project. (And it becomes even less intimidating when you eventually break each of those subtopics into smaller areas.) Later I'll explain how you can write an adequate introduction from such an outline in just a few minutes.

Developing Ideas and Expanding the Outline

Once you have a preliminary outline, it's time to begin developing your thoughts in more detail and to record and organize those thoughts in an expanded outline.

First decide what you need to do to develop your material for each of the main subsections of your paper. For the summary section, of course, you need to review the reading until you understand it and have decided how best to summarize it. For the class material section, you need to review your texts, class notes, memories to find material that relates to the reading, particularly material that would help you explain or critique it. For the critique section you need to present your own ideas on the reading.

You'll note that none of these activities needs to be done at a word processor or in the library or at a desk in your room. The first two steps require that you be able to read and take notes, which can be done during lunch, or while sitting on a bus, or while waiting for a friend. The last step requires only the thinking process, which can be done anywhere. These steps allow you the option of "working" on your paper at free, unconstructive moments of the day, rather than devoting time that could be used for other activities you would rather be doing. Also, I think you will find that your thinking will be more productive if you put in smaller amounts over a longer period of time. (It gives that unconscious a chance to work when you aren't.)

In summarizing a reading, it is important to clarify the structure of its presentation. (This is particularly important in philosophy, where what's being presented often is an argument.) In our sample reading the author presents an argument (he labels it such) and then two counterarguments (phrases like "the real fallacy," "assumption is completely false," and "don't have the value the arguments subscribes to them" should make it abundantly clear that these are counterarguments).

The argument, as given in the excerpted reading, isn't really an argument—it's a statement. However, from class material we know what argument is being alluded to—what the assumed premises are. This is the virtue defense (which should be included when relating reading to class material).

The first counterargument is that some virtues, like love, require no suffering. The second counterargument is that the value of the negative virtues is undercut by the fact that in the context of everyday life, we strive to eliminate the conditions that make them necessary.

In terms of relation to class material, we've already noted that the original argument is like the virtue defense. The first counterargument isn't covered in the text, but the second sounds somewhat like the text when it discusses the virtue defense as turning virtue inside out—"like kicking a man in the shins so you can feel sorry for him."

In terms of critical evaluation, your primary job is to evaluate the counterarguments in the reading (that's what it means to "critically evaluate the reading") and then perhaps give your views on the virtue defense in general. Look at the two counterarguments. The first says that some virtues require no suffering. Is this really true? What about the example of love? Would love really be love between two creatures who had never suffered in any way? What about the argument that the virtue ends up contradicting itself by promoting what we're supposed to eliminate? These are crucial questions you will need to think about as you develop the ideas in your paper.

As you begin to develop your ideas, you should record them on an expanded outline. The thoughts described above could yield an expanded outline like the following:

Introduction

Summary of reading
    Arg: phys. evil brings good into being (virtue defense)
    C-arg 1: Some virtues like love don't require evil
    C-arg 2: Neg. virtues don't have value commonly ascribed because all
        of us try to eliminate what makes them possible

Relation to class material
    (Could give overview of problem of suffering if need to fill up space)
    Arg = virtue defense (discuss)
    C-arg 1 = not discussed in text
    C-arg 2 = text: "virtue defense turns virtue inside out"

Critique
    Think about:
    C-arg 1: could love be possible without suffering?
    C-arg 2: does virtue defense contradict itself? (is there important differ-
        ence between God allowing suffering and our allowing suffering?)

I don't mean to imply that your expanded outlines should look this neat and formal. I do suggest that you keep a notebook with a couple of pages devoted to each subtopic, and just keep scribbling. When you arrive at a formulation you like, circle it, star it, whatever. Then keep working off that formulation, jotting down details of the argument or materials from class or your critique ideas.

If, as you move along, you discover serious difficulties in the way the material is beginning to flow, refer to your preliminary outline to see if a slightly different version will work better. Sometimes after a slight restructuring of the subtopics, the specific ideas will fall nicely into a logical order.

Drafting and Polishing

How far you take the outlining process is up to you. Like a lot of writers, I really don't like writing. Rather, what I really don't like is writing that first draft, of getting those ideas down on paper in sentence form for the first time. I like the *idea* of writing, I like playing with ideas, I like polishing what I've written, and I enjoy having written something. The better prepared I am for doing that first draft—the less work I have to do—the better I like it. So I try to keep my outline going until I feel that it has almost become a draft; others like to start drafting earlier. But don't abandon the outline until you have a pretty good idea of what you're going to write about—for instance, until you actually have answers for those questions you wrote in the critique section of the outline.

The burden of the drafting process is eased not only if you are prepared with an outline, but also if you demand less of that first draft. A standard writing tip is that you never try to polish and edit while you are drafting. One of the problems with my initial attempts at writing in graduate school was not only that I started writing before my ideas were clear, but also that I expected all the sentences to be well formed, clear, and grammatical. I was trying to do far too many things at once, and doing nothing well. Sit down with your outline, do a draft of each section without critically evaluating your own writing, then get up and go away, and come back to it later for refining and editing. If the draft is inadequate, take some time to read it over and evaluate what went wrong. Then write another draft using the same technique.

I mentioned earlier that an adequate introduction could be written in a few minutes using the preliminary outline. The minimum that an introduction ought to present is the topic (the general subject) and the subtopics (the main sections) in the order in which they will be presented. In most courses where the teacher is concerned with content foremost, and only with writing to the degree that it does or doesn't get in the way of the presentation of content, topic/subtopics are all you need. For most courses, the teacher would be quite happy if you simply filled in the following blanks: "This paper will discuss (topic). First there will be (subtopic 1), then (subtopic 2), and finally (subtopic 3). ("This paper will critically evaluate the assigned reading on the problem of suffering. First the reading will be summarized, then related to the class discussion, then critically evaluated.")

If that seems too bare bones to you and/or your instructor, or you need to catch someone's attention (as in a class discussion), you can elaborate on your ideas. Do make sure to mention the topic and subtopics within your introduction; and don't let the body of your paper "leak" into the introduction. A more elaborate introduction would sound like this: "Since before the time of Job, human beings have questioned whether a just God would allow them to suffer so. One attempted explanation has been that suffering brings into existence important goods that could not exist without it. The author of our reading considers and then rejects this argument. I will summarize the author's arguments, relate them to our class discussion, and then critically evaluate them."

As you go through your paper, signal the reader each time you introduce a new subtopic with the a phase that matches the subtopic—these phrases, plus the introduction, will help keep the reader constantly oriented. "Of the two counterarguments the author presents, one has been discussed in class, the other not" would serve to introduce the section on class material. "The two counterarguments seem to me cogent, but there are a couple of points that bother me" might serve to introduce the critique section.

Use subheadings if you wish, but a general rule is that the headings are not part of the paper; if they are removed, the structure of the paper should remain clear.

To summarize: Begin your paper by making sure you understand the assignment; once you do, develop a preliminary outline of subtopics to structure your thinking and writing. Giving yourself some time, think about and/or research the subtopics, jotting down the results in an expanded outline. Once you feel ready to write, produce a first draft without worrying about how polished it is; save the editing for a later time.

Questions and Exercises

1. Develop preliminary outlines for the following paper assignments. (Remember what a preliminary outline is; this exercise requires you to know nothing about the people mentioned below.)
   a. Present James's views on religious experience and discuss how he would assess the events presented in "The Vision." (Answer given below.)

Answers to 1a:
   Intro
   Summary of James's views
   Summary of "The Vision"
   Analysis of "The Vision" in terms of James's views
   Summary of paper

The introduction could go something like this:
   In this paper I would like to discuss how William James would be likely to assess the story "The Vision." First I will present James's views of religious experience, then summarize the story, then analyze the story in terms of James's views.

    b. Gassendi offers certain objections to Descartes's theory of mind. What are those objections? How do they relate to similar objections given in the discussion section?

    c. Compare and contrast the views of mind held by Ryle and Place.

    d. How might Barrington feel about the clinic in "Death on Demand"? How might Dyck feel about it? How do you feel about it?

2. Using the relevant preliminary outline, write an introduction for one of the papers outlined in b, c, or d.

3. As individuals or as a class, develop a preliminary, then expanded, outline for the following paper topic. (This exercise requires you to read "God and the Problem of Suffering.")

> Assignment:
> Summarize the passage below, relate it to your readings, and critically evaluate it.
>
> Passage*:
> [God] is omniscient. . . . He creates men with free will, with the natures men have, in the world as it is constituted, knowing that in His doing so He is committing many to moral evil and eternal damnation.
>
> In attributing such behavior to God . . . [we are] attributing to God immoral behavior of a serious kind. . . .
>
> We do not commend people for putting temptation in the way of others. If by modifying our own behavior, we can save someone else from an intense moral struggle and almost certain moral evil, for example, if by refraining from gambling or excessive drinking ourselves we can help a weaker person not to become a confirmed gambler or an alcoholic . . . we feel obliged to act accordingly. . . . How much clearer is the decision with which God is said to be faced. . . .

*From H. J. McCloskey, "God and Evil," *Philosophical Quarterly*, Vol. X, No. 39, (1960): 106, 108, 109, 113. Reprinted by permission of the author.

Glossary

The definitions below are convenient simplifications for quick reference; they are not meant to replace the fuller definitions presented in the discussions.

Agnosticism: Neither believing nor disbelieving in God.

Appeal to ignorance (fallacy):   Assuming that because a statement can't be disproved, it must be true.

Argument: A statement (the conclusion) and one or more additional statements (the premises) offered in support of the conclusion.

Atheism: The belief that there is no God.

Begging the question: Assuming what one is trying to prove; presenting a version of the conclusion as if it were an additional statement in support of the conclusion.

Behaviorism: A version of materialism, claiming that the mind is nothing but complex, overt, physical behavior.

Causal laws: Inevitable patterns in nature, such that when certain events occur ("the cause") certain other events must occur ("the effect.")

Cogito: "I think, therefore I am."

Consequentialist ethical theories: Those ethical theories which claim that what makes actions right or wrong are their consequences.

Cosmological argument (The):   Attempts to show that given the existence of a world (in motion), God must exist as First Cause (First Mover).

Deductive argument: (see "Valid argument")

Deontological ethical theories: Those ethical theories which deny that what makes actions right or wrong are simply their consequences.

Determinism: The theory that all events, including mental events, are governed by causal laws.

Dualism: The view that the world is composed of two radically different kinds of things: physical objects and nonphysical minds.

Ducking the question: Avoiding answering a question.

Euthanasia: Deliberately bringing about, either by action (active) or by inaction (passive), the painless death of people with certain incurable conditions.

217

External world (The):   Everything outside of one's own mind.

Fallacy: A type of erroneous reasoning.

Fatalism: The view that some specified events must occur in a person's life, no matter what that person may choose to do.

Free will: The concept that (at least some) human choices are not governed by causal laws.

Free-will defense (The):   Claims that it would be contradictory for God to give people free will and guarantee that they not cause suffering; further, that free will and suffering is better than no free will and no suffering.

Freedom of action: The ability or opportunity to perform whatever physical actions one might choose to perform.

Identity theory: A version of materialism, claiming that the mind is nothing but the (physical) brain.

Indeterminism: The theory that not all events are governed by causal laws.

Inductive argument: (see "Valid argument")

Interactionism: A version of dualism, claiming that the (physical) body and (nonphysical) mind are causally related.

Invalid argument: A deductive or inductive argument which does not meet the appropriate conditions for validity. (See "Valid argument.")

Libertarian: One who believes people have free will.

Logical implication: If statement A logically implies statement B, that means that if A is true, then B must also be true.

Logical incompatibility: Two statements are logically incompatible if the truth of one implies the falsity of the other and vice versa.

Materialism: The view that everything that exists is physical, including minds.

Metaethical: Relating to the nature of moral judgments, especially their meaning and justification.

Moral objectivism: The view that where there is a moral judgment and its negation, one of those judgments must be false; that there is such a thing as *the* moral truth.

Moral subjectivism: The view that where there is a moral judgment and its negation, neither judgment need be false; that there is no such thing as *the* moral truth.

Normative ethical: Relating to questions about what is morally good or bad, right or wrong, required or not required.

Ontological argument (The):   Attempts to prove the existence of God from the concept of God.

Parallelism: A version of dualism, claiming that the (physical) body and (nonphysical) mind are not causally related.

Principle of nonidentity: If the thing referred to by one phrase has characteristics differing from those of the thing referred to by another phrase, the two phrases do not refer to the same thing.

Problem of suffering (The):   The question of whether the existence of a God who is omnipotent, omniscient, and perfectly good is compatible with the existence of suffering in the world.

Slippery slope fallacy: Assuming, without specific evidence, that any move in a certain direction will inevitably lead to some terrible extreme.

Solipsism: The view that, with the exception of the belief in one's own mind, one cannot justify any beliefs about the world.

Sound argument: An argument that is valid and has true premises.

Tautology: A trivial, purely verbal truth.

Teleological argument (The):   Attempt to prove that given the complex orderliness of the world, God must exist as designer of that world.

Theism: The belief that there is a God.

Utilitarianism: The moral view that only happiness is good in itself and that one ought to promote the greatest happiness of the greatest number.

Valid argument:

    Deductive: An argument such that if the premises are true, then the conclusion is necessarily true.

    Inductive: An argument such that if the premises are true, then the conclusion is probably true, but not necessarily so.

Veridical: True; genuine; nonillusory.

Virtue defense (The):   Claims that it would be contradictory to have virtues and no suffering; further, that virtues and suffering are better than no virtues and no suffering.

Further Materials

FREEDOM, FOREKNOWLEDGE, AND TIME

Philosophy

Sober, Elliott. *Core Questions in Philosophy*. New York: Macmillan, 1991. Lectures 23–25.

Hook, Sidney (ed.). *Determinism and Freedom in the Age of Modern Science*. New York: Collier, 1961.

Taylor, Richard. *Metaphysics*. 3d Ed. Englewood Cliffs, N.J.: Prentice-Hall, 1983, chapters 4 and 6.

Other

Borges, Jorge Luis. "The Secret Miracle" in *Ficciones*. New York: Grove Weidenfeld, 1987. A man facing execution gets his wish that time stop for awhile.

A Clockwork Orange (video). Warner Home Video, 1971. The main character goes through a conditioning process that forces him to be "good."

Dostoevsky, Fyodor. *Notes from the Underground*. New York: E. P. Dutton, 1960. An expression of a man's hysterical insistence on free will.

Heinlein, Robert A. "—All You Zombies—" in *The Unpleasant Profession of Jonathan Hoag*. New York: Ace Books, 1989. The story presents the ultimate in time-travel complexities: A man manages to become the mother and father of himself.

Star Trek: Episode 28, "The City on the Edge of Forever" (video). Paramount, 1966. Time travel plus Joan Collins.

GOD AND THE PROBLEM OF SUFFERING

Philosophy

Hick, John. *Philosophy of Religion*. 4th Ed. Englewood Cliffs, N.J.: Prentice-Hall, 1990, chapters 3 and 4.

Pike, Nelson (ed.). *God and Evil*. Englewood Cliffs, N.J.: Prentice-Hall, 1964.

Sober, Elliott. *Core Questions in Philosophy*. New York: Macmillan, 1991. Lectures 4–11.

Other

Bedazzled (video). CBS/Fox, 1967. There are some delightful discussions between Dudley Moore and Peter Cook (as the devil) on why God allows evil.

The Book of Job. A Biblical exploration of the problem of suffering.

Dostoyevsky, Fyodor. *Brothers Karamazov.* New York: Norton, 1976. The chapter entitled "Rebellion" contains an outcry against a God who would allow suffering.

Huxley, Aldous. *Brave New World.* New York: Perennial Classics, 1989. The discussion between Mustapha Mond and the Savage at the end of the book parallels the discussion between God and Martin in "Surprise! It's Judgment Day."

Stoppard, Tom. *Jumpers.* New York: Grove Weidenfeld, 1989. The main character, a philosopher, presents an amusing discussion of the first-cause argument.

Voltaire. *Candide.* New York: Bantam, 1959. A satire of the claim that this is the best of all possible worlds.

MORAL PROOF AND MORAL PRINCIPLES

Philosophy

Frankena, William. *Ethics.* 2d Ed. Englewood Cliffs, N.J.: Prentice-Hall, 1973.

Satiris, Stephen. *Taking Sides: Clashing Views on Controversial Moral Issues.* Guilford, Conn.: Dushkin, 1990. Issues 1–4 & 6.

Sober, Elliott. *Core Questions in Philosophy.* New York: Macmillan, 1991. Lectures 27–33.

Other

Huxley, Aldous. *Brave New World.* New York: Perennial Classics, 1989. Mustapha Mond defends a quasi-utilitarian morality, distinguishing between his personal preferences and moral perspective.

Sartre, Jean-Paul. "The Flies" in *No Exit and Three Other Plays.* New York: Vintage, 1989. The "freedom" exalted in the play is not so much free will as the freedom to choose a morality without any possibility of being in error. In other words, the play primarily is concerned with moral subjectivism.

Stoppard, Tom. *Jumpers.* New York: Grove Weidenfeld, 1989. The characters discuss moral subjectivism with some sophistication.

ONE MORAL ISSUE: THE RIGHT TO DIE

Philosophy

Gorovitz, Samuel, and Maklin, Ruth. *Moral Problems in Medicine.* 2d Ed. Englewood Cliffs, N.J.: Prentice-Hall, 1976.

Satiris, Stephen. *Taking Sides: Clashing Views on Controversial Moral Issues.* Guilford, Conn.: Dushkin, 1990. Issue 13.

Other

Whose Life Is It Anyway? (video). MGM/UA, 1981. Richard Dreyfuss as a paralyzed sculptor fighting for the right to die.

THE NATURE OF THE MIND

Philosophy

Flew, Antony (ed.). *Body, Mind, and Death*. New York: Macmillan, 1964.

Shaffer, Jerome A. *Reality, Knowledge, and Value*. New York: Random House, 1971, chapters 11–14.

Sober, Elliott. *Core Questions in Philosophy*. New York: Macmillan, 1991. Lectures 18–22.

Taylor, Richard. *Metaphysics*. 3d Ed. Englewood Cliffs, N.J.: Prentice-Hall, 1983, chapter 1–3.

Other

Asimov, Issac. *Robot Visions*. New York: ROC, 1990. A compilation by the master of robot stories.

Ghosts (video). Paramount, 1990. Ghosts can interact with the world in certain ways. It's fun to try to figure out what the rules are and whether they're consistent.

2001: A Space Odyssey (video). MGM/UA, 1987. Of particular interest here is the revolt and death of HAL, the computer.

Vonnegut, Kurt, Jr. "Epicac" and "Unready to Wear" in *Welcome to the Monkey House*. New York: Dell Publishing Co., 1970. The first concerns a computer who falls in love, and the second is about a group of people who have learned to step in and out of their bodies.

APPEARANCE AND REALITY

Philosophy

Descartes. *Meditations*. New York: Macmillan, 1960.

Shaffer, Jerome A. *Reality, Knowledge, and Value*. New York: Random House, 1971, chapters 1–6.

Sober, Elliott. *Core Questions in Philosophy*. New York: Macmillan, 1991. Lectures 12–14.

Other

Borges, Jorge Luis. "The Circular Ruins" in *Ficciones*. New York: Grove Weidenfeld, 1987. In this story, a man discovers that he is only an illusion.

Calderon, Pedro. *Life Is a Dream*. New York: Hill & Wang, 1970. The main character has difficulty distinguishing dream from reality.

Total Recall (video). Live, 1990. Schwarzenegger on an adventure in which dream and reality become confused.

LOGIC

Philosophy

Kahane, Howard. *Logic and Contemporary Rhetoric*. 5th Ed. Belmont, Calif.: Wadsworth, 1988.

Salmon, Wesley. *Logic*. 3d Ed. Englewood Cliffs, N.J.: Prentice-Hall, 1984.

Other

Any "whodunit" can be helpful in the analysis and exercise of reasoning. Agatha Christie's mysteries are, of course, among the more sophisticated, and Rex Stout's are among the most enjoyable. But the Ellery Queen novels containing his characteristic "Challenge to the Reader" provide the most legitimate opportunity to reason out the solution.

Index